Cambridge Studies in the History and Theory of Politics

Texts concerning the
Revolt of the Netherlands

Texts concerning the Revolt of the Netherlands

EDITED WITH AN INTRODUCTION BY

E. H. KOSSMAN

Professor of Modern History
Rijksuniversiteit, Groningen

AND

A. F. MELLINK

Senior Lecturer in Modern History
Rijksuniversiteit, Groningen

CAMBRIDGE UNIVERSITY PRESS

Published by the Syndics of the Cambridge University Press
Bentley House, 200 Euston Road, London NW1 2DB
American Branch: 32 East 57th Street, New York, N.Y. 10022

© Cambridge University Press 1974

Library of Congress Catalogue Card Number: 73-83103

ISBN: 0 521 200148

First published 1974

Printed in Great Britain by
Alden & Mowbray Ltd
at the Alden Press, Oxford

Contents

CONTENTS

Preface

The purpose of this book is to introduce the reader to material which although not easily accessible ought to be more widely known. Most of the texts published in the following pages were written in Dutch and it was evident from the start that they should appear in translation. We were less certain about the French and Latin texts. When we decided to translate these too we did not underrate the erudition of those who will use this book but merely hoped to achieve a greater measure of uniformity. As we have only in twelve cases thought it necessary to print documents in full (Documents 3, 4, 7, 8, 15, 23, 24, 28, 29, 37, 49, 66), specialists may want to know more than we can offer and thus in any case have to turn to the originals.

The series in which our collection appears is devoted to the history and theory of politics. This obliged us to touch upon the religious issues which played, we think, a decisive part in the Revolt of the Netherlands only in their political form, that is, only insofar as they caused the problem of toleration to be discussed. It obliged us, in the second place, to concentrate on theoretical aspects and to reduce to a minimum the factual and narrative elements that make the history of the Revolt so absorbing an epic.

Obviously the selection of fragments remains somewhat arbitrary. W. P. C. Knuttel's catalogue of pamphlets in the Royal Library at The Hague shows how overwhelming the quantity of available material is. There are hundreds of catalogued pamphlets covering the years 1565 to 1588, many of them rare, some unique. We have read a large number of them and tried to select only those fragments that pertained to the subject matter of the series. If the reader feels nevertheless that he has to struggle through a mass of facts and dates he must not accuse us too hastily of an insufficiently developed power of abstraction. It was not always easy and sometimes impossible to separate narrative and theory for contemporaries did not distinguish these categories as neatly as we do.

The first draft of most of the translations was prepared by Mrs A. C. Mellink. We have tried to translate into readable English texts which are sometimes complicated and long-winded. The reader who finds himself stumbling over some English passages may take comfort in the fact that in the original the going is harder. We are grateful for the help of our friend and colleague Mrs Alice C. Carter of the London School of Economics, and we would like to thank the staff of the Cambridge University Press for their assistance in preparing the typescript.

Groningen   E.H.K.
                                                                             A.F.M.

Introduction

Like most historical discussions, that on the Revolt of the Netherlands is complicated, even chaotic, and inconclusive. It remains extremely difficult to assess the impact of such factors as religion, economic depression, nationalism and so forth on the long series of disturbances which we are accustomed to include under the general label of the 'Revolt of the Netherlands'. Even this term, incidentally, is open to criticism. It would, in the first place, not have appealed at all to sixteenth- or seventeenth-century Netherlanders. Revolt, after all, was an activity which most sixteenth-century people, educated in the discipline of strict loyalty to the natural sovereign and suspicious of systematic attempts to change the existing pattern of society, regarded as impermissible, ungodly and bound to be disastrous. The opposition to Charles V's successor in the government of the Netherlands emphatically denied being rebellious. Moreover, even if we permit ourselves to use the word 'revolt' as such, we may doubt whether we are justified in using it in the singular. In fact, it would perhaps be better to revert to the practice of sixteenth- and seventeenth-century historians many of whom, whether pro- or anti-Dutch, whether writing in Latin, Spanish, Dutch or French, entitled the books bearing on this much studied subject: The Wars (or: The Civil Wars) in the Netherlands. This terminology has the additional merit of avoiding the third fallacy inherent in the conventional usage. For not the whole of the Netherlands rose in revolt; some men, some groups, some towns, some areas did, at different times and for different reasons. Some persisted in their opposition; others submitted again to the legal sovereign after a short while. Some were Roman Catholic; others were Protestant. Their motives were as varied as their actions. At no time was it possible to distinguish an openly insurrectionary party that could truly make the claim that it was supported by the majority of the people and in which all the regions constituting the Netherlands were fairly, even if at all, represented.

After age-long discussions about whether the fundamental motives of the Revolt were religious, economic or political, today's sceptical historians tend to give up the search for 'main causes'. A series of disturbances stretching over various decades cannot, they think, be explained in such a simple way. The opposition of the 1560s was essentially different from that of the 1580s, inspired by other ideals, prompted by other resentments. And it is equally vain to distinguish in the Revolt the 'stages' which, on the analogy of the French Revolution, we have come to expect in all other revolutions. It may be that in some areas of the Netherlands there was a development away from moderation through extremism and terrorism towards the compromise represented by the final settlement; in other areas there was nothing like it and it would be most arbitrary to take one or another region as typical and the rest as exceptional. The Revolt was a long drawn out process of estrangement not only between the Low Countries and the sovereign residing in Spain, between Protestants and the established Church, between the poor and the bourgeoisie or the bourgeoisie and the landed aristocracy, but also between the various areas of the Netherlands. The result was anarchy, disintegration, and civil war. It was to these challenges that small groups of people reacted by setting up orderly governments of their own in some provinces, capable of organising life more satisfactorily in the compass of a reduced territory and with more limited responsibilities. They broke away from Spain as well as from their neighbours, entrenching themselves in an old-fashioned particularism that it would be far-fetched to characterise as the climax and fulfilment of revolutionary endeavour.

The discussion which started in the nineteenth century as to whether the Revolt was modern and revolutionary or conservative in its nature has led us nowhere. The antithesis makes no sense in a sixteenth-century context. Insofar as the events of the 1570s and 1580s produced a new state out of which the Dutch Republic gradually developed, the disturbances were decidedly revolutionary. But of course it cannot be said that the leaders of the movement consciously set out to build up a new nation. It just happened to emerge out of failures and mistakes, as a *pis aller* rather than as the realisation of a positive ideal. Conservative and revolutionary elements were inextricably mixed. Misinterpretation of historical precedent, moreover, enabled the opposition to feel perfectly safe in their conservative attitudes, although in the light of modern research it is clear that they were innovating. But this much is certain: the Revolt was not made by theorists; it was not based upon a solid set of political doctrines. If in fact it was at times revolutionary and produced in some areas a form of society and government which might be called modern in comparison with those of other states such as the Southern Netherlands or Spain, this was a result of economic and social forces not controlled, nor even clearly distinguished by the opposition.

The abdication of Charles V in 1555 represented the end of an era. His son and successor as sovereign of the Netherlands, Philip II, was not only quite a different personality, educated in Spain instead of in Flanders, more naïve and self-centred than his father, whose constant travelling and endlessly varied responsibilities had prevented him from becoming doctrinaire; his functions and the possibilities open to him were also different. Of course it mattered greatly to the inhabitants of the Low Countries that their sovereign was no longer German emperor, for the imperial dignity had shed lustre on Charles and on his subjects. Moreover, Charles's handling of religious affairs in Germany had given Dutch dissidents room to hope that in their country too some measure of toleration would perhaps be granted. Under Philip II however there was little chance that the non-conformists would be left the means of survival which were then, or were soon to become, available in a major part of Central and Western Europe: in Germany, in France (where from 1562 various edicts were issued defining limited religious freedom), and in England. On the contrary, Philip's counter-reformation zeal was likely to impose upon his northern domains a way of life which would isolate them and divorce their development from that of their neighbours. The Low Countries were to become a bulwark of strict orthodoxy, carefully closed to influences from abroad, with its own hierarchy and its own university.

Of course this ideal did not originate with Philip II. It was a corollary of what we used to call Burgundian centralising policies, and Charles V had greatly accelerated the growth to autarchy. Philip II merely continued what Charles V had begun. It was Charles who started in the 1520s the persecution of the various heretical sects – Sacramentarians, Anabaptists and, much later, Calvinists – that found broad support in the Netherlands. When in 1558 Philip II lay before the Pope a detailed project containing a complete reorganisation of the episcopacy in the Low Countries – in 1559 the Pope issued the bull in which he ordered the proposal to be carried out – he was presenting a project which had been in the making since 1525 and was acting at the instigation of his father. The new arrangement was designed in such a way as to make the bishops in the Netherlands independent of foreign prelates. Instead of the five bishoprics of the old régime, supervised by a German and a French archbishop, the Pope instituted four bishoprics in the Walloon areas (under the archbishop of Cambrai), six in the Dutch-speaking parts of the Southern Netherlands (under the archbishop of Mechlin) and five in the Northern Netherlands (under the archbishop of Utrecht). From a purely administrative point of view this was an admirable and carefully considered measure which could be expected to enhance the efficiency of the episcopacy.

Yet it was one of the main factors in the dangerous movement towards anarchy. In August 1559 Philip II left for Spain and gradually became absorbed in the dramatic struggle with the Turks. The government in the Netherlands, though well organised on paper, was in fact very weak. It had little coherence and less money. The newly appointed regent, Margaret of Parma, was somewhat helpless and sought the regular advice of men like Antoine Perrenot de Granvelle (1517–86) or Wigle van Aytta (Viglius, 1507–77), both from far outlying areas, Franche Comté and Friesland, and deeply loyal to the dynasty to which they owed their career as *noblesse de robe*. This made the high nobility and the clergy of the central areas suspicious; they feared that government instead of being exercised by the three so-called collateral councils established by Charles V – the Privy Council, the Council of Finance and, loftiest of all, the Council of State – was in fact concentrated in the hands of a small number of persons directly dependent on the regent. From the start the fierce debate on the ecclesiastical organisation was partly political. With undisguised distrust many of the towns chosen to become episcopal sees protested against this honour. Antwerp especially was afraid that the activities of a local bishop would make the port inaccessible to German, Lutheran merchants and thus ruin its trade. This reaction typifies the character of the opposition arising against the new, inward-looking, self-centred system. Moreover the decrees impaired all kinds of local interests. In the first place the clergy in the duchy of Brabant felt humiliated by an arrangement which imposed upon them the masterly figure of an archbishop (Granvelle) and deprived some big monasteries – destined to be ruled by the new bishops who would thus find the financial means they were in need of – of their right to elect their own abbots freely. At the same time the nobility, used to exercising various forms of patronage and to obtaining for their younger sons fat ecclesiastical posts or prebends, rightly saw that the Council of Trent's precise regulations about Church appointments and the standard of learning required for high position, regulations which the new, efficient episcopacy would undoubtedly enforce, were bound to make them lose their influence over the Church. In Brabant clergy and nobility, almighty in the provincial States, were united in their reaction to Philip's measures.

Inevitably the Protestants feared the new organisation as it would strengthen the Church but they did not yet themselves play a decisive part in the opposition. However, it was their anxieties, their unrest, their profound distrust of the king's government that the clergy and the nobility exploited in order to emphasise the seriousness of the situation.

The king was duly impressed. He was moreover involved in his Mediterranean preoccupations to an extent which did not allow him to take firm initiatives in the Netherlands. Without abandoning any of his principles he was cautious enough to withdraw some particularly offensive innovations provisionally (for example, the Antwerp bishopric) and to send away the servant whom he had charged with the execution of his decrees and made primate of the Church of the Netherlands, Cardinal Granvelle. When this much-hated man left the country in March 1564, the opposition, now supported by the regent herself, was apparently the victor.

From the beginning of 1564 to the middle of 1566 those among the nobles who disliked the tendencies of which Granvelle, the royalist and absolutist, seemed the living symbol, themselves controlled the government. After nine years of constant wrangling between the king and various groups of his subjects, years during which the sovereign had, however cautiously, stuck to his own methods, one wing of the opposition was allowed to grasp and exercise power. The leader of this group was William of Orange (1533–84). He was born in Germany, the eldest son of Count William of Nassau-Dillenburg, but was educated at Brussels as one of Charles V's favourites. He owed his great status among the Burgundian noblemen to his title of sovereign prince of the minute principality of Orange in France and to his large domains in the Netherlands, specifically in Brabant. Both came into his possession in 1544 when his cousin René of Chalons died in battle, twenty-six years old and with no legitimate children. It is significant that the count and countess of Nassau who were Lutherans or on the point of becoming Lutherans allowed their eldest son to be turned into a Catholic nobleman loyal to, and dependent on, the emperor, for it indicates that in 1544 and following years some sort of understanding or compromise between the reformers and the Roman Catholic authorities in Germany and the Netherlands did not yet seem altogether impossible. Tense though the situation had become it had not yet run into a complete deadlock.

During the 1550s and the early 1560s William's outlook was a reflection of early-sixteenth-century uncertainties. He was a Catholic but in a rather easy-going, pre-Tridentine manner. He had as yet no fundamental objections to the persecution of heretics but was sceptical about the results and deplored its cruelty. It seemed to him just as unwise to withdraw the anti-Protestant edicts of Charles V as to enforce them. The first would mean religious chaos but the second – if at all possible – national ruin. Politically he was by no means a reactionary. In fact, he could not be. His social group was traditionally dependent on the

Burgundian dynasty. It was to Charles V and his predecessors that he and his colleagues owed their high positions, their offices, their prestige and their immense pride at being the wealthiest nobles of the wealthiest country in Europe. William of Orange was not the representative of a 'feudal' outlook although as a matter of course he used, when obliged to define his attitudes in words, the terminology of the 'feudal' Middle Ages and emphasised his duty, as a vassal of the king, to oppose measures which he thought detrimental to the welfare of the king's possessions. But insofar as the dynasty stood for moderate modernisation of the state, a moderate form of centralisation and for order, William of Orange and his adherents loyally and scrupulously supported it.

Although Philip II did not radically alter the policies of Charles V he was a different man with a different background and lived in a rapidly changing climate of opinion. Problems left unsolved for decades, questions left unanswered, attitudes left vague, called for more definite direction. It became clearly impossible to control religious development if the courts were allowed to enforce the edicts only haphazardly and according to their whims. Equally it was impossible to improve finances if the provincial States and the States General were allowed to take advantage of the king's absence and of his being far less popular than his father, and to refuse subsidies. Royal prestige, manifestly on the decline during the 1550s, had to be enhanced. During the late 1550s and the early 1560s Philip II tried to strengthen central government. He failed, perhaps not so much because his rule was really more oppressive than his father's, but because his obvious weakness, his vacillations and his slowness destroyed confidence, leaving the impression that this man was far less able than Charles V to bring prosperity and order.

If the opposition to whom power automatically lapsed after Granvelle's departure held to any principle at all, it was that the uncertainties of the early sixteenth century should be preserved whatever the cost. From the point of view of the king and his followers the cost was of course unjustifiably high. But general opinion about the rule of the nobles has been very unfavourable, too, even among those historians who are in sympathy with the aims of the Revolt and acclaim its achievements. The nobles are criticised for their lack of administrative capacity as well as their failure to grasp the essentials of the situation and to appreciate the merits of radical Protestantism. Their government has been characterised as medieval and reactionary, as frivolous and egoist, as totally and dismally irresponsible. Yet it should be remembered that if they failed, so did such highly praised administrators as Granvelle, whom they drove away, and Alva, by whom they were crushed. It should also be realised that their aim was to revert to the system of Charles V and not to that of the long-forgotten, pre-Burgundian era. The weakness of their rule was not caused primarily by their lack of skill or public spirit but by their lack of power. They inherited the weaknesses of Philip's rule for which they had partly to blame themselves: they had too small an army and too little money. Moreover, order in the sixteenth century was based upon a careful system of patronage. Philip had wrecked this system, estranging those men upon whose goodwill the régime rested. Of course, he was not prepared to let the nobles who, he felt, were hostile to him, exploit the means of patronage in his possession with the result that the promises made by the nobles to people whose support they hoped to enlist, could not be carried out. It had been possible for Charles V to keep the situation in balance in spite of, or thanks to, its appalling uncertainties. Now that imperial prestige had vanished and royal prestige was withering away, the uncertainties which the nobles still tended to regard as a stabilising factor turned into complete anarchy.

Just as anarchy made it possible for Calvinism to spread rapidly, so the religious development intensified anarchy. Granvelle's departure was the signal for many militant emigrants to return from their refuges in Germany and England. Though the nobles did not issue toleration edicts (for obviously they could not do this without royal orders) many lawyers and judges and the public in general considered the old *placaten* to have lost validity and were not prepared to apply them any longer. Persecution was gradually stopped. At the same time Calvinism made its entry into the Netherlands, imported mainly by French ministers who took advantage of the circumstances to enter the French speaking areas in the south, and rapidly drew large audiences, especially in the industrial towns and countryside of Southern Flanders. This abruptly altered the religious situation and added immeasurably to the complexity of the problems. For here was a sect which, quite unlike Lutheranism which was adopted by German princes, was learning the hard way how to oppose princes. Here was a creed probably in principle not more revolutionary than any other sixteenth-century creed but, latecomer as it was, in almost all countries exposed to the systematic hatred of the rulers and thus obliged by dire necessity to develop means of resistance unknown to the 'heresies' which had emerged some decades before and could hope to achieve worldly success more easily. What none of the older sects in the Netherlands had aspired to achieve was for the Calvinists an obvious and immediate prerequisite: the organisation of a disciplined and militant community. For them this clearly represented their only hope of survival.

The expansion of Calvinism in the Southern Netherlands, particularly in Flanders, took place long before it achieved success in what were later to become its strongholds: Holland, Zeeland and Friesland. Perhaps the social and economic conditions in the more industrialised southern provinces contributed to the rapid spread of the new doctrine among the lower middle classes and the workmen in urban centres like Tournai, Valenciennes and, somewhat later, Antwerp. It is also possible that thanks to the poor relief organised by the reformed congregations a number of destitute people were led to join them but this did not substantially alter their social composition which remained predominantly lower middle and working class. This makes one somewhat sceptical about the hypothesis that in the events leading to the riots of 1566 the Calvinist 'poor' should have played the role of a revolutionary vanguard which wished to bring about social reform. In the Northern Netherlands, at any rate, where Calvinism did not firmly establish itself before 1572, this element was not of vital importance. In fact, the Calvinist congregations reflected the normal social composition of urban communities because big merchants and entrepreneurs also often exercised important influence. Although Calvinism in the Netherlands gradually adopted some original characteristics, both its confession and its organisation owed much to the French model with its presbyters, synods and local consistories uniting together into classes and church provinces. Thanks to this system the local congregations maintained a fairly large measure of autonomy. But as the consistories filled vacancies by co-option not by new elections it was not a democratic organisation.

By the end of 1565 the situation got out of control. Philip, who had kept silent for a long time, abruptly declared that he did not accept any of the proposals of the Council of State. He reaffirmed his decision to maintain the inquisition and refused to raise the Council of State above the other councils. When the king's letter (Document 1) was made known in the Netherlands the reaction was intense. It was this time not the office-holding nobility sitting on the Council of State that took the lead but the so-called 'lower nobility', some of them of the same families and rank as the councillors but without high offices. The aims of the 'Compromise' of the nobles were made clear in a declaration (Document 3) and in an important pamphlet (Document 2) by the French Calvinist François du Jon (Junius). The emphasis was now entirely on religion. Junius advocated religious freedom for the organised Protestant churches and warned against attempts to delay this any longer. Experience, he stated, showed that it would come anyhow as no authority is able to stop the process. But continued and in the long run in any case fruitless attacks on organised Protestantism would, he feared, further the spread of all sorts of un-organised, undisciplined, socially and politically disturbing opinions and sects. In this way Junius presented Calvinism as a politically and spiritual-ly safe alternative to Catholicism that it would be wise to tolerate in order to prevent atheism, libertinism and anabaptism from developing further. A short while later William of Orange was to adopt the same attitude (Document 8). In the well-known Request (Document 4) the same prob-lem was considered but without reference to the dangerous sects. The nobles asked for all persecution to be stopped until the States General were convened to study more appropriate means to deal with the question. This was a far from unexpected but still highly important proposal. The nobles who stated in 'feudal' fashion that it was their duty as vassals of the king to inform him of what was really happening, suggested at the same time that decisions on religious matters ought to be taken with the consent of the representative States General which Philip II had not called since the unpleasant experiences he had had with them in the late 1550s.

The proposals of the Request were only partly put into effect. The regent agreed to send them to Philip II and to order the inquisitors to proceed 'discreetly and modestly in their office' but this was not enough. In his interesting narrative of events in 1566 (Document 5) Wesenbeke emphasises the deep disappointment arising in the Netherlands when it became known that the States General was not to be consulted. Instead the local States and councils of the Walloon provinces – considered to be much less 'accustomed to freedom' than the others – were informed of the regent's decisions without being given the opportunity to discuss them. Only after they had been forced to approve did the government bring the matter before the States of Brabant and Flanders. This, the writer sug-gests, was a totally inadequate manner in which to consult the inhabitants and they were right to protest violently and not to heed government measures. Once again it was clear that broad sections of the population were now convinced that religious policies should be decided upon by the States General and not by the sovereign alone. Philip II objected that all this was unnecessary as he had in no way changed his father's religious legislation (Document 6). He was probably right. However, the debate had moved into new areas. The nobles and the opposition generally argued that because the traditional religious policy had failed – of course they were right in thinking that it had failed – it was the duty of the people's representatives to advise the sovereign about new policies. Although they were careful not to state bluntly that the sovereign's religious policy had always been subject to approval by the States General they vaguely hinted that there were ancient privileges and freedoms which seemed to suggest such a possibility and that anyhow the persecutions were bearing heavily on the country for the prosperity of which they were responsible to the inhabitants as well as to the king. In this way the religious problem was associated with the constitutional problem that confronted all sixteenth-century governments; for decades it had been left uncertain whether the sovereign, the 'parliaments' or both would eventually profit from the increase in state power which had been developing since the late fifteenth century.

In his letter of 31 July 1566 Philip II made some concessions; although limited – religious freedom was not granted – they still constituted a recognition of defeat. The recognition was half-hearted – on 9 August the king declared before a notary that his concessions were extorted by force – and the practical effect was nil. When the letter arrived in the Netherlands disturbances, radical to an unprecedented degree, were taking place that wrecked both the king's policy and that of the opposition. The 'Iconoclastic Riots' started on 10 August 1566 in the industrial areas of South-West Flanders; they spread rapidly through Antwerp northwards to various towns in Holland and reached Friesland and Groningen in the first half of September. Priceless Church treasures – from images, mass vestments, organs to unique manuscripts – were destroyed. When the storm had blown over it was impossible to estimate the losses. The central government was powerless; many local governments, dependent on Brussels, were unable to put up even a semblance of resistance. Perhaps more important still was the indifference of the majority of the population. What seems to characterise the situation in all places where the iconoclastic fury occurred, was the failure of the Roman Catholic clergy to muster effective help. The rapid success of the movement was proof not only of the relative popularity of Calvinism but most of all of the profound anti-clericalism rampant in all sections of society.

It is still impossible to explain the whole phenomenon satisfactorily. Of course economic factors must have contributed to the exasperation in a general way. All over Europe the economy ran into difficulties during the 1560s. However, in the summer of 1566 food prices in the Netherlands were not particularly high and there is no reason to assume that misery was more acute than previously. It was not misery, it was rather the fear of misery or reduced prosperity that made the lower and middle classes nervous. After a steep rise in wages in the early 1560s, due to the boom following upon the peace of Cateau-Cambrésis in 1559, the economy showed signs of slackening. With grain prices rising and unemployment spreading wages tended to diminish. The middle classes were afraid that the period of rapid and continual expansion that had characterised the early part of the sixteenth century was running out. Economic crisis was felt to be imminent. This may help to explain why the middle classes hardly tried to stop the iconoclastic movement. They felt no loyalty to a Church, a government and a social order so obviously unable to control development and so ignominiously helpless in the face of universal discontent. If anything the riots proved that broad sections of the lower and middle-class population of the Netherlands had become radically estranged from tradition.

It is impossible to generalise about the number of people involved in the act of image-breaking. When taken together the number must of course have been large but except perhaps at the very start in Flanders the disturbances did not take the form of a spontaneous rising of the masses. In some places it is even possible to detect efficiently organised action by fairly small groups of Protestants. However, the suspicion that the whole movement was methodically organised according to a masterplan designed either by the nobles or the Calvinist consistories on a nation-wide scale, has never been substantiated. Furthermore, it is illogical and improbable. Was the actual work of destruction carried out by the Calvinists exclusively? In this matter too it is hard to generalise. What is certain is that in some localities not Calvinist bourgeois but religiously fairly undecided members of the lower classes went to the churches or monasteries and pulled down the images. They did this only rarely for plunder. Of course one must assume that occasionally church property was simply taken away by individuals merely for profit. Essentially, however, the movement was inspired by religious motives which prompted people to destroy, not to steal, valuable pieces. Destruction however was not the ultimate and not the only purpose. After all, churches bared of treasures and images were fit as places of worship for the Calvinists who, in spring and summer perhaps content to gather in the open field, were desperately in need of cover for the coming winter.

The events were perplexing, even for the Calvinists. In 1567 Marnix of St Aldegonde, a young man in his late twenties, a versatile, cosmopolitan humanist converted to Calvinism, who left the Netherlands shortly before Alva's arrival, made an effort to justify them and to reconcile them with Calvinist political doctrine (Document 9). His complicated and revealing argumentation shows the frightening difficulty of the task. But one thing is certain: the movement entailed disastrous consequences both for the Calvinists and for the government of William of Orange. It wrecked the system of the *status quo* which was all the ruling nobles were capable of opposing to Philip's designs. The nobles themselves were aware of this and with few exceptions they joined the regent in hurriedly gathering forces to counter the disorder and social upheaval they feared. In the course of only a few months Margaret succeeded in reinforcing her prestige by carefully and patiently working towards a new understanding with the nobles who, discredited as they were by the events of the summer, she was eager to enlist as supporters of her anti-Protestant policies of law and order. She knew that the nobles had not organised the iconoclastic riots. She found that the majority of those who held government posts were shocked and dismayed by the disorders. She expected that they would be prepared to strengthen her power so as to render similar outbreaks impossible in the future. Document 10 gives a lively picture of the extent of the reaction that set in after the image-breaking.

However, Philip II and his advisers at Madrid interpreted the situation in an altogether different way. In their view the deplorable excesses were obviously planned, and ultimately the political opposition was held responsible for them. As the sovereign's goodwill and his numerous concessions had led to the events of August 1566 it was imperative radically to alter policies. In the autumn of 1566 it was decided to send experienced Spanish troops to the Netherlands where they would be joined by German and Netherlands soldiers; it was intended in this way to gather an army of no less than 60,000 men. The duke of Alva was invited to serve as commander and he agreed to punish mercilessly but justly all political and religious rebels. As usual, however, preparations were slow. In June 1567 Alva and his army left for the Netherlands. On 22 August he arrived at Brussels. Some modern historians tend to regard Philip's policy and Alva's methods of executing it as not only logical and inevitable in view of the circumstances but also legally perfectly correct within the generally accepted standards of that age. This is perhaps true. At any rate, sixteenth-century standards may well have been sufficiently pliable to allow also of the interpretation put upon them by Spanish jurists and soldiers. Yet there are at least three weaknesses in the argument. In the first place, the whole decision to treat the Netherlands in this way was based on a wrong assessment of what had happened. Secondly, large groups (and by no means only Protestant groups) in the Netherlands considered Alva's interpretation of sixteenth-century standards altogether unjustified; to them his rule was a long nightmare of illegal despotism. And finally, whatever the theoretical basis of the new policies, the practical results show with all possible clarity that they were misguided. For in fact they utterly failed.

Ferdinand of Toledo, duke of Alva, soon superseded Margaret, who offered her resignation. He ruled the Netherlands arbitrarily. His principles were simple. Catholic orthodoxy and obedience to the natural sovereign constituted for him self-evident necessities, to depart from which amounted to rebellion. A rebellion having taken place, the sovereign who so far had heeded the privileges of his subjects, now disregarded them in his rightful anger. Of course, he was justified in doing so; privileges after all are not contracts between sovereign and people but gifts generously granted that may be withdrawn should the subjects' behaviour make that advisable. As native officials and judges were unlikely not to abide by what they wrongly considered their ancient rights, Spanish specialists were sent to assist Alva. They worked hard and not inefficiently. A new law court (the notorious *Conseil des Troubles*) was charged with examining all persons involved in the recent disturbances and all heretics. More than two hundred assistants were appointed to assemble material and prepare the lawsuits. At least 12,000 people were summoned; probably thousands were executed or banished; the property of many others was confiscated. But this was no summary jurisdiction. The interminable proceedings of the court which, acting quite fairly within its terms of reference and its prejudices, patiently went through masses of paper and carefully listened to witnesses and informers, added the torture of delay to the cruelty of what many were unable to regard as the law.

It was more difficult for Alva to suspend the traditional checks of consultation and procrastination in the sphere of government and politics than in the administration of law. Some great nobles were arrested and executed; some important towns were forced to have citadels built so as to make it easier for the government to subdue them; old local law was pruned of elements not in accordance with 'the spirit of the time' and an attempt was made to bring all these local laws together into a coherent system. The new episcopal hierarchy was at last established. But as long as taxation was impossible without the consent of the provincial States, the government remained vitally dependent on the goodwill of the subjects. Therefore Alva designed a system of permanent taxes which however he did not succeed in getting entirely accepted by the States. The most important new tax – a ten per cent levy on the sale of all goods – from which Alva expected enormous benefits, was so unpopular that the duke hesitated to force through its introduction. When in 1571 he did so, it not only produced nothing at all, for nobody paid, but contributed to the outbreak of open revolt. The fact is that Alva's system of government, so superficially simple, logical and 'modern', was impracticable and unrealistic because sixteenth-century statesmen did not possess the instruments to impose it. Moreover its implications were considered incompatible with the fundamental needs of the country. The new system isolated the Netherlands, and the effect of the new taxes on trade was greatly feared. It is not surprising that resistance to Alva's regime grew stronger and more effective in proportion as it became more complete and firmly established.

This resistance was essentially different from the opposition to Granvelle during the early 1560s. But it was led by the same man: William of Orange, who fled from the Netherlands to his native Dillenburg in Germany in 1567 and, keeping as closely in touch with the inhabitants of the Netherlands as was possible, tried to increase and organise the fairly widespread but largely latent hostility to Alva. He no longer acted as the greatest noble of the country, or as a man holding responsible posts and as the natural leader of the other noble office-holders. For none of his former colleagues shared his exile. The counts of Egmont and Hoorne who had been his most intimate helpers stayed in the Netherlands. They were immediately arrested and sentenced to death (June 1568), to their complete bewilderment for they had not fully understood the difference between Alva's attitude and that of Margaret. Others, less compromised, collaborated with the duke, although soon with reluctance. It was clear that nearly all the great office-holders were prepared to submit, unwilling to forgo position, wealth and ambitions for the sake of an opposition inevitably becoming more radical.

However, the large body of nobles, not all of them necessarily lower in rank, who held no offices and thus were emotionally as well as practically less closely linked to the government in power, provided William of Orange with many men eager to fight the king's despotic minister. They fled to Germany, to France or to the sea. They formed gangs in the woods. They undertook innumerable raids, robbed churches and monasteries, occasionally cruelly murdering priests and monks, and on the seas they came to be feared as redoubtable privateers (the Sea Beggars). Of course they were not all Calvinists or even Protestants. Neither were they all concerned with high politics or positive ideals. But whatever their motives (and they were doubtless extremely mixed), whatever their social status, whatever the means they used, they all claimed to fight Alva because he was a foreigner trampling upon ancient liberties whether social, political or religious. Although obviously constituting only a small minority of some thousands of men in a total population of two millions and by no means representative of the country's attitudes in general, they developed interesting forms of patriotism that went beyond narrow social pride and particularist conservatism. In the many 'Beggars' Songs' (*Geuzenliederen*) rhymed and sung by members of all creeds and classes in praise of resistance (among them the *Wilhelmus* which was to become the Dutch national hymn), the old, noble, dearly loved fatherland, now deprived of its ancient freedom, was bemoaned and glorified.

The Beggars were not popular. Nor at this time was William of Orange. Various endeavours made by him and his brothers to rouse the population dismally failed; his raids into the Netherlands supported by relatively large but undisciplined mercenary troops were unsuccessful, meeting with practically no response from the people. He was clearly a Protestant now, a sort of Lutheran but surrounded by Calvinist advisers and helpers. Although not yet a Calvinist himself he began to appreciate the vigour and tenacity of a sect that in easier days he had despised. Was he a revolutionary fighting his natural sovereign? He denied this. He did not fight his sovereign but the sovereign's evil adviser, Alva. He had not only the right but the duty to do this because as a loyal vassal of the king he was under an obligation to keep good order in the country for which in his capacity of great nobleman he was responsible and obviously there is nothing more disastrous for a sovereign than to see his dominions being ruined. Thus by fighting Alva, William of Orange did not sever his feudal tie with Philip II. On the contrary it was this feudal connection which justified his taking up arms against Alva whose government was unconstitutional and thus rebellious (Document 11).

Even if this is an acceptable argument it clearly did not serve as a means to justify armed resistance by the inhabitants generally and neither could the *Joyeuse Entrée* be used in that way. In that famous document of 1356 the duke of Brabant allowed his subjects to suspend obedience to him as long as he did not govern them according to the conditions they had mutually agreed upon. William of Orange referred to this document repeatedly but never to explain why he took up arms. When he left the Netherlands in 1567 he emphasised that he suspended obedience and responsibility – he gave up his offices provisionally – because Alva's system was a departure from traditional rule. But if the *Joyeuse Entrée* could not be used as propaganda for William of Orange's attempts to win the population of the Netherlands for his policy of armed resistance, what arguments were then thought relevant? A characteristic attempt to justify violence is found in Document 12 (1568) in which various contradictory arguments appear. After a hasty reference to the *Joyeuse Entrée* the author states that there are urban privileges which permit the towns to resist by force not only the servants of the sovereign but also the sovereign himself if he is waging war upon them. But the author then finds that it is the Spanish intruders who are waging war upon the benevolent sovereign and that the inhabitants of the Netherlands are obliged to interfere in this struggle and support him against Alva. This was a promising line of attack. If pushed somewhat further, or rather, if translated into abstract terms, the argument might run thus: the prince is the personification of sovereignty; sovereignty and constitution are not opposites, indeed they are identical. If a man acts contrary to the constitution, as Alva was obviously doing, he undermines the basis of sovereignty and attacks the sovereign. It is then the duty of the loyal subjects – subjects to the sovereign constitution personified by the king – to punish him for this and to prevent him by all possible means from perpetuating his crimes.

Geldorp, the author of the memorandum of 1571 entitled *Belgicae liberandae ab Hispanis hypodeixis* (Document 13) did not concern himself with such theoretical subtleties. Here Alva appears in the role of the god-less tyrant sent by God to punish the people for their sins. But this is past history; tyranny is meant by God to be temporary and short-lived. After allowing the tyrant to perpetrate his misdeeds God helps the repentant people to overthrow him by debilitating his power. The prince of Orange is called by God to serve as deliverer of the Netherlands and all his acts, whether successful or unsuccessful from the limited viewpoint of human observers, may be trusted to be necessary steps towards the ultimate liberation. It is the people's duty to deliver the final blow and the moment has come. Geldorp developed a detailed plan of attack. For strategic and more general reasons he advised concentrating on Holland and with remarkable, almost prophetic lucidity but in desperately pedantic Latin, he foresaw the emergence of a free, independent and prosperous community that would lead the other provinces to throw off the yoke or to decline. Obviously his simplistic belief in God's support, his refusal to worry about constitutional complications, his firm conviction that God had already started wrecking Alva's and probably Spanish rule in general inspired Geldorp with a vivid sense of reality.

In 1572 Alva's régime collapsed, although the general attack on the Netherlands planned by William of Orange and his brothers in collabora-tion with the French Huguenots could not be carried out after the

massacre on the eve of St Bartholomew's day at Paris (23–4 August 1572).
Already well before that night a number of towns had, to use the expres-
sion of the time, gone over to the prince of Orange. The first was Brill in
the province of Holland where on 1 April some hundreds of Sea Beggars
established themselves, after being forced by Queen Elizabeth to leave the
English ports. Soon they captured a number of neighbouring towns, and
in the course of the following weeks and months towns in all the northern
provinces; some in Flanders and Brabant also received rebel garrisons.
North of the big rivers about fifty towns were at some stage involved in the
movement. It would be rash to make generalisations about the way in
which they decided upon their defection, for obviously there was a great
variety of motives and methods, depending on the local situation as well
as on the very rapidly and wildly changing circumstances in the country
generally. Yet despite many local differences it seems possible to detect a
sort of common pattern.

One major factor without which the whole movement would have been
altogether impossible is just as manifest as it is difficult to describe with
any precision. It is the general disillusionment with Alva's system of
government. Not only Protestants, but Catholics also who had welcomed
him as a vigorous statesman capable of bringing law and order after the
excesses of the iconoclastic riots, were now eager to see him depart.
Everywhere the Spanish troops were felt to be an unbearable burden, not
merely because they were Spanish but simply because they were troops.
The new taxes were thought to prove Alva's utter indifference to the
welfare of the country. It was humiliating to see Spanish officials taking
the crucial decisions, often overriding ancient customs. In many towns,
especially in those where the iconoclastic riots had occurred late and only
in a mild form so that Alva had not found it necessary to purge the urban
administrations and appoint people dependent on him alone, there was no
important group which felt itself really tied to his cause.

However, the urban rulers acted hardly anywhere as the initiators of the
revolt. Frequently the stimulus setting the process in motion came from
outside the towns, just as in 1566 when the iconoclastic epidemic was
carried by enthusiasts from area to area. But apparently Sea Beggar bands
appearing before the gates of the various towns commanded sufficient
support within them to leave most administrations no choice but to open
the gates or risk potentially dangerous disturbances. Although in many
cases some force was needed to persuade the magistrates of the seriousness
of the situation, their reluctance to fight and their willingness to compromise with the rebels gave the whole development the semblance of

spontaneous revolt and prevented it from taking the form of outright civil war. This fact was of momentous importance. In this way the local patricians escaped the social revolution which might well have occurred had they shown greater determination to offer resistance to the Sea Beggars and the very mixed groups in the towns – Calvinists, petty bourgeois, fishermen, workmen, unemployed – who supported them. Unwittingly they thus prepared themselves for the preponderant rôle they were destined to play in the aristocratic Dutch Republic.

Alva's reaction to the revolts was fairly slow. From May to September he was busy reconquering Mons in the Southern Netherlands which William of Orange's brother Louis had taken. With the fall of Mons – a town which would have opened the way for the French if the St Bartholomew's eve disaster had not occurred – Louis's campaign was abruptly terminated. Meanwhile the prince himself, not yet informed of the massacre in Paris, crossed the river Maas on 27 August, was welcomed by some southern towns but had to retreat hastily when Alva turned to attack him. He dissolved his army, and the Spaniards had no difficulty in taking Mechlin which was punished for its defection in an 'exemplary way'. The army then moved to the Northern Netherlands where it was left to Alva's son Frederick to restore order. In the beginning Frederick did not meet with greater obstacles than execrable autumn weather and impracticable roads. The towns of Overijssel and Gelderland which, willingly or unwillingly, had sided with William of Orange submitted at the approach of his formidable army. Zutphen was systematically plundered. From there Frederick led his troops to Holland. After taking Naarden and killing its inhabitants he reached Amsterdam at the beginning of December. Amsterdam was still loyal to the government and had not opened its gates to the Sea Beggars. Meanwhile the prince of Orange had decided to take refuge in Holland and Zeeland, a desperate decision, in his own view, for he expected to die defending his last stronghold. Going by ship from Kampen over the Zuyder Zee he arrived on 20 October in Enkhuizen.

By far the most remarkable element in this confusing series of events was the speed and the determination with which the opposition in Holland managed to set up a government of its own. This can only be explained by the long tradition of particularism and the old-fashioned pattern of the so-called Burgundian state which, while superimposing a federal structure upon the old institutions, had refrained from destroying or providing substitutes for them. The institutions, regulations, instruments and habits of mind needed for the provincial government to act independently were available and the rebels – to use a term wholly un-acceptable to them – readily took them over. But it was to William of Orange, a tactful as well as a most obstinate man, to his pride as a great nobleman and his experience in government and in international affairs that they owed the knowledge of how to take advantage of the possibilities open to them.

In June 1572 William of Orange addressed himself to the inhabitants of Holland and Zeeland in a highly rhetorical pamphlet (Document 14) in which he claimed to be responsible for the fatherland generally and the patrimonial provinces in particular, and for Holland, Zeeland, and the bishopric of Utrecht in the first place. Alva was once again depicted as a foreign despot whose rule could not legally be regarded as emanating from Philip II's sovereign will. Moreover William had already hinted that he should still be considered stadholder of the three provinces since he had never received an official letter of dismissal after his departure in 1567. He promised freedom of religion in those areas where his troops were allowed to enter and a representative form of government under the king's direct guidance. Meanwhile he asked the inhabitants to swear allegiance to him not so much as stadholder but in the most general possible way as 'patron of the fatherland and champion of freedom'. In July 1572 his position in Holland was more precisely defined. The States of the province met at Dordrecht and allowed Marnix of St Aldegonde to attend as William of Orange's deputy. Representatives of the nobility, the Sea Beggars, and no less than twelve towns – more than usual – were present, but the meeting was nonetheless necessarily incomplete: Amsterdam and other towns usually taking part in meetings of the States were absent. On behalf of William of Orange Marnix read a long and detailed paper (Document 15).

Both the meeting of the States and William of Orange's attitude to them have been differently interpreted: some historians consider the procedure revolutionary and praise it for that while others emphasise the legal basis on which the opposition to the government still sought to place itself. This discussion is somewhat unnecessary. Obviously the king, still recognised as sovereign, did not want the States to meet without his permission, but there were precedents for the States to refer to; and no States of any province had ever admitted being totally subject to the sovereign's will and command. William of Orange, on his part, confined himself to restating the position he had taken in previous years. As a grandee of the realm he was obliged to protect the Netherlands and even to act as its chief in the king's absence. Two new elements, however, appeared.

William of Orange now explicitly asked to be recognised as governor of the provinces which he had ruled as the king's stadholder before 1567 and moreover he refused to admit the legality of what had happened since. But secondly he asked for a formal alliance between himself and the States of Holland as representatives of the people. This was a remarkable request and perhaps difficult to justify constitutionally. If in Holland he was only taking up his old office as the king's lieutenant or stadholder again, what then permitted him to enter into a kind of contract with the king's subjects?

There was another vital point upon which the States had to decide: religion. Marnix was instructed by the prince to make a proposal which had been left out of his written instruction. The States endorsed this and declared that both Protestants and Catholics should be allowed to hold private and public religious services in their houses and in churches allocated to them by the urban administrations and that the ecclesiastics should be left in their state and not molested unless they proved hostile. For this, of course, there was no constitutional precedent. The States may well have reasoned that toleration was somehow in accordance with the spirit of the constitution and that, as sovereignty and constitution were inseparable in the Netherlands, their edict was in accordance with sovereignty too. Thus in an abstract way it emanated from the sovereign, Philip II. In a document of 1573 (Document 17) in which William of Orange and the States of Holland write that they go down on their knees and pray the sovereign in all humility to listen to their supplication, they state explicitly that they are fighting for freedom of conscience. Obviously, humility, obedience, and some form of religious freedom ordained by the States were even then considered reconcilable. Moreover in July 1572 the States were careful to add that their toleration edict was provisional until – as was stated in a rather obscure phrase – matters might later be arranged differently on the advice of the States General of the country. This was in line with the policy of the nobles before 1567, when they had repeatedly asked for a meeting of the States General to discuss religion.

From 1572 to 1576 Holland and Zeeland fought an apparently hopeless war in almost complete isolation. They were extremely small. Holland's population is estimated at 260,000 inhabitants in 1514 and 700,000 a century later, but the most rapid increase occurred probably well after the 1570s; Zeeland was of course much smaller. How could such tiny states withstand the attacks of the Spanish Empire? Yet the Spanish troops which in December 1572 arrived at Amsterdam and were able to take Haarlem in 1573, thereby cutting Holland into two halves, failed even after long sieges to capture either Alkmaar or Leyden. The relief of Leyden in October 1574 was made the more remarkable by the decision of the stadholder and the States to establish in 1575 a university in that town as a reward for its courage. In various ways this was highly characteristic. The University Charter stated that the new institution was being founded by the only person legally entitled to do so, the sovereign, Philip II, whose stadholder William of Orange was merely acting on his behalf. The university was designed to compete with the two universities already existing in the Netherlands, Louvain and Douai, both of course Catholic. Naturally one of its main functions was to be the training of Protestant ministers and theologians but this was not its sole or even its primary task. It was explicitly stated that the institution would serve as a firm support of the liberty and legal government of the country not only in matters religious but in all matters of common interest to the population. Thus Holland created a School, truly humanist in character, which it was hoped would turn out the many-sided, broadly educated men who were needed to administer the emerging state. In the midst of a war, the nature of which remained uncertain as long as Holland and Zeeland refused to claim independence, Holland decided to train an élite by which it could be ruled competently. Calvinism and classicism, joined into a Calvinist humanism which was felt to constitute a harmonious unity of history and religion, made a small provincial university and the state that was gradually but almost unintentionally taking shape, characteristic products of the Northern Renaissance. Indeed the Northern Netherlands remained loyal to the Renaissance, its literary style and its language, well into the nineteenth century, long after other European nations had abandoned it. For centuries to come Humanism was to be the tissue of Dutch national existence.

Appallingly alone among men absorbed by local affairs and unwilling to look beyond the narrow boundaries of their towns or provinces, William's vision of future autonomy for the whole or the greater part of the Nether-lands remained so broad that he was never really in danger of degenerating into a mere guerilla leader or *condottiere*. However, occasionally he seemed to identify himself completely with his environment, seemed so sceptical about the possibility of winning a foothold in the other provinces that he was prepared to abandon them to the French king if France helped secure Holland's and Zeeland's virtual independence and Protestantism (1573), and was so proud at Holland's perseverance that the tones in which he praised the nation sound truly patriotic (Document 19). But ultimately the obvious need to expand the revolt and to break Holland's isolation, as well as his status as Brabant nobleman and the whole nature of the federal Burgundian government (to the traditions of which he remained faithful throughout his life), made him an ardent anti-particularist, if this word, merely used to avoid the anachronistic term 'nationalist', is permitted.

During these years the war, initially fought by Holland against a Spanish general, often took the form of a struggle between Holland and the rest of the Netherlands. The term 'domestic war' actually appears in a document of 1573 (Document 16) which was addressed by the States of Holland to the States General of the 'obedient' provinces meeting at Brussels and in which the terrible effects of the situation were depicted in some detail. In 1573 the problem of civil war was also discussed in letters exchanged between William of Orange and Marnix. The latter had been taken prisoner by the Spaniards, that is, by troops commanded by the Walloon nobleman, Noircarmes, whom William of Orange knew very well before 1567 as a member of the Golden Fleece. Marnix was obviously totally discouraged and deeply impressed by the fact that he found himself among compatriots. He advised the prince to make peace and tried to prove with numerous historical examples assembled with great humanist scholarship that civil war has always led to material destruction and spiritual degeneration. William of Orange refused to consider capitulation (Document 18); moreover he refused to keep to himself this personal correspondence with one of his most intimate collaborators and declared that he would make his decision depend upon the advice of the States of Holland. Shortly afterwards he wrote to Noircarmes, who had offered to act as an intermediary between the rebels and the Brussels government, that he and his friends should have offered such virtuous services long ago. Meanwhile Philip II changed his tactics. He dismissed Alva and ordered his successor, Requesens, to bring about a reconciliation through moderation in all except religious matters. This was obviously intended as an attempt to enhance confidence in the 'obedient' provinces and to persuade them to fight the Hollanders or at any rate to provide financial and diplomatic means for such a war.

The Hollanders attacked Requesens in a pamphlet addressed to the States of the loyal provinces (Document 20). They praised William of Orange highly as a man much more dignified and of much nobler lineage than Requesens and thus more acceptable as a ruler. They depicted the king as totally dependent on the inquisitors who prevented him from carrying his personal plans into effect. In doing so the States made a clear distinction between the king as a person – a sovereign whose sovereignty was doubtful because he was not free – and the king as the sovereign guarantee of the ancient constitution. This was a brave attempt at clarification and could, if carried on consistently, have led to theoretically coherent conclusions. However, the author of the text did not need to go further. He did not ask the loyal provinces to start armed resistance but merely not to obey and not to support Requesens. And this he was entitled to justify by the usual reference to the *Joyeuse Entrée*. In the same year another author put forward an interesting theory about the ancient unity of the Netherlands and their right to hold meetings of the States General, emphasising both their common constitutional laws and their solidarity (Document 21).

Thus the supporters of William of Orange tried to prove that they were not fighting a civil war against the provinces loyal to the legitimate and conciliatory government of Requesens but were defending a constitution common to the whole of the Netherlands which notwithstanding its often disturbed history and its inner conflicts did form one country. All this served as a basis for negotiations with the Orangist party which were started by Requesens in February 1575 in Breda. He started them without the authorisation of Philip II but thought them necessary because the loyal provinces refused to support him effectively and Spanish finances were once again in a most terrible plight; in fact in September 1575 Philip II declared himself bankrupt and thus wrecked the little credit he might still have had in financial circles in the Netherlands. Requesens's desperate attempt failed; it could only have succeeded if Philip II had admitted defeat, sent away the Spanish troops and granted toleration. Of course the Orangists knew this well enough. For them the negotiations were a marvellous opportunity to make propaganda (cf. Document 22), especially as the emperor had sent an ambassador to attend the discussions and even to plead in favour of the so-called rebels.

In July 1575 the States of Holland considered for the first time a proposal 'that one ought soon to abandon the king as a tyrant who sought to oppress and destroy his subjects, and to seek another protector'. On 13 October they decided unanimously 'that one ought to forsake the king and seek foreign assistance, referring the choice to the prince who with regard to the form of government was previously to take the opinion of the States.'[1] In November the States appointed some deputies to go to England and offer Queen Elizabeth sovereignty over Holland and Zeeland under certain conditions later to be decided upon. It is most interesting to compare this first attempt to obtain foreign assistance by offering a form of 'sovereignty' with the various occasions later when this was done in a more sophisticated way. Of course Queen Elizabeth refused the offer and soon circumstances changed so dramatically that it was unnecessary to repeat it.

On 5 March 1576 Requesens died suddenly. The position of the king's officials in the Netherlands, with no money to pay the army, no prestige and no prospect of rapid success in any sphere, was extremely weak. The Spanish troops, left unpaid for a long time, mutinied, ransacking Flanders and Brabant. By the end of July they had concentrated their forces in Alost, from where they threatened both Brussels and Ghent. Meanwhile William of Orange made the most effective possible use of his old connections. He carried on an extensive correspondence with leading personalities in the Southern Netherlands while his agents launched a veritable propaganda campaign for the defence of the common father-land. In September the Orangists of Brussels, most of them Roman Catholics who were now prepared to oppose the king, forced the Council of State, which might be considered entitled to take up the government in the absence of a governor, to call the States General. In October representatives of this body went to Ghent to discuss with representatives of Holland and Zeeland ways and means of driving the dangerous Spanish troops away. Holland's position was very strong. Indeed the mainly Roman Catholic States General (to which Holland and Zeeland sent no delegates) badly needed the Calvinists' experienced troops to control the mutineers whose excesses, especially those perpetrated on 4 November at Antwerp, convinced even the most reluctant that something ought to be done. Thus on 8 November the so-called Pacification of Ghent was signed, a real peace between the two Protestant provinces and the rest.

The Ghent peace (Document 23) was a declaration by the majority that they would join Holland and Zeeland in their fight against the Spanish military. It brought to an end the civil war which had disrupted the Netherlands since 1572 and which it was too dangerous to continue in the catastrophic circumstances of 1576. Its weakness was that it neither could, nor did solve any of the fundamental problems. For it was left to a future meeting of the States General, to be called after the actual purpose of the Pacification had been achieved – that is, after the departure of the Spanish troops – to take decisions about how to organise the Netherlands and how definitely to settle the religious disputes. Provisionally all edicts against heresy were suspended. For the time being both groups of provinces remained essentially separate, Holland and Zeeland being allowed to keep the authorities and the form of government which had developed there since 1572 but not to spread either its religion or its political idiosyncrasies over the territory of the States General. William of

Orange's success, immense though it was, remained dangerously restricted.

The next three years showed how fatal the restrictions were in fact. It turned out to be relatively easy to get rid of the Spanish troops; at any rate, Don John of Austria, the newly appointed governor who, though with reservations (see Documents 24 and 25), subscribed to the Peace of Ghent, was prepared to send them away. At the same time however the States General allowed him to interpret the religious paragraphs of the Pacification in a way wholly unacceptable to Holland and Zeeland. Not that they suffered from such an anti-Calvinist interpretation; Don John had no power to prevent them from perpetuating their own religious policy which had developed rapidly since 1572 in an anti-Catholic direction. The principle of toleration originally accepted in July 1572 was not put into effect and the Roman Catholic majority of the population had not been granted the freedom to hold public services. Thus Holland and Zeeland feared not so much that Don John would attack them but that the precarious compromise of Ghent would break down immediately after the departure of the Spanish troops and they would then be driven back into their isolation. Document 25 shows how cautiously they reacted to the unpleasant information from Brussels in February 1577; it also shows their disappointment when the States General failed to take advantage of the situation to follow ancestral examples and wring further constitutional concessions from the impotent sovereign. It is interesting to see how, after all the discussion of the previous years about armed resistance, toleration and other subjects, it was still possible in an official document written by, one would have thought, mature rebels, to adopt such a naïve, almost childishly innocent attitude towards constitutional issues.

It was humiliating for Don John to be recognised by the States General only after subscribing to their conditions; from his point of view moreover the whole procedure was probably unconstitutional. He soon found that his concessions served no worthwhile purpose and did not increase his prestige and power. He remained in Brussels for only a short time, then went to Mechlin, and on 24 July 1577 took the citadel of Namur by surprise with his bodyguard. Waiting for the return of troops he had sent away at the beginning of the year, he ordered the States General in Brussels to expel suspect people – that is, Protestants – from their meeting and to help him fight William of Orange. He justified this policy in a document of August 1577 (Document 26) which, although by no means unrealistic, was much too simple to increase the number of his supporters. Of course he was right in stating that ultimately, to oppose him was tantamount to

opposing the sovereign and the maintenance of Roman Catholicism as the
only tolerated religion, but if that was true, what then was the significance
of the treaties and accords which he had concluded with the States
General and repeated that he was willing to stand by? In Document 27
Marnix of Saint Aldegonde refuted Don John's arguments. Not only had
the governor broken the treaties he referred to, he was also shown to have
misunderstood the position of the States General. They appear in Marnix's
text – as they do in the important and elaborate pamphlet of 1579 printed
here as Document 41 – as the lower magistrates of French Calvinist
theory, representatives of the three estates and thus of the body of the
common people and called not only by men but also by God to protect
the constitution. This emphasis on the divine origin of the States General
as well as on its representative character on the French pattern is interesting. In fact of course the States General of the Netherlands formed
a meeting of representatives not of the estates but of the provinces;
and in some provinces all three of the estates were not represented. Long
before 1572 the clergy had ceased to attend the States of Holland; in
Flanders the nobility did not send deputies to the States. Marnix simpli-
fied matters considerably in order to inflate the importance of the States
General and to justify the thesis that even in matters of war and peace the
sovereign was dependent on their decision. Finally Marnix drew from the
Joyeuse Entrée the conclusion that it was the duty of the States General to
take arms against a stadholder of the sovereign who attacked the country.
This adventurous conclusion was not this time accompanied by the assurance that of course royal sovereignty and the royal person was left
out of all discussion. Political theory was slowly abandoning the old
positions.

So did political practice. Don John's display of determination had the
effect of increasing William's popularity in the provinces taking part in
the States General. In September 1577 the prince left Holland; he was
rapturously welcomed in Antwerp on 18 September and five days later in
Brussels. But he was not without enemies. For more than ten years the
high nobility had been divided into groups either loyal to the royal
government, indifferent to it, or openly hostile. William of Orange did
find far more support among men of his own rank in 1577 than he had in
1567 but the majority still refused to go as far as he did. The noble
families which had traditionally been supported by the Burgundian
central government and owed to this their position in the state, now found
that the eclipse of Burgundian power symbolised by the Pacification
brought their own decline. The Walloon nobility in particular, used to

playing a preponderant rôle in the Burgundian state, was alarmed to see how after 1576 power reverted to the towns of Flanders and Brabant and to the 'rebels' in Holland, that is, to what they called 'democracies' and Calvinists, both of them Dutch-speaking. William of Orange was obviously the leader of that 'democratic' party and he was profoundly suspected even by those nobles who did not dare to side with what remained of the Spanish government. They tried to solve their dilemma by calling Archduke Matthias to the Netherlands. Matthias, a rather incompetent boy of twenty, but a brother of the emperor and a cousin of Philip II, was persuaded to come and preserve the Netherlands for the Habsburg dynasty and for the Roman Catholic faith. Although this was intended as a move against William of Orange, the prince arranged for the archduke to be officially installed by the States General as governor of the Netherlands after Don John had been declared an enemy of the country. Politically this was ingenious but fundamentally it was unsatisfactory manoeuvring on a small scale; the constitutional consequences and implications however were of decisive importance.

On 8 December 1577 the States General voted the resolution by which they recognised Matthias as governor general – although only provisionally until the king's consent was received – if he subscribed to a number of conditions (Document 28). The list of conditions was formidable. Matthias was made much more dependent on the States General than any governor before him. All his initiatives, political, fiscal, legislative, needed the approval of the States General or the provinces which sent delegates to the States General. The States appeared in the treaty as a truly independent body provided with extensive rights not only of control but of government. It was they who appointed and dismissed the governor's council; it was they to whom the ultimate decision on all matters of any importance reverted. Of course much of what was achieved here on paper was part of the whole set of traditional claims put forward by late medieval and sixteenth-century parliaments; but on the other hand it is quite clear that the States went much further than sixteenth-century practice in the Netherlands allowed. The new system was obviously incompatible with the form of government inaugurated by Charles V. In this respect it is significant that Marnix, who used to write down what he actually thought, told one of his correspondents in February 1577 that as far as he was concerned the reign of Charles V was far from satisfactory, and was on the contrary, the origin of most evil. How great indeed had the distance between the late and the early sixteenth century become was shown by the resolution voted by the States General on 10 December 1577 (Document

29). This pertained to the religious issue that had been carefully omitted from the proposed treaty with Matthias. If he wanted to be accepted as governor he would also have to approve of the new resolution even though it was highly favourable to the Protestants. In effect the Catholic members of the States General agreed to interpret the Pacification of Ghent in the widest possible sense as implying that the Catholic provinces would not allow anyone – and of course Don John was meant more specifically – to attack Holland and Zeeland on religious grounds; in other words they promised to help the Protestant provinces with armed force, if necessary, to maintain their Protestantism. Even if this was a logical consequence of the Pacification of Ghent it was nevertheless rather an improbable one.

Meanwhile Don John waited impatiently for the Spanish soldiery; as soon as a few thousands had returned he marched from Luxemburg, where he had taken refuge, in the direction of Brussels. At Gembloux he met a much larger army raised by the States General, but thanks to the genius of his commander, Alexander Farnese, prince of Parma, the only son of the former regent Margaret of Parma, and the dismal incompetence of his enemies, he had no difficulty in crushing it (31 January 1578). On 13 February Louvain allowed Spanish troops to enter its gates; on 14 February the States General and Matthias were persuaded by William of Orange to follow him to Antwerp. Parma marched into the Walloon provinces and achieved success after success. In Artois the States started considering ways to secede from the States General and make peace with the king. On the other hand the opposition was also hardening its attitude in the field of theory. In March 1578 Marnix answered one of Don John's declarations with a furious pamphlet in which he emphasised the absurdity of trying to maintain Roman Catholicism by force (Document 30). Marnix was probably also responsible for a declaration of the States General published on the same day by Plantin's (Document 31). This was a diatribe of unusual violence not because its rhetoric or argument differed from innumerable previous declarations and pamphlets but because the traditional clear distinction between king and evil ministers was omitted. Apparently the king had taken the wrong side in the conflict between his loyal subjects and his bad advisers. Facts showed that contrary to all that had been said previously he was actually capable of doing wrong. This was further developed in a booklet so daring that it was thought safer to pretend that it was written by a German nobleman (Document 32). Loyal Netherlanders, it seems, were not yet supposed to be so radical; they confined themselves to printing, circulating and pondering such ideas. The author stated implicitly what the States General suggested discreetly: Philip II was a tyrant who was in the process of being deposed by public authority. The logical consequence was to look no longer for a governor agreeable to the States General – that is Matthias – but for a new sovereign – that is the duke of Anjou with whom William of Orange and the States General were indeed negotiating at that time. The author asked whether this was rebellion and naturally answered that it was not. Rebellion is anarchy, it is the negation of sovereignty. The inhabitants of the Netherlands could not be accused of attacking the principle of sovereignty for they were merely trying to get the right sovereign.

The fundamental infirmity in such an argument is of course that it fails to indicate the content of sovereignty. Anjou was represented as a particularly suitable candidate because his weakness and his lack of knowledge would prevent him from giving his government a personal character. On such a low level of abstraction it was clearly impossible to reach firm conclusions of a more general nature. Here the question arises why indeed the problem of sovereignty was dealt with so indifferently in the Netherlands whereas in France it was in similar circumstances discussed with clarity and perspicacity. Perhaps one among many reasons needs some emphasis. For French jurists, particularly Bodin, the reinterpretation of sovereignty as a dynamic concept was essential in justifying the enactment of toleration edicts. If the sovereign were to be allowed to introduce toleration, by definition a departure from tradition, it was imperative to enquire in what capacity he exercised such a novel right. Judicial sovereignty in the old sense with its implied conservatism obliged the sovereign to preserve religion in its ancient form; however, the French sovereign was obviously doing more than this. Here the concept of legislative sovereignty was extremely useful. If the main characteristic of sovereignty is the right to make new law, it is not difficult to see why the king has the right to enjoin toleration. However, for obvious reasons, in the Netherlands the problem never presented itself in this manner as the sovereign persisted in opposing any form of toleration. This prevented his subjects from studying the matter in the French way. For them toleration, rationalised in political terms, was supposed to flow from the ancient constitution and to be one of the manifold traditional rights and liberties enjoyed by the inhabitants and guaranteed in contracts with the sovereign. In Documents 33, 41, 43, 48, 53 etc. toleration is defended as an old privilege, as a practical solution to a difficult problem, as a fundamental right given by God to all men, but it was not seen as a legal issue needing profound analysis in political theory.

In practice the religious problem grew to unmanageable proportions; the tortuous interpretations of the Pacification of Ghent – there are various striking instances in the texts – indicate the complexity of the situation. Document 34 makes the confusion, intellectual as well as material, into which matters were falling almost palpable. It comes from Ghent where the Calvinists succeeded in 1578 in establishing a Protestant administration with semi-dictatorial power. They gradually conquered the major part of Flanders. Such a development was not foreseen in the Pacification of 1576. According to that treaty the Calvinists of Holland were forbidden to propagate their religion outside their province; apparently this was then considered a sufficient guarantee for the preservation of Roman Catholicism in the other provinces. But everywhere the edicts against heresy were suspended. Both articles now proved inadequate. Ghent Calvinism was of a radicalism politically and spiritually more intransigent than that of Holland. Document 34 shows how deeply the rulers of Ghent distrusted even William of Orange and his association with the Catholic Frenchman, the duke of Anjou. In Document 35 one of the Ghent Calvinists objects to the interpretation of the Pacification as implying the exclusive maintenance of Roman Catholicism outside Holland and Zeeland. But in doing so he went a long way towards ruining the principle of toleration itself. Meanwhile William of Orange desperately sought to establish what was called a *Religions-vrede* or *Religions-Frid*, a half or wholly German word meaning religious peace (cf. Document 36).

Possibly the reason why this technical term was derived from the German was simply that the concept was not yet familiar in the Netherlands where no federal authority had until then made any positive pronouncement on the religious issue. In the summer of 1578 William of Orange tried in vain to make the States General promulgate an edict allowing the public exercise of both religions in all villages if the majority of the population wanted this and in all towns if it was desired by a hundred families. It was – as appears clearly from Documents 38 and 40 – far from certain that this was reconcilable with the Pacification of Ghent. But undoubtedly it was an interesting compromise between imposing toleration by the States General (which William of Orange endeavoured to transform into a parliament overruling the legal and political autonomy of the provinces), and making it dependent on the will of the inhabitants themselves: those who wanted toleration had to ask for it and to prove that they were numerous enough to come within the terms of the law. But the States General categorically refused to play the rôle William of Orange tried to prescribe for them. They had no ambition to act as a federal legislative and confined themselves to inviting Governor Matthias to lay William of Orange's proposal before the various provincial States. This was virtually the end of the initiative. Neither the Protestant nor most of the Roman Catholic provinces were prepared to forsake their preference for religious uniformity.

Not only religious disputes, but also social forces, old political idio-syncrasies, antagonism between Walloons and Flemings, feuds between rival noble families were potent factors that ruined William of Orange's vision of the Netherlands as a sort of federal state ruled by the States General under the guidance of a benevolent and virtually powerless sovereign. It was a generous vision but impossible to realise in the cir-cumstances. Its essential weakness was that the state to which William of Orange was seeking to give substance was not at all intended by him as a peaceful 'liberal' society but as an instrument of bitter war. The unity upon which he laid so much emphasis was a means to carry on hostilities with greater determination and effect (cf. Document 39); but in that very respect it was totally inadequate. At the beginning of 1579 the well-known Unions of Arras and Utrecht formalised the process of separatism which had set in earlier. On 6 January 1579 the provincial States of Artois and Hainault and the city of Douai signed a solemn declaration known as the Union of Arras, in which they swore allegiance to the Pacification of Ghent interpreted in the strictly Roman Catholic sense Don John had also given it; in May they negotiated peace with the duke of Parma who had acted as governor of the Netherlands since the death of Don John in October 1578. Of course this was a capitulation but on terms highly favourable for people who had after all taken part in what the Spanish court doubtless still considered a rebellion. Parma was willing to exclude all 'foreign' interference in local business; posts and responsibilities were reserved for native people; it was even ex-plicitly stated that the system of government prevailing under Charles V and highly idealised in the early stages of the Revolt would be restored. This was a re-enactment of the success of 1564 when Philip II had given in to the noble opposition and sent Granvelle away but with the decisive difference that there was no question of dismissing Parma. On the con-trary, the peace greatly strengthened the power of that remarkable man. The attempt to return completely to the situation of 1564 and to reappoint Alexander of Parma's mother, Margaret, as regent was thwarted by her son who refused to abandon power. Document 46, inspired by this plan which was, ironically enough, strongly supported by Granvelle who was again in favour at the Madrid Court, is an example of the sort of propaganda forthcoming from the loyalist camp and it is characteristic in that it shows that polemics and argumentation of that party were much lower in quality than those of the 'revolutionary' party. (Compare Document 56.)

The Union signed at Utrecht on 29 January 1579 (Document 37) was a totally different affair although it also purported to be an extension of the Pacification of Ghent. It was joined by all the northern provinces with Flanders and Brabant as associate members. It was a formal alliance of provinces acting as if they were independent states, and deciding to integrate their foreign policies and war efforts through a fairly loose federation in order to defend their individual independence and traditional customs. It is noteworthy that the first article according to which the provinces should hold together as if they were only one province goes on to state that the purpose of this is to preserve their separate identity. Even the ancient rights and customs were recognised as essentially local and were not supposed to be parts of one general abstract constitution as had been done in the period when William of Orange's propaganda endeavoured to sustain the unity of the country. On the other hand, this restricted number of provinces, associated in a union freely entered upon, sought ways to establish a more coherent form of federal government than the States General had achieved. The most striking innovations, however – majority decisions, full powers of delegates to the assembly, federal taxation etc. – were in fact not put into effect. What did indeed happen soon after 1579 was that Parma succeeded in occupying most of the Southern Netherlands with the result that the provinces which remained members of the general Union were virtually the same as those associated in the Union of Utrecht. As early as the summer of 1580 the States General recognised the Treaty of Utrecht as binding upon them: Gradually the Union of Utrecht was merged into the general Union, and in the process the attempt to revise and simplify the method of reaching binding decisions was largely abandoned. It was the traditional methods of the States General rather than the innovations of the Union of Utrecht that were consecrated as constitutional dogma in the state of the Northern Netherlands although, to complicate matters, the Utrecht Treaty was often later regarded as fundamental Dutch law.

Meanwhile it had become almost impossible to maintain that the States General, the Union of Utrecht, their officials and army were still acting as loyal subjects of the king. In 1579 it was stated in an authoritative pamphlet (Document 38) that it was unnecessary to respect the king's opinions in matters relating to the Low Countries. At the same time negotiations with the duke of Anjou were going on (cf. Document 42) and they explicitly concerned the appointment not of a new governor as in the case of Matthias but of a new 'sovereign'. Obviously in 1579 the prevailing view was that Philip II had lost, or was rapidly losing, his sovereignty because as a tyrant he had become an enemy of the state. As a result the sovereignty in the Netherlands was somehow vacant. It is not altogether clear what actually happened then. Probably the States General argued that they, allegedly elected by the people to guard the constitution, were entitled to hold in trust a sovereignty which, as it was inseparable from and possibly identical with the constitution, was something permanent that did not evaporate with the person who lost it. In no way did they suggest that Philip II's lost sovereignty reverted to the people and their representatives, the States General. This would have implied a concept of sovereignty still alien to this generation not so much because it approached the idea of popular sovereignty – after all, a sufficiently traditional theory – but because it was too precise and definitive. Even popular sovereignty in this sense and form can be more coherent and creative than what the States General were looking for at this time. In fact they merely wanted a French protector who would provide them with military, financial and political means to carry on their war. Characteristically the practical reorganisation of government on which William of Orange and his advisers repeatedly insisted (see especially Document 45) was not immediately connected with the discussion about the new sovereign. Sovereignty and government were apparently seen as distinct matters in distinct spheres of life. Whether the Netherlands had a sovereign or not mattered enormously from a legal and diplomatic point of view, but it did not materially interfere with the working of the government and the independence of the ruling institutions and persons.

After long negotiations and morose hesitations on the part of the individual provinces Anjou was at last offered a treaty (August 1580) which would promote him to the quality of 'prince and seignior of the Netherlands' – not to that of sovereign. When Anjou asked why he was not to be called 'sovereign' – Jean Bodin was Anjou's councillor – Marnix, who explained the proposal in a personal conversation with Anjou in Tours, answered that the French word had no equivalent in Dutch. This was, though in a sense true (in Dutch the French word is used), a sophisticated diplomatic reply but at the same time much more than this. Very interesting from a constitutional point of view was article XXVI:

His Highness and his successors will not only swear a general oath to the States that they will keep to this treaty but also swear the usual solemn oath in each province. In case His Highness or his successors infringe any point of this treaty the States will *de facto* be relieved of their duty to obey him and of their allegiance to him and will be allowed to take another Prince or arrange matters differently as they think best.[2]

This represented a considerable extension of the *Joyeuse Entrée* which only allowed suspension of obedience for a certain length of time (as was clearly and objectively stated in 1580: Document 44). Nevertheless the delegates whose task it was to persuade Anjou of the reasonableness of this article declared with somewhat exaggerated optimism that 'the princes of the Netherlands have never been reluctant to have themselves restrained by similar clauses, even sometimes by clauses still more stringent than the present one, as might be substantiated by innumerable old charters'.[3] Notwithstanding Anjou's strong protests the article was maintained because, according to the delegates, 'it was an ancient privilege, indeed the basis and foundation of all our liberties and privileges'. However, when Anjou proposed that 'as this was an ancient privilege of the country and His Highness intended to maintain the privileges in all respects and at all times...the clause "according to their old privileges" should be added',[4] the delegates refused this too. Possibly they suspected that examination of the old charters would not bear out the interpretation put by them on articles of this kind – there was some doubt among pamphleteers in 1581 about the value of privileges (Documents 50 and 51) – although we may perhaps assume that they considered it the only one which was fundamentally correct.

In September 1580 Anjou signed the document without intending to respect it, for in return for the large amounts of money and soldiers he was made to promise, he received little effective power. Formal ratification on his part took place in January 1581 at Bordeaux (Treaty of Bordeaux). When after much delay and a visit to Queen Elizabeth he arrived in the Netherlands (February 1582) and swore the required oath to the States General at Antwerp, he rapidly managed to make himself unpopular by his preposterous manners and his male harem. In January 1583 he tried to perpetrate a *coup d'État* and to overthrow both the States General and William of Orange by force. However, in a determined and efficient manner the people of Antwerp drove away the French soldiers Anjou had introduced into the city. Although in spite of all this William of Orange remained loyal to the French alliance (Document 53) and pre-

34

vented Anjou's formal dismissal it was obvious that the problem of sovereignty remained unsolved.

Document 47, which must be read in the context of these events – it was published in spring 1581 – gives an interesting impression of the sort of theoretical and practical problems then visualised, the sort of argumentation then used in an attempt to solve them and the quandary into which people were led by circumstances. What strikes the modern reader is the mixture of abstract schematisation and pragmatic realism. Acute awareness of the fact that the States General did not rise to the intellectual level required for governing the country instead of merely mitigating the government of the king and withstanding his orders – the same point was emphatically made in William of Orange's eloquent speech to the States General of 1 December 1581: Document 52 – was coupled with the inadequate and rather pedantic hypothesis that aristocratic government was necessarily a government exercised by nobles and doomed to failure in the Netherlands because of the glaring deficiencies in the character of the nobility. In fact of course the States General were not dominated by the nobility. Moreover it is difficult to see how the benefits of monarchical government, described in the traditional way as bringing order and unity into the divided and corrupt state and praised here in defence of Anjou's candidature for the sovereignty, can be derived from the system the author obviously had in mind. Undoubtedly his interpretation of popular sovereignty deprived the monarch of the very power he would need for doing that for which the author was hoping.

In the eyes of the Spanish court, especially Granvelle, the negotiations with Anjou proved that William of Orange was committing high treason. In an edict dated 15 March 1580 and rather reluctantly published by Parma in June, William of Orange was held responsible for all the unrest in the Netherlands and declared to be the only cause of the troubles, the man who with his cunning and brutality forced people in the Netherlands to abandon Roman Catholicism, who ruined the Church, perturbed the whole state, the 'public plague of the Christian republic', a traitor and enemy of king, country and humanity; thus he was outlawed and a price was put on his head. In December 1580 William of Orange sent a remonstrance to the States General in which he refuted the king's accusation (Document 48). In the accompanying letter he told the States that he addressed his Apology to them because he 'acknowledged only them for his superiors' – a remarkable statement intended of course as an answer to the imputation of the Spanish court that he was the sole originator and leader of the whole movement. The States naturally

35

accepted a share of the responsibility for what had been done and emphasised in their reply to William that he was indeed 'lawfully elected and chosen' to his offices both of lieutenant-general of the Union and stadholder. This too was an interesting statement. The States however were not prepared to print the Apology under their own authority; apparently they were careful not to identify themselves completely with William's plight. It was therefore on his personal initiative that the prince finally published his Apology in January 1581; soon after copies were sent to kings and princes all over Europe with a covering letter which contains the following passage:

> But further the king of Spain, having all the world through published, that I am a public plague, an enemy of the world, unthankful, unfaithful, a traitor and a wicked person, these are such injuries that no gentleman, no though he were of the basest of the king of Spain's natural subjects, can or ought to endure, in so much that though I were one of his simple and absolute vassals...yet so it is that by such a sentence, so unjust in all and every part thereof – I also having been by him spoiled of my lands and lordships in respect of which I should heretofore have taken an oath to him – I might have held myself absolved and free from all my bands towards him, and have essayed also (which thing even nature has taught every one) by all the means I could to maintain my honour, which ought to be to me and to all noblemen more dear than life and goods. Notwithstanding, seeing it has pleased God to show me this great grace that I am born a free Lord, not holding of any other but of the Empire, as do the princes and other free lords of Germany and Italy, and further seeing that I bear the title and have the name of *an absolute and free Prince*, though indeed my Princedom be not very great, yea whatsoever it be, I not being his natural subject neither having held anything of him but by reason of my seigniories and lordships of which notwithstanding he has wholly dispossessed me, it has seemed unto me that I could not defend my honour and satisfy or content my near kinsfolk, sundry princes (to whom this is my honour that I am linked) and my whole posterity but in answering by public writing to this accusation which in the presence of all Christendom is published and set out against me.[5]

Apparently therefore the argument of William of Orange was two-sided. On the one hand he was a servant of the States General, responsible to them and dependent on them, and in that capacity the executive of constitutional government. On the other hand he was a sovereign prince in his own right. The feudal connection with the king on which the justification of his policies had previously been based was broken by the king himself when he took away William's possessions. The first argument was used to prove that William's acts were justifiable from a purely legal point of view, the second to establish the nature of William's new attitude towards Philip II. As he was no longer a vassal bound by oath to him it was necessary to emphasise that he was more than just an individual deprived of the link with a feudal lord but that he was in fact an independent sovereign himself making war against another foreign sovereign.

The famous edict of the States General of 26 July 1581 (Document 49) in which they confirmed that Philip II had forfeited the sovereignty of the Netherlands adds nothing new to what had already been said many times before. The document contains no exclusively Protestant views and the religious question was not emphasised. There is an intentional flatness in the resolution, there are occasional obscurities – particularly in the theoretical passages at the beginning where the author refers to positive and natural law, to popular sovereignty and the appointment of kings by God without making clear that he is using contradictory, or at any rate totally different, concepts that need further development before they would add up to a coherent doctrine; but it is all the same an extremely efficient piece of work with its judicious mixture of fact and fancy. It was not bitter propaganda in the sense in which the Apology was; it was a relatively calm explanation of what had happened and why these events had for a considerable time made it illegitimate for the inhabitants to regard Philip II as their sovereign any longer. Of course Philip II did not forfeit his sovereignty on 26 July 1581; he had clearly lost it well before that date. On 26 July the States General confined themselves to stating this as a fact; they did not proclaim independence, they did not decide on any revolutionary innovation, they passed the resolution as a routine matter, by way of a mere formality and without drawing special attention to it.

Was the constitutional puzzle now solved? Matthias had left the Netherlands just before July 1581; Anjou was expected to take up government soon; Philip had lost the sovereignty. It would seem that in theory matters had become clear enough although, because of practical circumstances, in reality they still remained terribly confused. But even in theory the situation was less satisfactory than it looked on the surface. From 1572 Holland and Zeeland had been the most important agents of resistance to Philip II; even in 1580 and 1581, before Parma completed his reconquest of the Southern Netherlands, it was obvious that for any ruler in the Netherlands the character and size of his power depended to a large extent on the position he acquired in Holland and Zeeland. Anjou received no authority in these provinces. Article XIII of his treaty with the States General was phrased thus: 'Holland and Zeeland will remain as they are now, especially in religious but also in other matters. However in matters concerning the coinage, war, taxes and privileges which involve various provinces or towns, they are subjected to His Highness and the Generality'.[6] William of Orange thus retained his very special position in the two provinces and this constituted a vital qualification of the authority with which Anjou was charged. In 1572 William of Orange had been recognised as stadholder but soon it turned out to be necessary to define somewhat more precisely what power he was supposed to hold not so much as *locum tenens* or stadholder of the king but in his own right.

In the course of the years this was attempted at various times. In 1574 the States of Holland declared that thanks to their benevolent 'collation' William of Orange was entitled to act as governor and regent and they granted him 'absolute power, authority and sovereign command' for the duration of the war. In 1575 they formalised this further, recognising him as 'principal person of these Netherlands and as a principal and the first person in the States of the country' with the title 'Lord and highest authority'. In 1576 Zeeland did the same. But throughout the negotiations it was carefully added that the States elected and chose him to that quality 'as far as was in them'. This probably meant that as far as they were concerned William was entitled to this office but that the king ought to ratify such a decision. It was a far from elegant solution; for what is the constitutional position of States that claim to be capable of granting absolute power to the king's *locum tenens* in some provinces provided the king allows this? Moreover in practice such words as 'absolute' and 'sovereign' turned out to mean virtually nothing. The States did not dream of creating a new form of absolute power and William of Orange had no ambition to possess it. Possibly this reckless terminology was used to increase William's prestige; it also served as a sort of incantation to ward off imminent anarchy without changing anything fundamentally.

In 1580 it was evident that the negotiations with Anjou would oblige the States General formally to declare Philip II an enemy of the country. It therefore became necessary to examine what was going to happen to William of Orange's offices. In any event his function of stadholder of Philip II lost the little constitutional significance it still had. Theoretically it would have been neat to perpetuate the office and to recognise William of Orange as Anjou's stadholder but this was unacceptable to the States of Holland and Zeeland. Some members of the States considered the possibility of appointing William as 'absolute overlord and protector' of the two provinces and having him in that capacity make an alliance with Anjou, the overlord of the Netherlands. The discussion about this and similar ideas however dragged on without leading anywhere. In July 1581 the States finally confined themselves to emphasising that circumstances had in no way impaired the power granted to William in 1575 and 1576. Once again he was given 'high authority and government' over Holland and Zeeland and the right to exercise 'full authority and power as sovereign and overlord' for the duration of the war. On the other hand Anjou was obviously considered to have succeeded Philip II in the latter's capacity as count of Holland and Zeeland. This makes the construction embarrassing. Whereas William's elevation to such high functions was in 1575 and 1576 logical at least from a practical point of view because the legitimate sovereign, the count of Holland, was waging war on the country, it was not particularly elegant to adopt the same attitude in relation to Anjou who was supposed to be their friend and protector.

Notwithstanding the pompous and inaccurate terms used it is not difficult to see what Holland and Zeeland wanted the Prince to do and to be. He was to be a war-time leader with a narrowly defined authority, just sufficient to give him confidence that the financial and political means needed for carrying on the war would be forthcoming with some regularity. But the course of events which in 1577 made William leave Holland to take up residence first in Brussels and then in Antwerp was detrimental to his influence in Holland, where the towns increasingly sought to act independently and where republican sentiments and ideas were being broached by responsible and weighty men. At the same time, however, William was needed to serve as a counter-weight to Anjou; his authority in the two provinces was to be emphasised to prevent Anjou's influence penetrating there. In 1582 or 1583, so it seems, Holland dropped the time limit – for the duration of the war – attached to the prince's authority. In August 1582 a delegation of the States of Holland went to Bruges, where William then was, to ask whether he would be prepared to accept the dignity of count of Holland, and he answered that he was willing to do so. In September Zeeland made a similar offer. Soon however opposition to this initiative, both in the two provinces and outside them, slowed down proceedings considerably. Amsterdam above all was reluctant to subject itself to such a form of sovereignty. In June 1584 C. P. Hooft, one of the

members of the Town Council – he had an important career as burgomaster – made a speech in which he said characteristic things:

> If you talk about this with the citizens you find how difficult it is for
> many of them to approve of it; I think that many prominent citizens
> will choose rather to go away than stay with us under such circum-
> stances and this will cause great unrest in the lower strata of the
> population. If His Excellency had shown at the start of this war that
> he intended to become count he would, I think, not have achieved
> much and the people who everywhere opened the town gates for him
> would not have been willing to do this. But at the time everyone was
> repeating *pro Lege, Rege et Grege* (for the law, the king and the
> people), nice words surely, and telling the people that it was the
> liberty of the countries which one was striving for without ever
> mentioning, as far as I know, the idea of making His Excellency
> hereditary lord of the countries.[7]

Both the bitter tone of this speech and its contents show clearly that in
Amsterdam the problem was taken seriously and that the haphazard
improvisations leading up to the offer of sovereignty were resented. Or
did this display of republican pride disguise more worldly and therefore
more immediately important motives? Amsterdam was said to fear the
elevation of William of Orange to the dignity held by Philip II because it
expected the king in his wrath at being offended in the crudest possible
way to impede all trade between Holland and Spain and thus to wreck
Amsterdam's profitable trade with the enemy.

But in spite of Amsterdam's attitude negotiations went on, and in
December 1583 the States of Holland and Zeeland agreed on terms of a
treaty with William of Orange which were acceptable to him. In reality
the quality of count of Holland did not add substantial authority to the
limited power he possessed according to the arrangements of 1576 and
1581. The vital point was that what had been provisional was now made
permanent. But this did not increase his power; in a sense it actually reduced it. In 1576 and 1581 William was appointed with the purpose of
protecting the constitution in conjunction with the States, and he derived
his authority from this task. Now, however, the States became the protectors of the constitution against William of Orange who as count ought
to be prevented from encroaching upon ancient rights and privileges. The
result was that the treaty of Holland with William of Orange did not
essentially differ in character and content from that of the States General
with Anjou to which explicit reference was indeed made: William of

Orange granted the States of Holland and Zeeland, it was said, all rights conceded in the *Joyeuse Entrée* of the duke of Brabant and the treaty with the duke of Anjou. Even clause XXVI of the Anjou treaty was taken over. All this however was fruitless. In July 1584 before he could be inaugurated as count, William of Orange was murdered.

What remained obscure in all these proceedings was their legal or constitutional basis. Nobody ventured to ask whether the States of an individual province were entitled to appoint a sovereign. Moreover it would have been logical for people who offered the dignity of count to William of Orange to take the trouble of dismissing Anjou (cf. Marnix's ingenious but unsatisfactory argumentation in Document 54). Circumstances however were not such that much attention could be spared for constitutional subtleties. No coherent constitutional plan had been worked out. The treaty with Anjou was just as much an improvisation as that with William of Orange. If these treaties or contracts look like modern constitutions, this is in a sense accidental and moreover only partially true. For what was still lacking was a definition of sovereignty. Clarity about its contents had not been provided nor was it ever decided where sovereignty was ultimately to reside.

Discussion about the best form of government became general in 1583. The selected fragments (Documents 55, 57, 58, 59) give an impression of its size and style and show at the same time the disarray to which events had led. In 1584 the total collapse of the rebels' front was far from unlikely. Not only did Parma's offensive in the Southern Netherlands achieve success after success with the fall of the major cities of Flanders (cf. Document 60), the death of Anjou in June and the assassination of William of Orange in July undermined both the theoretical and the practical basis of the governmental system. Attempts to strengthen government by creating yet another Council of State which it was suggested should be given 'all power and sovereign authority' (Document 61), were only half-successful. A man like Marnix who had been appointed burgomaster of Antwerp by William of Orange and in that capacity was defending the city against Parma's troops, repeated in a pathetic pamphlet (Document 62) the rhetorical arguments and the unsuccessful solutions of the past. With the death of his great friend and leader he lost his self-confidence and nerve and in August 1585 he surrendered Antwerp without, perhaps, exhausting all means to perpetuate resistance.

Meanwhile the States General were trying to re-define their position in an effort both to obtain foreign help and to clarify the governmental situation. Circumstances were singularly complicated. Just before his death on 10 June 1584 Anjou had agreed to the principles of a new treaty with the States General as the value of the original Treaty of Bordeaux had become doubtful after the events of January 1583. Although the States General were rightly considered the offended party after Anjou's failed *coup d'État* they nevertheless sought to win Anjou's favour again and it was the dramatic development of the war that made them willing in 1583 to concede to Anjou substantially more power than in 1580. In the new draft treaty, article XXVI of the Bordeaux Treaty was not taken over. The States General no longer appeared as they did in 1580 as the high and mighty power benevolently granting some restricted authority to the French duke. Their desperate need for foreign help was so dominating that they were prepared to declare that in case Anjou died without legitimate offspring the Netherlands would be 'perpetually united with and annexed to the crown of France on the conditions which the States agreed with the duke of Anjou in the Treaty of Bordeaux and with the understanding that the laws, customs, usages, contracts and ancient privileges of the countries remain valid'.[8] This was more than mere phraseology. The States gave Henri III permission to take two cities by way of a guarantee whereas Anjou was allowed to put his troops in all towns where he took up residence except in Antwerp and Ghent.

The draft which naturally needed ratification on the part of both Anjou and Henri III was not yet sealed and sworn to when Anjou died. Nevertheless the States decided to act as if the treaty were valid and they thus informed the French king that the provinces had now gone to him and that they would like to swear an oath of loyalty to him and obey him 'so as it suits good vassals and subjects to do in relation to their sovereign seignior'. However, Henri III would not dream of accepting a form of sovereignty as narrowly defined as that of the Bordeaux Treaty. Not unreasonably he considered the help he was expected to give the Netherlands, implying open war with Spain, poorly rewarded by the distinction of calling himself prince and seignior – or even in spite of the Bordeaux Treaty: *sovereign* seignior–! of the Netherlands without power to act as such. The Netherlanders on their part did not understand the nature of his refusal to regard the draft treaty as binding. They failed to realise that the French king would not be satisfied with a position reached in long negotiations between virtually equal partners and based on a set of constitutional limitations. Notwithstanding the desperately critical circumstances they started once again in provinces and towns to deliberate about possible alterations in the Bordeaux Treaty and new concessions to the king with the result that it was not until January 1585 that a deputation of the States General arrived at last in France to offer the sovereignty to Henri III. They used interesting terminology. They no longer referred to the draft treaty with Anjou but stated:

> As by the death of His Highness, prince and seignior of the Provinces, these are vacant and again at the disposal of the States ('sont vaccantes et retournées en la disposition desdictz Estatz'), and because the king of Spain and his adherents continue the war and invade and oppress them cruelly, they have found it appropriate and in accordance with justice and natural law to take refuge in, and to throw themselves into, the arms of His Majesty so that they be joined to the kingdom of France from which they, or most of them, were separated in the past, and be ruled and defended as his very humble vassals and subjects on certain reasonable conditions...[9]

It is not easy to define what theory was behind the idea that at the death of Anjou the provinces were again at the disposal of the States, but the terminology does not, it seems, indicate that the States considered themselves to be sovereigns in the period between the disappearance of one sovereign and the arrival of the next. The idea was rather that as guardians of the constitution they held in trust the authority needed for protecting it as long as there was no one else to perform that task (cf. also Document 63 for a somewhat ambiguous or incomplete exposé of what happens in such a situation). When they were considering the instruction to be given to the deputies to Henri III they anticipated that the king might well ask them what power the States had to hand over the provinces to him and decided to answer that the law of nature and history as well as ancient privileges allowed oppressed nations to seek the help of generous princes whose royal duty it is to defend the weak and poor against the mighty and rich. This of course was no answer at all but it had the limited merit of carefully eliminating the conception of popular sovereignty or sovereignty of the States. Although tactful it was all the same dangerous and naïve. If Henri III had accepted sovereignty on such a basis he would certainly have interpreted it in the modern French fashion the significance of which the Netherlanders had not grasped or did not wish to grasp. But Henri III did not accept the proposal. In March 1585 he refused to support the Netherlands in an open war with Spain and put an end to the negotiations.

A few days later the States General decided to approach Queen Elizabeth with a similar proposal but it was three months before all preparations were completed and a fully authorised deputation could set sail for England. Made wiser by Henri III's attitude, the States had provided three sets of instructions. The deputies were first to offer the sovereignty of the Netherlands to the queen, on 'reasonable conditions', in fact almost the same as those proposed to the French king; if the queen declined this, they were to ask her to become 'protector' of the countries and if this too was refused, they would make a request for military assistance only. It is well-known that the queen did not want to be sovereign or protector of the Netherlands but felt obliged under the circumstances to provide military aid. From the very start she made it quite clear that she refused the 'principality and property' of the Netherlands. But the Dutch envoys insisted. On 11 July they presented the English with a remonstrance in which they stated:

> The Netherlands are all duchies, counties and separate seigniories, governed by their own magistrates, laws and ordinances, each so independent that no province possesses authority over the other. This is the reason why they need the supreme power of a prince or sovereign seignior who commands all of them. Such a prince will care for the public well-being of the generality and not for the private profit of an individual province; he will oblige all of them to execute and obey readily and generally the commands and ordinances made for carrying on the war and reducing society to order according to the circumstances, the available opportunities and the season...If each province retains the sovereignty and supreme command over the population, it will be impossible to ensure that the orders of Her Majesty's lieutenant general or his Council will be obeyed so promptly and completely...10

When the English asked the envoys what securities they were prepared to give for the restitution of the advance money which the queen was expected to spend before Dutch taxes yielded enough to finance the war effort, they were told that 'if Her Majesty accepted the sovereignty or perpetual protectorship such restitution would not take place for Her Majesty would then possess the whole country'.11

It is remarkable that 'perpetual protectorship' was considered to be in practice equivalent to sovereignty. That this was indeed more than a manoeuvre during the negotiations in order to obtain financial advantages appears from the resolution of the States General on 6 June 1585 in which they defined at length what was to be understood by protection. If the queen refused sovereignty

Her Majesty will be asked by the States General of the United Provinces, that is, by Gelderland, Flanders, Holland, Zeeland, Utrecht and Friesland, to accept and receive for herself and the legitimate successors to the kingdom of England, protectors of the reformed religion, the said United Provinces under her perpetual protection and to maintain and defend them against the king of Spain..., under good and reasonable conditions, to wit: that Her Majesty will be declared protector of the United Provinces and of all their privileges, rights, freedoms and laudable customs and usages, both general and particular, and that in that capacity she will be respected, honoured and obeyed...The said provinces, their members and towns, will remain united in one body and association as far as this protection and their common defence are concerned...[12]

It is not surprising that according to the Dutch with their traditional conception of the relation between sovereignty and constitution, protecting the constitution amounts to being sovereign. The difference was one of form and title, not of substance.[13]

On the level of practical government the States General proposed that Queen Elizabeth, agreeing to protect the Netherlands, would send a lieutenant general who was to rule the country together with a Council of State appointed by the States General, and according to an instruction drafted by the States General. It was explicitly stated that neither the lieutenant general nor his Council could ever make any changes in the religion or the privileges of States General and provinces. Obviously the States tried thus to sketch what they thought the ideal arrangement in a situation they had known well in the recent past. The idea of making the protector delegate a lieutenant general was evidently taken from the model of the governors general sent by Charles V and Philip II with the result that in this respect too the difference between sovereignty and protectorship was very slight.

The queen remained adamantly opposed to such suggestions. When this was realised some important men at the Court, among them the earl of Leicester, advised the Dutch deputies to go beyond their instruction and to ask for an English governor with military and political functions even though the queen did not want to be either sovereign or protector. Even though what they were doing was illogical the Dutch envoys politely asked the queen 'to grant (*verleenen*) the countries some lord of quality to become leader and director in the Netherlands because matters had run into disorder since the death of His Excellency [William of Orange]'.[14]

It must be emphasised that this compromise solution was not proposed by the Dutch who had originally been consistent enough to connect the request for an English governor with the request to be accepted as the Queen's subjects or protégés.

In the definitive treaty of October 1585 the position of lieutenant general was left largely undefined although he clearly received more authority than the 'prince and seignior' Anjou some years previously. His duties were extensive; he was commissioned to restore public authority, reform the financial and military situation and generally to serve the Netherlands as well as he could. Apparently the intention was that more precise arrangements about the governor's competence and power would be made by him in direct negotiations with the States General. This at any rate was the opinion of both the queen's Privy Council and the States General. The queen herself however either disagreed from the start or changed her mind afterwards for shortly before his departure she forbade the earl of Leicester, who was appointed to the post, to accept further commissions by the States General. Officially he was merely to be the general of the English army; if he helped to restore order in Dutch affairs that would be nice and even necessary according to the treaty but he should not do so in the capacity of governor sent by the queen. Constitutionally this was a correct point of view. Elizabeth was giving military assistance; she was neither sovereign nor protectress. The States however did not know of this secret order to Leicester. Obviously they thought – and this was far from unreasonable – that if she sent a governor, she wished him to do business and accepted responsibility for this, in fact, acted as if she were protectress *sine titulo*. Thus they literally showered honours and powers upon the earl on his arrival in the Netherlands in December 1585. They did this in a manner that had implications which were probably not clearly realised. In February 1586 they resolved

that His Excellency (in addition to the title, charge and commission given him by Her Majesty, and in addition to the authority which he possesses by virtue of the Treaty concluded between Her Majesty and the above-named States General, which His Excellency will keep and have kept in all its points and articles, which shall retain their original force, each in its respective regard) shall be commissioned Governor and Captain General of the aforesaid United Provinces...; and that His Excellency...shall have full power and absolute command in the matter of the war and all matters concerned with it...; Item. His Excellency shall have full and absolute power in the afore-

said Provinces and associated regions, in the matter of civil government and justice, such as the Governors General of the Netherlands
have in all times legally possessed, and particularly in the time of
Charles V of beloved memory...And his Excellency shall be empowered to summon the States General of the said Provinces at any
time and place within the said Provinces, or wherever he wishes;
and on the summons of His Excellency they shall be bound to appear
at the designated time and place. In addition, the said States, both
general and particular, shall assemble when they wish and act as they
deem proper for the welfare and service of the country: All this
without prejudice to the rights, freedoms, preeminences, privileges,
treaties, contracts, statutes, ordinances, decrees and customs of the
above-mentioned provinces in general, or of each province, city and
member of each in particular, which, notwithstanding anything
above, shall remain in their full vigour.[15]

This is an extraordinary document. Did the States really accept that
the governors general had always possessed 'full and absolute power' and
if so, what might they have thought this meant? Obviously such power
was not allowed to encroach upon the existing constitution, which was
interpreted in the widest possible way as including total freedom on the
part of the general and provincial States to meet and act as they wished.
But even so the commission granted to Leicester by the States implied
much more than the queen had granted him. She was furious. This was
exactly what she had not wanted to happen. To the outside world
Leicester would probably appear as her governor, and this would involve
her in the affairs of the Netherlands to a much greater extent than she
thought wise. The States did not understand this. They had been very
careful to state with so much precision that it was they and they alone who
were responsible for the appointment. Leicester was becoming not the
queen's but their own governor. It was caution which prompted them to
do so, not presumption. But nevertheless, in doing it they at last openly
accepted that they possessed sovereignty. They had not done so before.
In their dealings with Anjou, William of Orange and Henri III they had
refrained from claiming sovereignty. Now inevitably they had to. It was
not what they had wished. They would have preferred having a governor
general appointed by Queen Elizabeth in her capacity as their sovereign or
protectress. But she had refused such honours. Leicester himself had then
suggested the illogical compromise which led to his mission to the Netherlands. In the absence of a sovereign to perform the task of appointing him

as governor general the States took this upon themselves. During the States General's negotiations with Leicester in January 1586 this attitude was clearly formulated. On one occasion the provincial States were mentioned as institutions 'with which the sovereignty of the country is now residing' ('bij denwelcken nu de souvereineté van den lande was'). This was the extraordinarily paradoxical beginning of Dutch independence.

A wiser man even than Leicester would probably have been unable to cope with his task. His position was ambiguous in the extreme. Though only a delegate of the English queen and an official of the States General he was asked to rule the Netherlands more arbitrarily even than William of Orange was ever allowed to. No wonder he failed. His military, economic, financial and religious policies were unsuccessful and rapidly made him lose the support of the province of Holland. An extremely complicated process of polarisation led to the formation of what was regarded as Leicester's political party. Its opponents suspected this party of having a set of political aims that amounted to a real programme. It was considered to be centralist, democratic, Calvinist and eager to expand the war with the purpose of reconquering the Southern Netherlands for Calvinism. There was undoubtedly some truth in this although these political objectives formed in reality less of a consistent whole than was suggested. But even if for example the democratic tendencies of the party were not as strong as was suspected, there was no doubt that Leicester's adherents were in favour of governmental reforms detrimental to the superiority and autonomy of the provincial States, particularly those of Holland. Their policies were directed against those elements in the system of government which ensured the provincial States a firm hold on the reformed churches and the unchallenged power of the urban oligarchies. Instead of this Leicester hoped to establish centralised government under his own undisputed leadership.

It was thought that he would be in a better position to achieve his aim if the queen were induced to accept the sovereignty in spite of her previous refusal. Document 64 gives an impression of the arguments and implications. Here indeed a new definition of sovereignty was considered that differed substantially from the traditional one. Prouninck (Document 64 and cf. Document 47) obviously visualised a Calvinist monarchy that was no longer based on the ancient constitution but formed a dynamic, charismatic sort of government which had no precedent in the Netherlands. He was apparently convinced that the queen might be persuaded to assume the sovereignty if it was offered without conditions. But the States of Holland could not dream of defining sovereignty in such a way. At the beginning of 1587 they and the States General reluctantly consented to ask the queen once again to take up sovereignty but it was, as in 1585, a conditional and limited sovereignty in which little room for the 'absolute' royal prerogative was left. Meanwhile the whole matter was irritating the States and causing them serious anxiety. When Leicester was temporarily called back to England in November 1586 they immediately started to undermine the power of the Council of State to which he had delegated his authority. This inspired one of its English members, Thomas Wilkes, to write a remonstrance of real importance although of a highly paradoxical nature (Document 65 and cf. Document 67).

The paradox was that Wilkes referred to the doctrine of popular sovereignty in order to refute the sovereignty of the States. This was a clever move, especially as he introduced Bodin's new definition of sovereignty in a country still unprepared for it. But fundamentally it made little sense. In the first place it must be repeated that if the States had learned to claim sovereignty, this was because they needed such sovereignty when obliged to take the responsibility for Leicester's appointment as governor general. In the second place it was far from clear that the sixteenth-century concept of popular sovereignty was opposed to that of States sovereignty. One of the things the States of Holland, answering Wilkes in a long Deduction written by Francis Vranck (Document 66), tried to show was that there was no conflict between the two doctrines. What mattered more to them, however, was to demonstrate in a long and scholarly though highly selective historical analysis that the urban administrations, together with the nobles, had for the last eight centuries been in possession of sovereignty which they had often entrusted to counts and countesses. Wilkes's theory was therefore meaningless.

Vranck's Deduction not only gave a realistic picture of the form of government that had emerged – in a letter of 22 July 1587 to the queen Wilkes recognised Vranck's view to be perfectly accurate – it also became a major source of Dutch constitutional thought. It may indeed be interpreted as the logical conclusion to the development of Dutch political thought during the Revolt. But there are qualifications. Vranck did not really define the nature of sovereignty. There is in his prose no echo of Bodin's phrase quoted by Wilkes. Sovereignty in his sense was not isolated or separated from the constitution and from constitutional rights as it was later by Dutch seventeenth-century theorists who raised the sovereignty of the States to the level of that of absolute kings. In the second place it was still not clear whether sovereignty resided with the States of the individual provinces or collectively with the States General.

If eventually it was monopolised by the provincial States this was caused by political events; it was not implied in Vranck's theory.

Looking back on the history of Dutch political thought during the Revolt what strikes one is its unadventurous character and its precision. The Netherlanders apparently felt compelled to justify all their acts and decisions as based on law. Of course they strained law and precedent to the point of misrepresenting them perhaps wilfully; and of course they failed to put forward a consistent theory of constitutional government. But notwithstanding that, there was something moving and impressive in their sometimes desperate and sometimes extraordinarily pedantic attempts to prove that all they did was legitimate. Ultimately their ideas and their actions form a link in the development of European constitutional thought and practice that was in danger of being broken by the hard innovations of modern absolutism.

Endnotes

(1) Resolutions of the States of Holland quoted in [J. Wagenaar], *Vaderlandsche Historie*, vol. VII (2nd ed., Amsterdam, 1770), pp. 79–80.
(2) G. Griffiths, *Representative Government in Western Europe in the Sixteenth Century* (Oxford, 1968), pp. 495–6.
(3) *Ibid.* p. 502.
(4) *Ibid.* p. 503.
(5) Contemporary English translation reprinted in H. Wansink ed., *The Apologie of Prince William of Orange against the Proclamation of the King of Spaine* (Leyden, 1969), pp. 3–4.
(6) Griffiths, *Representative Government*, p. 494.
(7) H. A. Enno van Gelder ed., *Memoriën en Adviezen van Cornelis Pieterszoon Hooft*, vol. II (Utrecht, 1925), p. 7.
(8) P. L. Muller and Alph. Diegerick eds., *Documents concernant les relations entre le Duc d'Anjou et les Pays-Bas (1576–1584)*, vol. V (Amsterdam, 1899), p. 698. This draft dates from 25 April 1584.
(9) N. Japikse ed., *Resolutiën der Staten-Generaal van 1576 tot 1609*, vol. IV (The Hague, 1919), p. 495.
(10) 'Rapport van de Nederlandsche gezanten, in 1585 naar Engeland gezonden', *Kronijk van het Historisch Genootschap*, 5th series, vol. II (Utrecht, 1866), p. 221.
(11) *Ibid.* p. 232.
(12) Japikse ed., *Resolutiën*, vol. V (The Hague, 1921), p. 59.
(13) In 1575 the queen had already been asked to act as protectress; this was thought to be legally possible on condition that the States abandoned Philip II.

That, at any rate, is the impression left by the documents. In relation to the duke of Anjou, however, the term protector meant something quite different from sovereign. When Anjou was declared to be 'protector of the liberty of the Netherlands against the tyranny of the Spaniards and their adherents' (1578), this did not, according to the theory of the States General, reduce the sovereign rights of Philip II. It may have been easier to make the distinction in the case of Anjou who was not in possession of a sovereign title, than in that of Queen Elizabeth, who was.

(14) 'Rapport', p. 252.

(15) The translation is by Griffiths who prints the document in full, pp. 528–31.

Philip II to the duchess of Parma, 17 October 1565[1]

The letters of Philip II from the Segovia woods written in October 1565 arrived at Brussels at the beginning of November. They were not however made known to the provincial and local authorities until 18 December.

Madame my dear sister, I answer your letter of 22 July in which you told me, as you did in your preceding letters, how you have started to comply with the instructions transmitted by my cousin the prince of Gavre,[2] and have been trying to remedy the religious problems. I understand that, as I had ordained, you have convoked at Brussels the bishops of Ypres, Namur and St Omer and the presidents of Flanders and Utrecht with the councillor, Muelerus, and also the theologians and Doctors Tiletanus and Jansenius, nominated as bishop of Ghent, and with them Doctor Wulmarus, canonist,[3] whose statements in Latin, signed in their own handwriting, you have sent me together with the minutes. I am very pleased to learn that the assembly was constituted by men of such quality and such zeal for our religion and I value their advice on various points, and also on matters in which it does not seem suitable to make innovations, as you will see from the enclosed answers to their statements. I have added some other points which I think are important in the matter of

---

[1] J. S. Theissen ed., *Correspondance française de Marguerite d'Autriche avec Philippe II* (Utrecht, 1925) pp. 99ff.

[2] Lamoral count of Egmont, prince of Gavre, was a delegate sent to the king by the government at Brussels at the end of January 1565. He returned with a royal instruction in April. This suggested that a meeting of bishops, theologians and councillors with the Council of State be called in order to consider the religious situation in the Netherlands, to which the problem of promulgating the decrees of the Council of Trent was closely related. This meeting assembled at Brussels at the end of May.

[3] The nine participants were Bishop Martin Rithovius of Ypres, Bishop Anthony Havet of Namur, Bishop Gerard Hamericourt of St Omer, James Martens, the president of the Council of Flanders, Hippolyta Persijn, the president of the Council of Utrecht, Anthony Meulenare, councillor of the Great Council of Mechlin, Cornelius Jansenius, appointed bishop of Ghent, and Just Ravesteyn of Thielt (Tiletanus) both doctors of divinity, and the lawyer Vulmarus Bernaerts.

religion and I instruct you to have these executed without fail in the best manner possible. I rely upon you in this.

You say that I did not make it clear in the afore-mentioned instruction that it was not my intention to ask you or the seigniors of the state council in the Netherlands for more advice in this matter but in fact you were made to understand my definitive intention. As to whether I would wish to ask the advice of the private and great councils and of the governors and provincial councils, this would be a considerable waste of time since my mind is made up. I have not asked others at all but followed the advice of the above-mentioned assembly as much as possible and as seemed fitting, and I have been very pleased to hear that you have already begun to apply the other canonical remedies, such as having good preachers and pastors, founding good schools and reforming the ecclesiastics in accordance with my instruction, and, moreover, publishing the decrees of the council and all that is connected with it...

As to the proceedings of the inquisitors of Louvain,[4] you must endeavour to support them as well as the others in all that concerns the exercise and administration of their charges. For this makes for the strength and maintenance of religion.

I cannot but be very much affected by the lampoons which are continually spread abroad and posted up in the Netherlands without the offenders being punished. This, of course, happens because the authors of earlier ones were not punished. You should consider what remains of my authority and yours, and of the service of God, when it is possible to do such things with impunity in your very presence. Therefore I pray you, take the necessary measures so that this does not remain unpunished. These things are not so secret but that several men hear of them and if some are not seen to be punished, the daring increases daily and in the end so much liberty is taken that we must fear most dangerous consequences...

As to the resentment you have noticed at some of the things which the prince of Gavre says I told him and which don't seem to correspond with my letters from Valladolid[5] and with the negotiations in progress over the matter of religion, I don't see or understand that I wrote anything different in these letters from what was entrusted to the prince of Gavre. For as to the inquisition, my intention is that it should be carried out by the inquisitors, as they have done up till now and as it appertains to them by virtue of divine and human rights. This is nothing new, because this

[4] The theological faculty of the university of Louvain had played an important part in the fight against heresy.

[5] Dated 13 May 1565.

was always done in the days of the late emperor my seignior and father, whom God has in His glory, and by me. If one fears disturbances there is no reason to think that they are more imminent and will be greater when one does allow the inquisitors to perform their proper duties and when one does assist them. You know the importance of this and I command you urgently to do in this matter all that is so necessary and not to agree to any different policy. You know how much I have these things at heart and what pleasure and satisfaction this will give me.

I have heard how insubstantial are the objections raised by the inhabitants of Bruges against Titelman;[6] you would do well not to permit anything to be done to undermine his authority. I am sure that being well-informed of what happens (as I believe you are) you won't fail to take the necessary steps.

As to the Anabaptists, what I wrote to you about them was in answer to what you asked me about the punishment of some prisoners.[7] This did not differ from what the prince of Gavre reported. For though you have to deliberate about proposals for altering punishments, this does not mean that they should cease until a resolution is taken. These prisoners must be punished as I told you in my letter from Valladolid. This also answers your representations to me in your letter of 22 July about state-affairs. I cannot refrain from telling you that considering the condition of religious affairs in the Netherlands as I understand it, this is no time to make any alteration. On the contrary, His Majesty's edicts should be executed; I think that the cause of the past evil and its subsequent growth and advance has been the negligence, leniency and duplicity of the judges, about which I will give you more particulars later. I told the prince of Gavre that since the men condemned to die advance to execution not in silence, but as martyrs dying for a cause you should consider whether they ought not to be executed in secret in some way or other (though it is true that a public execution also serves to set an example)....

For the rest I can only thank you for all you propose to me, but assure you that my orders are designed for the welfare of religion and of my provinces and are worth nothing if they are not obeyed. In this way you can keep my provinces in justice, peace and tranquillity. Now that you know the importance of this, I pray you again to take steps to bring this state of affairs into being. Thus I shall be most satisfied with you and with the seigniors who are with you. You must pass on my wishes to them.

6 Peter Titelman, a notorious inquisitor in Flanders.
7 This concerned a lawsuit against repenting Anabaptists, for whom the assembly of nine had advocated milder penalties.

I trust that they won't fail to do what I want as they know what satisfaction this will give me. Thus they will do their duty according to their rank and to the obligation they have to serve God and me, and to further the common welfare of the provinces in the Netherlands on which they are themselves dependent.

So far, etc.

From the Segovia woods, 17 October 1565

2

A brief discourse sent to King Philip, our prince and sovereign lord, for the interest and profit of His Majesty and in particular of his Netherlands, in which are expounded the means that should be applied to obviate the troubles and commotion about religion and to extirpate the sects and heresies that abound in the Low Countries, 1566[1]

The brief discourse was written by Francis Junius (François Du Jon), a Frenchman by birth, afterwards a university professor at Leyden. He was an officiating Calvinist minister at Antwerp in the years 1565–6. This discourse was drafted when the Compromise of the nobles was set up at the end of 1565, in close personal consultation with Louis of Nassau, William of Orange's brother.

As all judicious people agree, no physical violence can rectify faith and inner belief and it is through conscience that people should recognise their errors. We must now pass on to the second point that we have proposed, to wit whether one could not prevent at least the public worship of their religion [viz. Calvinism] by prohibiting them to assemble, to preach, to catechise and to profess openly what they believe in their inmost hearts. And if this should be somehow feasible, whether this is good and necessary.

In fact, can any religion exist without the public worship and ceremonies, by which it is maintained? The emperor Gratian[2] was right in

---

[1] *Brief discours envoyé au roy Philippe nostre sire et souverain Seigneur, pour le bien et profit de sa Maiesté, et singulierement de ses pays bas, auquel est monstré le moyen qu'il faudroit tenir pour obvier aux troubles et emotions pour le faict de la religion, et extirper les sectes et heresies pullulantes en sesdicts pays 1566* (L. D. Petit, *Bibliotheek van Nederlandsche pamfletten*, I, no. 115).

[2] Roman Emperor, 375–83.

emphasising that people must be kept under the outward discipline of some religion, whatever it may be, whether good or bad. For, as the nature of man is such that he desires to ease his conscience and to cast off the yoke of God, it is necessary that he should be bridled and kept under discipline, otherwise he will become as a horse that has bolted, indulging in uncurbed licentiousness and rejecting the fear both of God and men.

Thus as we cannot extirpate the faith which these men cherish in their hearts, it is little use (even if it were feasible) preventing them from attending their public worship, and the services by which they are maintained in their religion and in the fear of God and authority. For instead of being taught in their assemblies to be honest people fearing God and respecting the king and his officers, they would then become vile atheists and libertines stirring up seditions and disturbing order and peace.

That this is true, daily experience clearly shows. For today we see a large number of people who have rejected the yoke of obedience to the Roman Church and deride the mass and priests. But for fear of losing their possessions or offices they do not want to attach themselves to the discipline and worship of some other religion and have become absolute atheists without faith and without law. There is even no small number of vile libertines who form separate sects, teaching that one should not serve God outwardly in any form or discipline, but only in spirit and liberty.[3] And under this pretext they indulge in every possible villainy and abomination, in murder and plundering, in incest and adultery, thinking that such things do not matter as they merely pertain to the external side of life. What does matter, they claim, is the purity of their hearts. Things have gone so far that some even boast of being Christ, whereas others think they are the Spirit of God, or God's charity. In a word, their impiety is boundless, they despise God and the authorities, asserting that it is wrong to use the sword or to give orders to people, for, they say, it is the spirit that should govern and be allowed to move the heart of man whither it wishes.

It is not difficult to indicate the reasons for this situation. These people see that there are grave abuses in the Church but they are not permitted to adopt any other discipline or religion. In such circumstances they consider it legitimate to conform outwardly to the rules of a Church which they reject provided their hearts are pure. But this amounts to not taking religion seriously at all and inevitably makes them lapse into evil atheism. That there are no more seditious individuals and no greater disturbers of

[3] This passage could refer to Anabaptistical sects like those of David Joris or Hendrik Niclaes.

every order in the world than such people, is clearly shown by the example of the Anabaptists in Münster and their likes.[4] There is no better means (if one considers the matter without prejudice or passion), to exterminate such heresies than to permit, nay expressly to command that all who profess the religion called reformed or evangelical, assemble openly and keep a strict discipline in accordance with the obedience due to God and the authorities, and correct all vices and licentiousness.

If this is done we shall no longer see new and abominable sects full of sedition and mutiny, and horrible blasphemies against the majesty of God spring up every day. Instead there will be only two ways of public worship in public sight, each of them keeping to the obedience due to God and the king. Even if there were no other benefit, this would be valuable enough in the maintenance of public order. And as soon as a new opinion arises, it will be very easy to show by the word of God that it is false.

But should some people think it unacceptable to give heretics the liberty to disseminate their heresies, let us now consider whether it is possible to stop them assembling. If we take experience, the perfect counsellor, into account, it will certainly be found that it is indeed possible to prevent them from assembling but absolutely impossible to prevent them from believing what they think to be in keeping with God's word. Have we not seen the late very victorious emperor, Charles, of very blessed memory, possess such great power that it made the world tremble? Have we not seen with what almost incredible ardour he sought to prevent the spread of this religion? Have we not seen the great rigour of his edicts? And what else did he want but to prevent the new religion from being publicised and to make it impossible for the people who profess it to assemble (for he knew quite well he could not convince them completely of their error). Yet he made no progress, in spite of all the prohibitions he issued.

Did he fail because the heretics assembled in some foreign country, where they enjoyed greater liberty? No, on the contrary,[5] all the princes of Christendom, together with the Pope, were determined to exterminate them, and to give them no place where they might find refuge. And yet all this was in vain. How can we possibly think that the power of the king, surely no greater than that of the emperor, could suffice to stop the

---

[4] A reference to the events of the years 1534-5 at Münster and their repercussions in the Netherlands.

[5] In point of fact even during the reign of the Emperor Charles V many people emigrated from the Netherlands to other countries for reasons of faith, especially to Germany and to England.

heretics? For are not France, Germany, England and all the countries around now open to them? They might go there and enjoy the liberty which is denied them here. And are there not now many princes and kings who side with them? Are not their numbers multiplied by a thousand and one? Are not their books read and seen by everyone? Truly those who offer this advice to His Majesty, show beyond question that they have either lost their reason or that they are trying to establish their own grandeur at the expense of the king and to the ruin of the country.

3

Compromise, January 1566[1]

The real originators of the Compromise of the nobles at the beginning of December 1565 were the Calvinists John Marnix, lord of Tholouse and Nicholas de Hames, herald-at-arms of the Order of the Golden Fleece. Shortly after, Louis of Nassau and Henry Brederode gave it their approval and on this basis some hundreds of nobles were to unite.

Every one who has this paper before him must know that we, the undersigned, have been duly and sufficiently warned and informed that there is a great crowd of foreigners[2] – men without any concern for the safety and prosperity of the provinces in the Netherlands, with no care for God's glory and honour or for the commonweal, driven only by private avarice and ambition, even to the disadvantage of the king and all his subjects – who pretend to be zealous for the maintenance of the Catholic religion and the union of the people and have managed to persuade His Majesty by their well-turned remonstrances and false information to violate his oath[3] and to disappoint the expectations he has always let us cherish, by

---

[1] G. Groen van Prinsterer ed., *Archives ou Correspondance inédite de la Maison d'Orange-Nassau*, le série, II (Leyden, 1835), pp. 2ff.

[2] The reference here is above all to Cardinal Granvelle, but Philip's Spanish counsellors may also have been included.

[3] Made at his investiture in the Netherlands in 1549, while his father Charles V was still reigning.

not only failing to mitigate the edicts already in force,[4] but by reinforcing them and even by introducing the inquisition in all its strength. Not only is this inquisition iniquitous and against all divine and human laws, surpassing the worst barbarism ever practised by tyrants, it will also most certainly lead to the dishonouring of God's name and to the utter ruin and desolation of these Netherlands. Under the veil of only a few men's false hypocrisy, it will inevitably destroy all law and order, do away with all honesty, wholly weaken the authority and force of the old laws, customs and ordinances observed from time immemorial. It will deprive the States of this country of all freedom to express their opinion, it will do away with all ancient privileges, franchises and immunities, and not only make the burghers and inhabitants of this country miserable and ever-lasting slaves of the inquisitors, who are worthless people, but even subject the magistrates, officers and all nobles to the mercy of their investigations and visitations, and finally endanger the lives and possessions of all the king's honest and loyal subjects perpetually and openly. Not only will the glory of God and the holy Catholic religion (which they pretend to maintain) be very much affected, but so too will the Majesty of our king and lord. He will be in grave danger of losing the whole of his estate, because normal business will cease, people will leave their trade and be continually incited to sedition, the garrisons of the frontier-towns will become untrustworthy. In a word, the only result will be horrible confusion and disorder.

We have carefully pondered all these matters and duly considered the duty to which we are all bound as faithful vassals of His Majesty and particularly as nobles, that is, as His Majesty's helpers whose function it is to maintain His authority and greatness by providing for the prosperity and safety of the country through our prompt and willing service. We have come to the conclusion that we cannot perform our duty but by obviating those disastrous consequences and by trying at the same time to provide for our personal safety and that of our possessions so that we may not fall a prey to those who would wish to enrich themselves at the cost of our lives and goods under the pretext of religion. Therefore we have decided to form a sacred and legitimate confederation and alliance by which we promise and bind ourselves mutually by solemn oath to prevent by all means the introduction of this inquisition in whatever shape, open or covert, under whatever disguise or mask it may assume, whether bear-

---

[4] As appears from Philip's letters from Segovia which had arrived at Brussels at the beginning of November (see Document 1).

ing the name of inquisition, visitation, edicts or otherwise, and to extirpate and eradicate it entirely as the mother and cause of all disorder and iniquity. We have the example of the inhabitants of the kingdom of Naples before our eyes: they wisely reject it to the great relief and peace of their country.[5]

We protest however before God and men with a good conscience, that we have no intention whatsoever of attempting anything that might eventually dishonour God or diminish the king's grandeur and majesty, or that of his estates; on the contrary our purpose is to maintain the king in his estate and to keep order and peace, suppressing, as much as we can, all seditions, popular risings, monopoly, factions and partiality. We have promised and sworn and now again we promise and swear to preserve this confederation and alliance forever holy and inviolable as long as we shall live. We take Almighty God as witness for our conscience that we will not contravene our alliance in any way, neither in deed nor in word, directly nor indirectly of our own free will. And to ratify this alliance and confederation and make it firm and strong forever, we have promised and do promise each other full assistance with our bodies and goods, as brothers and loyal companions, joining hands so that none of us or of our confederates shall be investigated, harassed, tormented or persecuted in whatever manner, for any cause resulting from the inquisition or on account of the edicts or of our confederation. And if any molestation or persecution does take place involving any of our brothers and allies, whatever and however it may be, we have promised and sworn and promise and swear now to assist them with our bodies and property, to the utmost of our ability without sparing anything and without any exception or subterfuge whatever, just as if it concerned ourselves; and we emphasise that we will not withdraw or absolve ourselves from this confederation, even if those molesters or persecutors try to conceal their persecution by some pretext (for example, by claiming that they only want to punish rebellion, or some similar pretext) provided it is clear that their action is occasioned by these causes. This is of great importance because we maintain that in these and similar cases it is wrong to claim that the crime of rebellion[6] has been committed because its source is the holy zeal and laudable desire to maintain the glory of God, the king's Majesty, the public peace and the safety of our lives and possessions. However, we agree and promise one

---

[5] The nobles and burghers of Naples formed a union against the introduction of the Spanish inquisition in 1547.

[6] From the onset it was feared that the action of the nobles against religious persecution might be construed as attempted revolt.

another that in such cases each of us shall follow the common opinion of all brothers and allies or of those whom we elect to take the decision, so that the sacred union be maintained among us and that what will be done will be the firmer and stabler thanks to our joint assent.

As witness and surety of this confederation and alliance we have invoked and invoke now the most holy name of Almighty God, Creator of heaven and earth, who sees into our consciences and thoughts, and knows that this is our firm decision. We most humbly entreat Him that by His heavenly power He will keep us firm and steady and endow us with such a spirit of prudence and discretion, that, always enjoying good and mature counsel, we may bring our design to a happy conclusion, to the glory of His name, the service of His Majesty the king and the public weal. Amen. H. Brederode. Charles, count of Mansfeld.[7] Louis of Nassau.

[7] Son of Peter Ernest Mansfeld, stadholder of Luxemburg.

4

Petition of 5 April 1566[1]

The text of the Petition was drafted by John Marnix of Tholouse and Louis of Nassau. It was presented to the governess at Brussels by Henry Brederode in the name of the assembled nobles on 5 April 1566.

Madame!

It is common knowledge that throughout Christendom the people of these Netherlands have always been praised for their great fidelity to their seigniors and natural princes, and this is still the case, and that the nobles have always been prominent in this respect, since they have spared neither life nor property to conserve and increase the greatness of their rulers. And we, very humble vassals of His Majesty, wish to do the same and to do even more, so that night and day we are ready to render him most humble service with life and property. And considering the condition of affairs at present, we prefer rather to incur some people's anger than to hide from your Highness something which might afterwards be to the

[1] Groen van Prinsterer ed., *Archives ou Correspondance inédite de la Maison d'Orange-Nassau*, le série, II pp. 8off.

prejudice of His Majesty and undermine the peace and quiet of his provinces. We hope that time will show that of all the services which we have ever rendered or shall in future render to His Majesty, this may be reckoned among the most notable and useful, and we are firmly convinced that Your Highness will highly value our action.

We are not in doubt, Madame, that whatever His Majesty formerly ordained and now again ordains regarding the inquisition and the strict observance of the edicts concerning religion, has some foundation and just title and is intended to continue all that the late emperor, Charles – blessed be his memory – decreed with the best of intentions. Considering however that different times call for different policies, and that for several years past those edicts, even though not very rigorously executed, have caused most serious difficulties, His Majesty's recent refusal[2] to mitigate the edicts in any way, and his strict orders to maintain the inquisition, and to execute the edicts in all their rigour, makes us fear that the present difficulties will undoubtedly increase. But in fact the situation is even worse. There are clear indications everywhere that the people are so exasperated that the final result, we fear, will be an open revolt and a universal rebellion bringing ruin to all the provinces and plunging them into utter misery. The extent of the danger that menaces us being, in our view, so manifest, we have hoped up till now that eventually either the Seigniors[3] or the States of the provinces would draft a remonstrance to Your Highness, with the purpose of remedying that evil by striking at its cause. But since for reasons unknown to us they have not come forward, and the evil is meanwhile daily augmenting, so that open revolt and universal rebellion are imminent, we consider it our bounden duty, incumbent upon us because of our oath of fidelity and homage as well as our zeal to serve His Majesty and our fatherland, to wait no longer but to be the first to come forward and do what we are obliged to do.

We speak the more frankly because we have sufficient reason to hope that His Majesty will not blame us at all for warning him. The matter concerns us more deeply than anyone else, for we are most exposed to the disasters and calamities, which usually spring from such rebellions. Our houses and lands are situated for the greater part in the open fields, and cannot be defended. Moreover, as a result of His Majesty's order to execute the edicts in all their severity, not one of us, or even of all inhabitants of the whole country, whatever his condition, will not be found

[2] The king's letters from Segovia of 17 October 1565 (see Document 1).
[3] When they met at Hoogstraten in March, the great nobles could not agree upon combined action, mainly because Egmont refused to take part.

guilty and sentenced to forfeit his life and property, as all of us will be subject to the defamatory testimony of whoever might like to accuse us on the pretext of the edicts in order to obtain part of our confiscated goods. Only thanks to the duplicity of the responsible officer shall we be able to escape this fate and our lives and property will be entirely at his mercy.

Because of this we have every reason very humbly to implore Your Highness, as we do in this petition, to put these matters right and to dispatch a suitable courier to His Majesty as soon as possible to inform him and entreat him most humbly on our behalf,[4] that he be pleased to take measures to prevent this happening now and in the future. This will never be possible, if the edicts are left in force, for they are the source and origin of all difficulties; thus His Majesty should be asked kindly to repeal them. This is not only very necessary to avert the total ruin and loss of all his provinces, but is also in keeping with reason and justice. And so that he may have no reason to think that we, who only seek to obey him in all humility, would try to restrain him or to impose our will on him (as we don't doubt that our adversaries will say to our disadvantage), we implore His Majesty very humbly that it may please him to seek the advice and consent of the assembled States General for new ordinances and other more suitable and appropriate ways to put matters right without causing such apparent dangers.

We also most humbly entreat Your Highness that while His Majesty is listening to our just petition and making his decisions at his good and just pleasure, Your Highness may meanwhile obviate the dangers which we have described by suspending the inquisition as well as the execution of the edicts until His Majesty has made his decision. And finally we declare with all possible emphasis before God and men that in giving this present warning we have done all we can do according to our duty, and state that if there should occur disasters, disorder, sedition, revolt or bloodshed later on, because no appropriate measures were taken in time, we cannot be criticised for having concealed such an apparent abuse. For which purpose we call God, the king, Your Highness and the members of your council together with our conscience to witness that we have proceeded as becomes the king's good and loyal servants and faithful vassals, keeping within the bounds of our duty. Therefore we are entitled to implore Your Highness to assent to this, before further evils ensue and to do what is right.

---

[4] John Glimes, marquis of Bergen, and Florence Montmorency, baron of Montigny were very shortly entrusted with this mission.

Apostil of the governess

Her Highness has noted the contents of this request and is firmly determined to despatch a courier to His Majesty, to present it to him. Her Highness wants to use her good offices to induce His Majesty to grant the request of the petitioners who may expect a reaction worthy of and in accordance with his innate and customary benignity. Before the arrival of the petitioners, Her Highness, with the assistance and the advice of the governors of the provinces, knights of the Golden Fleece and the members of the State and Privy Council who are with her,[5] had already drafted a plan to be laid before His Majesty for moderating the religious edicts. Her Highness hopes that this plan may be found to give everyone reasonable satisfaction. As the authority of Her Highness (as the petitioners will consider and understand well) does not allow her to suspend the inquisition and the edicts and as it is not becoming to leave the country without law in religious matters, Her Highness is confident that the petitioners will be satisfied with her decision to send a special envoy to His Majesty and, while awaiting the answer, to order the inquisitors, wherever they and the officers respectively are at present, to proceed discreetly and modestly in their office, so that no one shall have cause to complain. Her Highness expects likewise that the petitioners on their part will so conduct themselves that there will be no need to take other measures. There is room to hope that by reason of Her Highness's good offices, His Majesty will agree to stop the inquisition in the provinces where it has been established. The answer given to the request of the chief towns of Brabant that the inquisition should not be introduced there makes this not unlikely.[6] Her Highness is most willing to use her influence with His Majesty to this end, because she takes it for granted that the petitioners are firmly determined to make no innovation at all in the ancient religion of these provinces but will maintain and conserve it with all their power.

Written by Her Highness at Brussels, the sixth day of April 1566, before Easter. Margarita.

[5] This assembly of stadholders, knights of the Golden Fleece and members of the Council of State and the Privy Council took place at the end of March.

[6] On 24 March 1566 in answer to the protest of the four towns of this province of 22 January the Council of Brabant stated that the king did not intend to introduce any novelty and therefore they would not be oppressed by the inquisitors contrary to the prevailing privileges.

The description of the events which happened in the matter of religion in the Netherlands, 1569[1]

The author of the Description is Jacob van Wesenbeke, former pensionary of Antwerp, who emigrated to Germany in April 1567. He was very well-informed as to the events of the year 1566, described here. This work appeared in a French and a Dutch edition in 1569. The Dutch historian Robert Fruin called it 'one of the most accurate and credible accounts we have of the religious movement of the year 1566'.

All people were made to hope that the States General of the country would be called to draft a definitive and good ordinance concerning religion. Such an ordinance, intended to be really binding, to restore calm, to bring no harm to the country and give satisfaction to the inhabitants had been awaited, longed for and yearned for by every one. Shortly afterwards the hope and the satisfaction of the population turned to sadness, hatred and suspicion, because it was discovered that at court men had secretly devised a moderation or new edict which was sent to His Majesty in Spain. And although it had been hoped that the States General would be convoked thereupon, as had been asked in the petition of the nobles[2] and had moreover been promised them, some persons schemed so ingeniously and successfully that it was resolved to present this moderation, not to the States General convoked for that purpose but to the provincial States of every province one after the other and, in the same order, to the provincial councils. Learning this many people feared and concluded that no good would arise from such a procedure and that things would grow worse every day, for they were far from confident that the result would come up to the hope deeply cherished by the people. No one, it was feared, would like to be subjected to such private consultation and the population continued to favour the convocation of the States General as an alternative acceptable to everybody. This suspicion, this distrust and this embitterment greatly increased and took root in people's

[1] *De beschrijvinge van den geschiedenissen inder religien saken toeghedragen in den Nederlanden* (Knuttel, no. 147).
[2] See the text of the petition and the apostil of the governess, Document 4.

hearts when they saw clearly, that some provincial States were ordered to meet separately (according to the aforementioned plan) in the presence of their governors or other knights of the Order or lords of high rank who were sent there to persuade them to accept the proposed moderation. Moreover, people's perplexity and despair about the results were complete when it was found that the provincial States were left so little liberty in convoking the meeting that only a few selected members were summoned and many, who also belonged there, were omitted and in several places people were even excluded who usually attended the meetings. Moreover, discussion was almost impossible; members were not allowed the usual time or means to deliberate and consult others, and were made to swear that they would not notify anyone of the proceedings or inform any members of the councils in the towns they came from except the magistrates. In short the approval of States meeting in such circumstances was generally considered to be an extorted rather than a free and frank opinion. People who attended the discussions in the States of Artois, Hainault, Namur and Tournay know that this was the way it went.

A further important reason for scandal and discontent was the fact that the States were first convoked in the provinces which were least accustomed to show that they have some freedom and were most subject to the inquisition and the persecutions, while in the provinces which were most influenced by the novel developments, possessed the greatest privileges and had through words and deeds most boldly defended the freedom of the country, the States were not convoked at all. This was the case in Holland, Friesland, Gelderland, Luxemburg, Limburg, Zeeland, Overijssel and others (which have never been convoked since)[3] and above all Brabant, the principal and most important province.[4] As to the province second in importance, Flanders, this was only convoked after the States mentioned previously had met and passed judgment. And though every attempt was made to keep secret the contents of the new edict as well as the opinion of the States assembled to discuss it (which made things look even more suspicious to the common people), there were nevertheless some people who succeeded in discovering part of the truth and got to

[3] Holland and Zeeland belonged with Brabant, Flanders and others to the so-called patrimonial provinces. Friesland, Overijssel, Gelderland and Utrecht were acquired during the reign of Charles V; of these only Utrecht was normally summoned to the meetings of the States General. Luxemburg did not attend these meetings either.

[4] Cf. Document 4, note 6.

know still more about it when the States and Members of Flanders, told of the limitations prescribed for their meeting, with the utmost difficulty obtained at first four days' and later eight days' delay. And it became known that these States had given their approval to the new edict (though with some restrictions and conditions added by the secular States) without having, in the old way, convoked and heard all their members and councillors. All this caused a violent commotion among the people. Many different booklets and pamphlets were immediately written and distributed in various places arguing that the new edict was illegal, that it was no better than all the previous edicts, that the inquisition was still in force, that all this was the work of the adherents of Cardinal Granvelle, some of them mentioned by name,[5] and of the inquisitors who wanted to cause bloody disturbances, that it was done contrary to the promise made to the nobles and to the freedom of the country, that this way of assembling the States was an innovation never before witnessed, that this could not therefore be called approval of the edict and that it was entirely null. People were earnestly exhorted to oppose it forcefully and not to allow the enemies of the country to deceive the king and the governess and to give them false information any longer but to arrest and punish them. All this was accompanied by yet more strong and violent arguments and exclamations. It proved impossible to stop the flood of publications by prohibiting them, for the more the court issued edicts against them, the more the number of such booklets and writings increased. One complained that the commonalty was deprived of its liberty to explain and to discover the truth openly, whether in the councils of the provinces and the towns or in clear remonstrances and writings, although on this depended the prosperity of the country. People wrote that these outrages would very soon have all sorts of evil consequences and suggested that the men who thus wanted to keep the king and the country in servitude, were afraid that their treachery would be revealed if the States General were convoked in the proper fashion and allowed to give their opinion freely. Soon, because of the refusal and delay in convoking the States, the commotion, embitterment and grumbling that had existed among the people before the nobles presented their petition, began anew.

This, however, was much more serious than before because the inhabitants, made much more hard-hearted and embittered by the course of events, gave up all hope of improvement and redress since the dis-

---

[5] The supporters at court of Cardinal Granvelle who had left the Netherlands in 1564. Among them were Viglius of Aytta and Berlaymont.

tinguished assembly and well-founded petition of the nobles as well as the promises made to them had been of no avail, and because they saw clearly that it was not the intention of the court to convoke the States General, or, if it was its intention, that there would be people to prevent it from being brought about although the meeting of the States General was considered by all sensible people to be the only remedy against the troubles. What else could be concluded when neither the supplication of the nobles, nor the desire of various provinces and towns intimated long before,[6] nor the consent of many of the most important lords, including those who sat in the council and agreed to it and thought it necessary,[7] had succeeded in persuading the court to do it? There seemed nothing left to give them hope that the promises given to the nobles might be kept, or that the inhabitants might be released from the hated persecutions and odious inquisition, or might be given some relief or exemption from the slavery and servitude of their consciences which they had been enduring for such a long time. Despair made those who dissented in religion more obdurate and made them prefer to oppose the government openly and confess their belief frankly, rather than to remain for ever oppressed and subdued. This was the reason why they started to hold their meetings and services each day more openly,[8] thus getting so many more adherents. The others too now became embittered and opposed to the way in which the matter was being dealt with, and began to turn against the doctrines of the authorities who, in their opinion, were the cause of all these troubles, commotions and outrages.

[6] The States of Brabant insisted on this as early as 1565.
[7] The prince of Orange and his supporters (Hoorne, Bergen, etc.).
[8] Calvinist public services started in Flanders and near Antwerp as early as May 1566.

6

Philip II to the duchess of Parma, 31 July 1566[1]

In his letters to the governess Margaret of Parma from the Segovia woods dated 31 July 1566 the king finally answered the urgent mis-

[1] F. A. F. Th. de Reiffenberg ed., *Correspondance de Marguerite d'Autriche avec Philippe II* (Brussels, 1842), pp. 96ff; H. A. Enno van Gelder ed., *Correspondance française de Marguerite d'Autriche, duchesse de Parme, avec Philippe II*, ii (Utrecht, 1941) pp. 269ff.

sives about the actions of the nobles which the duchess had been sending to Spain since the end of March. They arrived at Brussels just as image-breaking began in the Netherlands (12 August). In the meantime King Philip made a notary public draw up a statement that the concessions in these letters were extorted from him and did not bind him in conscience.

Madame my dear sister,

Since my last letters of 6 May I have received several letters, to wit of the 4th and 29th of the same month brought by baron of Montigny and of 21 June and the 7th inst., with a duplicate of the one of the 4th which the marquis of Bergen, who has not yet arrived, was commissioned to bring me.[2] All of them tell me of the great troubles and disturbances stirred up in the Netherlands to my regret, on the pretext of religion, after some confederates presented to you a petition in which they called the inquisition in question and asked to abolish the religious edicts and to draft others in collaboration with the States General, and to suspend the execution of both inquisition and edicts until I shall have made my decision.[3] In these letters you also described to me the great danger and troubles into which the country would otherwise undoubtedly fall, as well as the daily increase in the numbers of the confederates and the boldness which the heretics and the sectarians have lately been displaying. Bearing arms and sticks for their protection they even dare to hold their sermons and meetings in public[4] in the neighbourhood of the great towns you mentioned in your letters. And they claim that this is allowed by the apostil which you ordered to be added to the petition, and in which you stated that you would inform me and would give orders that the inquisitors as well as the other officers should, wherever they had so far been performing their tasks proceed with discretion and modesty.[5] This they wrongly interpret as a provisional decision to stop the proceedings against heretics.

To remedy this you told me earlier that your advisers saw only two possibilities, namely to take up arms (which would be very difficult) or to give in on some points, to abolish the inquisition and to moderate the rigour of the edicts little by little. Some time later a memorandum was

[2] Florence Montmorency, baron of Montigny, arrived at Madrid as envoy from the Netherlands in the middle of June. John Glimes, marquis of Bergen, was delayed because of illness and arrived later on.

[3] See the text of the petition, Document 4, p. 64.

[4] See the Description, Document 5, p. 69.

[5] See the apostil of the governess, Document 4, p. 65.

drawn up containing this suggestion, so that the provincial councils and the provincial States (each meeting separately) might be asked for advice about it.[6] At the same time a general pardon would be announced for those who had taken part in the confederacy. And though it was impossible to guarantee that this would remove the dangers, yet it was thought that much would thus be gained. The league or confederacy would be broken, several honourable men would be satisfied and be given security, and the latter could afterwards be used against the others. I would hear further particulars about all this from the afore-mentioned marquis of Bergen and Montigny, whom you decided to send to me for this purpose. You added that if the proposal were refused, several seigniors in the Low Countries dare not rely on those who have to assist them in case of need, nor take up arms to maintain the inquisition and the edicts in all their rigour and you ended by insisting on the necessity for me to make a decision immediately (because otherwise religion and my lands in the Low Countries would both be in immediate danger of being lost) and to advance the date of my journey – which is so necessary to remedy the disturbances which go continually from bad to worse – thither. Your letters give a detailed account of all these matters and contain still other points which I will answer later, but which to avoid prolixity I will not dwell upon, because they are well-known to you.

I am certain, Madame my dear sister, that you can easily imagine the great sorrow this very important matter causes me. What is at stake is on the one hand the respect for our holy Catholic faith which I have always had at heart and furthered with due zeal and in accordance with the obligation I have to maintain it; on the other hand I fear that great difficulties and trouble might come to so many of the honest vassals and subjects whom I have in the Low Countries: I cannot forget the natural affection I have always had and still have for them. In truth I cannot understand how this great evil originated and why it has increased so much in such a short time. Since my departure from there,[7] I have not heard of any cruel execution or rigorous prosecution having been undertaken on the strength of the inquisition or the edicts, which might account for these difficulties.

In the old edict there was always the possibility of moderation or of grace. The letters I wrote to you from here last year[8] did not contain any innovation in the religious field; they only said that there should not be any innovations concerning the inquisition and the edicts and that every-

---

6 See the Description, Document 5, p. 66.   7 In August 1559.
8 Dated from 17 October 1565, Document 1, pp. 53ff.

thing should remain as it had been in the times of the emperor my lord and father whom God has in His glory, and in my own life time.

I took a long time to answer your letters, because those of 4 May referred expressly to further information which the seigniors of Bergen and Montigny would give me and, secondly, because you also told me that, as mentioned above, you had asked for advice. Under these circumstances it seemed to me that I neither should nor could take a decision before the arrival of the two gentlemen and before having received that advice, and I therefore thought it necessary to wait. As the baron of Montigny has not yet brought all the papers, I have been waiting all the time for those that are missing to be brought either by the marquis or in some other way. When I realised at last that it was useless to wait any longer for the arrival of the marquis (I have heard since, that he was held up on his way by ill-health) and that the papers he had with him and which he sent to me from his sick-bed did not contain the afore-said advice, I ordered the papers to be examined without any more delay because of the great urgency of the matter on which you insist in your letters and also in those of the 7th inst. I have now decided upon those three things: the inquisition, the moderation of the edicts as well as a general pardon, and my visit to the Low Countries, and everything connected with these things, as you will see. I should like to tell you that it is not only because of the necessity to act in this way (although your arguments are fully justified) that I have, without letting any other consideration influence my decision, complied with all requests so far as my good conscience and the obligation I have to serve God and to conserve the holy faith and the state allow me, but also because I am naturally inclined to treat my vassals and subjects rather with love and clemency than with rigour and severity.

Taking the various points separately and first of all that about the inquisition, I know how important this is. It is the only means the Church has at her disposal of making every one live and behave according to her commandments. It is an instrument which has been applied since ancient times and is fully legitimate according to canon and civil law, to Holy Scripture and natural reason. Its purpose is to see that those who don't behave as they should and fail to do as the Church commands, should be admonished and brought back to the right path and reprimanded, if necessary. If the inquisition were abolished, this would no longer be possible, and it would seem that then every one would be permitted to live almost as he likes. However, as the inquisition was originally introduced into my territories in the Law Courts because there were not enough bishops then and because the persons in charge were negligent,

I feel that the situation is now different.[9] The present bishops are good pastors and can give their flock the care to which they are entitled, so that they may behave in accordance with the ordinances of our holy mother Church and also with the moral conceptions upheld in that region, as can be concluded from the instruction given to baron Montigny. Taking also into consideration the wishes expressed by the seigniors, the character of the time we live in and especially the nature of this matter, I have decided after long and mature deliberation to acquiesce in this. As the episcopal jurisdiction is now fully and firmly established I am content for the inquisition to cease.

As to the request to moderate the edicts and to revise them accordingly, it is most improbable that this would be useful. The heretics and sectarians who as they daily give to understand in the booklets they distribute, demand absolute religious liberty, will be just as little satisfied as the confederates who, it seems from their petition, have a different end in view and desire that an entirely new edict should be framed on the advice of the States General. Add to this that for honest people it is unnecessary to 'make such or any other ordinance; even the four chief towns of Brabant have expressly declared in their request that they will obey the edicts.[10] Thus it seems to follow that a new ordinance is totally unnecessary or, at any rate not required immediately. However, in view of the arguments put forward in your letters and because in the Low Countries it is hoped that the confederation might be broken in this way and those gentlemen be enabled to deal firmly with the evil-minded, I think it right to agree to this now, and, the sooner the better...

I have therefore found it appropriate and necessary to moderate the edict in some way or another on condition that the holy Catholic faith and my authority be maintained and that special notice be taken of the points and articles mentioned. You must send the proposal to me and I shall take a decision without further delay, as I think right; and I shall do all that is possible.

As to the general pardon, there is reason to fear that hardly any profit will arise from it over there, because it is doubtful whether the sectarians and confederates will give up their malevolent attitude when they see that

[9] Before 1559 there were only a few bishoprics (Utrecht, Liège, Cambrai, Tournai, Arras, Münster, Osnabrück). By a papal decree of 1559 at the instigation of Philip II three archbishoprics were instituted under which fifteen bishoprics would fall henceforth.

[10] In their protest to the Council of Brabant dated 22 January 1566 against the introduction of the inquisition.

their plans for almost complete religious liberty are thwarted. I am not sure, moreover, what is meant by a general pardon, and whether it applies only to the confederates or rather to the conventiclers and in general to all heretics and those who broke the edicts...But I have always been inclined to treat my vassals and subjects with the utmost clemency, abhorring nothing so much as the use of severity when things may be remedied in another way. If therefore you see that the difficulties are being overcome by means of the above-mentioned measures and that a general pardon would be the final measure to pacify the country, I grant you permission to give it in the form and way you think best. You may make it applicable to the confederates only or to the others too; to people sentenced in the past and to people who have not yet been brought to trial at the date of the proclamation of this pardon. My condition, however, is that these leagues and confederations will be broken up and that those who have been guilty of taking part in leagues, confederations, conventicles and sects or of breaking the edicts in any other way, do not do this any longer and will behave in future as is becoming to good Catholics, vassals and subjects of mine. And as to the three points mentioned it is my intention that my orders be carried out in the prescribed form and manner. But before starting upon this course you must make certain that these seigniors will meanwhile do their utmost to maintain the holy religion and the peace of the state and oppose all leagues, confederations, assemblies, riots and similar things.

As for my journey to the Low Countries, I certainly have a great desire to be there before this winter, and I have examined all possible routes, even over the ocean, but there are several difficulties and it is already so late in the year that I do not see how I could do it. At the moment I am considering which of the two ways I had better take, either the one I have just mentioned, or by the Mediterranean. But by whichever way I go, I will not fail to come, please God. I expect to be with you at the latest next spring and if there is a way of going earlier, be sure that I won't fail to use it.

Meanwhile the situation there must be improved; the religious services and most pernicious and dangerous assemblies with all the troubles that may ensue from them, must be stopped. You had better send some troops of ordinance[11] to the places where they are held, and foot-soldiers from the garrisons, to hinder and disturb them. For the rest, do what should be

---

[11] The troops of ordinance as the nucleus of a standing army date from the time of the Burgundian duke Charles the Bold (d. 1477). They were composed of cavalry under the command of great nobles.

done....And if it becomes necessary to give you more assistance and troops, I am negotiating to send some cavalry and foot soldiers from Germany to support you; I shall give particulars in my later dispatches. I shall also take care to send you with the next dispatch a provision of 300,000 écus about which I shall then write to you in detail.

From the Segovia woods, the last day of July 1566

Post data. Before this letter was closed, your letter of the 19th inst. arrived with news about the state of affairs over there and among other things about the proposal to assemble the States General as the only solution at present; you add the arguments pro and contra.[12] Together with this letter I have also read the written considerations and I wish to answer you more fully in my next letter. Meanwhile I demand and instruct you not to tolerate in any way the holding of such a general assembly.

[12] See the Description, Document 5, p. 69.

7

The prince of Orange to the duchess of Parma, Antwerp, 4 September 1566[1]

The prince of Orange who had left Antwerp on 18 August 1566, returned at the end of the month. He then concluded an agreement with the consistory of that town which assigned three meeting-places within the walls to the Calvinists.

Madame, all the time I have been in this town, I have been continually hindered from putting things straight. On my arrival I found everything in great disorder because those of the new religion who are so numerous in this town, had become so licentious and audacious, that they tried to subject everything to their will. Finally after several discussions and despatches from both sides, it was considered fitting to come to an agreement with them. I send a duplicate of this to Your Highness: you will see that I did not in any way wish to go beyond the points contained

[1] L. P. Gachard ed., *Correspondance de Guillaume le Taciturne*, II (Brussels, 1850) pp. 213ff.

in the accord made with the confederate seigniors and nobles.[2] There are even several additional articles which aim to maintain and assure the religion, our ancient and Catholic faith, the service of the king, the protection and safety of the town as well as the justice and public order in it. On the other hand, Madame, the agreement allows those of the townspeople who belong to the new religion to have their services within the town. Before taking leave of Your Highness, I explained at length why it seemed to me more expedient to let them have their sermons within the town than outside. To remind Your Highness of my arguments I shall repeat them here.

Whenever such sermons take place 18 or 20,000 persons leave the town through various gates, to listen to them. In Flanders and elsewhere trade as well as industry stagnate, so that the country is full of vagabonds and idlers. These might easily mingle with the crowd under the pretext of listening to the sermons, join them (of this we have been warned and are still being warned) and then enter the town together and pillage it. In fact they have said themselves that this is their intention, because it is the richest and most opulent town of the whole country and the one where the most plunder is to be found. They will unite with the great multitude of workmen in this town, who cannot earn wages to sustain themselves, their wives and children because of the troubles and stagnation of trade. Although we do our utmost here, Madame, at the gates and elsewhere, to ensure that strangers do not enter in great numbers, such a lot of strangers of all sorts and conditions have all the same got in and are still inside under pretext of some trade business, that I am greatly puzzled how to get them outside so that the town may be at rest and in order. For these reasons it is easy to imagine how all these vagabonds and others may increase in number and enter with those who go outside to hear sermons. But thanks to the new agreement the latter need no longer go outside the town to attend sermons. I wanted to inform your Highness of all of this and I beg you to approve my action in making this agreement. Thanks to it all churches will be opened to celebrate mass in the usual way without any fear and this is the chief thing we should work for. Your Highness is now informed of the very great number of people belonging to the new religion in this town.

[2] According to the agreement which the governess concluded with the delegates of the confederate nobles at the height of the image-breaking on 23 August public services would be tolerated at those places where they had been held up to that moment. On the other hand the nobles would help to uphold the law and dissolve the Compromise. The nobles were also promised impunity for their action.

I most humbly kiss your hand, Madame, and ask God to keep your Highness in good health and to give you a very good and long life. From Antwerp, the fourth day of September 1566

8

Second letter of the prince of Orange to the duchess of Parma, 4 September 1566[1]

Madame, since my last letter of to-day I have received the letters it has pleased Your Highness to write to me, and I cannot fail to thank you very humbly for approving all I have done here so far. Regarding your order not to permit in any way those of the new religion to preach within the town, and to concede to them nothing more than the declaration given to the confederate seigniors and nobles implies, Your Highness will have seen from my last letter why I decided to come to an agreement with them and, on conditions specified in the document, to allow them to hold their sermons within the town. But, Madame, in the resolution given to the nobles it is said that the sermons should not be held in places where they were not held before. And before this resolution was taken, those of the new religion did hold sermons here, not only within the town, but also inside the churches. I assure Your Highness that, when they expounded this to me it was very difficult for me to make them vacate all churches and monasteries but, contrary to their wishes, I have only given them permission to preach in the places mentioned in the agreement. I thought it right to do this, to avoid the grave difficulties and dangers which might otherwise arise. And about what Your Highness has written to me, that the other towns where the new religion is being preached will want to have the same licence, one town differs from another. Nowhere are there so many adherents of the new religion as well as so many strangers of all sorts and conditions as here and there is no other town which vagabonds and idlers are so eager to pillage. In the other towns it will therefore be easier to restrict oneself to the declaration given to the confederates. As far as my own provinces[2] are concerned, I had missives sent everywhere ordering the people to observe this resolution. I sent

[1] See Document 7, note 1.
[2] The prince was stadholder of Holland, Zeeland and Utrecht.

77

them a copy of it as well as of the edicts against the church-robbers, and I guarantee that, as I was charged by Your Highness, they will see that it is observed. I much regret that for the reasons and considerations mentioned in my preceding letter and to avoid greater evils and difficulties, it has been necessary to permit this here, with the restrictions specified in the agreement. I was led to do this by my great desire to conform to the will of His Majesty and Your Highness. I cannot fail to tell you that the Anabaptists are also beginning to preach not only outside this town, but in several places in the country-side. May it please Your Highness to forbid them by edict before they increase in number...

9

A true narrative and apology of what has happened in the Netherlands in the matter of religion in the year 1566. By those who profess the reformed religion in that country, 1567[1]

This was written by Philip Marnix of St Aldegonde, the younger brother of John Marnix of Tholouse. He moved from the outset in the circles of the confederate nobles and the Calvinist consistories. In this work, published anonymously in 1567, he looks back on the events of 1566.

The final point to be considered is the image-breaking, for which the adherents of the new religion are more severely reproached than for anything else. This is interpreted as an act of public violence and as a seditious act clearly intended to disrupt all political order. In short, some think this fact alone is of such a nature that only the ruin and extermination of the greater part of the subjects can represent sufficient satisfaction for His Majesty. But if those who pass such a judgment and give this advice to His Majesty, were inspired by the desire to see justice prevail and wished to further the public weal rather than their own profit and career, they would give closer attention to how this action came about and who gave the advice and counsel to do it, by whom it was executed, and where the fault that was committed chiefly lies. And then finally they

[1] J. J. van Toorenenbergen ed., *Ph. van Marnix van St Aldegonde: Godsdienstige en kerkelijke geschriften*, I (The Hague, 1871), pp. 98ff., p. 109.

would weigh the evil they think so great, against the difficulties which might arise if their advice were acted upon.

For even if breaking and cutting images is the most enormous and capital crime to be committed or imagined, yet they do not know whom to blame for it. It is still uncertain who the persons were who did it so promptly and it is still more uncertain who advised them to do it. To accuse the ministers, the elders or consistories of the churches or the assemblies of those who adhere to the reformed religion, would be shameless, for no one has ever succeeded in extorting a confession from the men executed for this crime, in spite of the torments and sufferings inflicted upon them. On the contrary one knows that the adherents of that religion have always been of the opinion that private persons must not cut down images erected by the public authorities. This they declared several times in public exhortations as well as in private remonstrances, always so that no one should be given offence. And no one who ever took the trouble to study their doctrine can be ignorant of this. But even if they had thought such action justifiable (which is not true at all), it is at all events certain that they never wanted to do it. Moreover, at the time it was done, it was useless to them. They had unanimously decided to send deputies to Brussels to beg Her Highness provisionally to grant them some churches or other public places in which to practise their religion, in order to avoid disturbances and riots.[2] They had great hopes of obtaining this because every one could see that it was the only way to keep the people quiet and tranquil. Would they not damage their cause and fall out of favour with Her Highness, if at the same time they ventured to perform a deed so prejudicial and contrary to their request? Thus it is obvious that they were never of that opinion and intention.

I concede that among the image breakers there were people who professed to be of the religion, but I also say that there were as many others who did not make and never made that profession. In several places one even saw only women and children busily destroying things. In several other places the bishops and priests began to hide their most beautiful rings and the citizens followed suit, thinking that orders had been given to hide whatever might be saved, until the children and street-boys de-

---

[2] At the end of July 1566 the confederate nobles handed a second petition to the regent after deliberations with the Calvinist delegates of the consistories at a meeting at St Trond (in the bishopric of Liège). In this they once more insisted that religious persecution should cease. The Calvinist synod at Antwerp intended to present a petition at Brussels towards the end of August asking that some churches be put at their disposal.

stroyed the rest. In some places the magistrates sent their officers to accomplish the task and they were followed by the common people. Even now one does not know who were the originators. There are, however, strong suspicions and clear indications that it was the priests who started this as a device to set the magistrates against those of the religion (in the past they undoubtedly often did such things to cause new persecutions), as well as to ruin the plan, unanimously accepted by all the churches to send a request to Her Highness. Time was short for the priests and their adherents realised that if the churches' plea were indeed accomplished, their own little schemes would be entirely wrecked. And indeed, after the troubles at Antwerp had died down another riot was instigated by some who forced their way into the Church of Our Lady.[3] Six of those responsible were apprehended and hanged the day after. There were four papists among them and one of these was a well-known nobleman who had urged the others on. So we have to presume that by means of such a stratagem they tried to wreck the churches' plan. This is proved by later events for, because of this, the request was not presented and those of the religion afterwards met with nothing but disfavour and hatred.

And yet, to tell the whole truth, these events were due not so much to such stratagems, but to the manifest providence of God who wanted to show how much He detests and abhors the abominable idolatry committed around these images to the disgrace of the name of Christ and the whole of Christendom. He wanted to stigmatise and ridicule the foolish imagination of people who always wish to contrive new ways to honour Him. For people who wanted to go on adoring and serving images contrary to God's commandment, sought excuses similar to those brought forward by the ancient pagans (which Justin, Lactantius, Origen, Augustine and other holy fathers criticised) and declared that they knew very well that the images were only wood and stone, and that they did not adore them but only what was represented by them. Notwithstanding this we see, I say, that the poor people committed and are still committing every day such horrible and abominable idolatries in connection with those statues, that every God-fearing man cannot fail to shudder with horror...

And certainly, considering the facts in all their detail, it is easy to see that God Himself intervened to lead the whole action and carry it out and men cannot resist God's power. How else could women, children and men

[3] The image-breaking raged violently at Antwerp on 19 August and the following days, especially in the cathedral.

without authority, without arms, in small numbers, for the greater part poor and humble people, pull down and destroy nearly everywhere in the country so many images, altars and church-ornaments in only four or five days? Various master masons assert that even with the help of fifty men they would not have been able to destroy in eight days what a small number of boys destroyed in one or two days in the most famous and bustling towns of the Netherlands, in full view of every one and without meeting with any difficulty or interference.

Who is so blind or so dull that he does not see and understand that the hand and the power of God brought all this about? Of God, I say, who struck the magistrates with stupor and tied their hands, lest they try to prevent His work? Certainly if a sparrow does not fall to the ground without His will and ordination, how can we think that such almost incredible work happened by chance or through the will and diligence of men?

10

Request of those of the new religion to the nobles confederated in the Compromise, 1567[1]

This request of the consistories was addressed to the few remaining nobles of the Compromise (Brederode and some others), who added it to the third petition that was handed to the governess on their behalf on 8 February 1567. This petition was stubbornly rejected by Margaret.

To the confederated seigniors and nobles,
My lords, because of the ardent desire we have always cherished to see the service of God and of the king in these Low Countries well and firmly established so that his obedient and faithful vassals and subjects might enjoy the state of prosperity they have so long been waiting for, we greatly rejoiced when we noticed that thanks to the agreement of 23 August such felicity had begun to be realised.[2] We hoped then that this excellent measure, inspired – as it has pleased you to declare to us – by

---

[1] *Requeste de ceulx de la religion nouvelle aux gentilzhommes confederez* (Knuttel, no. 151).
[2] See Document 7, note 2.

order of Her Highness and promises of the seigniors knights of the Order,[3] might be kept inviolate to the prosperity of the country and the satisfaction of His Majesty's subjects. But to our very great regret we have found for a long time now and are finding every day more and more through clear, pernicious and very dangerous experiences, that the assurance which was given to us by you, seigniors, served only to make us stop our activities and to lull us, while means were being prepared and set in train to ruin and overwhelm us completely. We thought, according to the promises which it pleased you to give us, that it was the intention of the king and Her Highness that the inquisition and the execution of the religious edicts should cease and that public preaching (by which, it was declared, was meant the entire practice of our religion) should be permitted until such time as His Majesty and the States General of these Low Countries, legitimately assembled, would make some other resolution.

However, now, contrary to our expectations – which were based on your promises – we have seen that the edicts have been rigorously executed, and that some people who refused to swear to persevere for ever in the faith of the Roman Church have been imprisoned and banished. The ministers of God's word have been persecuted, some even hanged, others have had their beards torn off, harquebuses were fired and discharged at them, and some, who were standing close by, were mortally wounded. The assembled crowd was assaulted, some were miserably killed for attending services, others for chanting psalms when they returned from services, some were banished for having had their children baptised in the reformed church,[4] and the children of others, baptised in this church, were seized and rebaptised forcibly in public by people who behaved in this respect as Anabaptists rather than adherents of the ancient canons. Letters were sent throughout the country prohibiting on pain of death all practise of the religion. The result was not only that in several places preaching was stopped but also that several of his Majesty's faithful subjects abandoned the country, their wives and their children because of these menaces. Hatred of the religion which we profess has also caused the people of Valenciennes[5] and the whole country around, to be more

---

[3] The accord of 23 August with the confederated nobles was concluded through the mediation of the knights of the Golden Fleece: Orange, Egmont and Hoorne.

[4] In the opinion of the Calvinists baptism, the Lord's Supper, and other ecclesiastical ceremonies formed as much a part of the practice of their religion as preaching.

[5] The town of Valenciennes had been invested since the end of 1566 by Margaret of Parma's newly levied troops under the command of Noircarmes.

grievously afflicted than they ever were by the avowed enemies of the country in the recent wars.[6] And it is beyond doubt that, if defeated, the same fate immediately awaits all the other churches. In Gelderland, Friesland and elsewhere,[7] similar attacks daily take place and in several parts of this country attempts are being made to extirpate the practise of our religion not only by secret tricks and practices through the magistrates and the provincial States but also openly and by force. The country is swarming with armed men, by whom those of the religion in several towns and villages have been and still are more roughly treated than ever before by foreign enemies. They are outraged, pillaged, ravaged, their wives and daughters raped and many other intolerable outrages which need not be specified, are regularly committed.

All this is, as your seigniors know, directly contrary to your petition of 5 April[8] and to the promises and assurances you have so often made to us. And though it is true that some professing the religion may have gone too far after your promises had been made, this was before there were any negotiations with them, and it ought not to be an excuse for punishing the others who very much regret those excesses. Moreover after negotiations had started, they willingly submitted to reason. If it is found that one of us does something that cannot be permitted, we accept, as is reasonable, that he be duly punished. It has always been our ardent desire and our intention to behave unpretentiously and unobtrusively, to practise all due obedience, and to perform all other normal duties because this is the way a just citizen must act and also because we hope that leave to practise our religion freely will be continued. Your seigniors may now ask themselves if we who thought ourselves safe thanks to your promises but find ourselves so outrageously afflicted, have reason to complain of being abused, and, so to say, led to the slaughter house, and, under the pretence of obtaining liberty, rendered utterly miserable.

[6] The French, against whom war had been waged until 1559.
[7] The provinces of Gelderland and Friesland were under the stadholders Megen and Aremberg, who were entirely loyal to the governess.
[8] See Document 4, pp. 62ff.

II

The prince of Orange's warning to the inhabitants and subjects of the Netherlands, 1 September 1568[1]

The Warning of the prince of Orange appeared when the prince, a refugee from the Netherlands since April 1567, was preparing to invade Brabant with the help of troops levied in Germany. The invasion actually took place in October.

Firstly, we would remind you of something that is clear to every one, that the Netherlands have always been ruled and reigned over by their princes and overlords with all gentleness, right and reason and wholly in accordance with their freedoms, rights, customs, traditions and privileges, which have always been observed there and were obtained in former times from emperors, kings, dukes, counts and seigniors by the inhabitants of the country, great friends and supporters of their liberty and enemies to all violence and oppression. The princes as well as the subjects of the country have always had to commit themselves by a formal contract and to swear a solemn oath that they would maintain these rights and realise them. The inhabitants therefore owe obedience to the rulers only on condition that the freedoms are maintained – and it should be added that respect for the privileges brought our dear fatherland all that power, richness and prosperity which one found there in the past.

Neither can it be denied, since it is so plain and definite, that for over fifty years since the time when the countries of Spain came by marriage together with the Netherlands under one sovereign[2] some grandees of Spain have been intent on somehow obtaining power to govern and tyrannise over so prosperous a country as they do elsewhere. And though the freedoms and privileges of the Netherlands always meant that their attempts failed, nevertheless they did not cease to be on the watch for opportunities to mislead the benevolent prince so completely that ultimately they would achieve their aim. It is also only too obvious that

---

[1] *Verantwoordinge, verklaringhe ende waerschowinghe des Princen van Oraengien*, ed. M. G. Schenk (Amsterdam, 1933), pp. 120ff.

[2] The marriage of Philip the Fair with Joanna of Aragon in 1496. She became heiress to the Spanish throne through the deaths of her brother and elder sisters.

Cardinal Granvelle and his adherents took an unfair advantage of the faith of the trustful and good prince and, seeking only to rule and dominate the Low Countries completely in order to satisfy their ambition, avarice and other passions, proposed all those leagues, practices and strange innovations that were to serve as means utterly to enslave the conscience, persons and possessions of the whole population, nay to rob them of all their freedoms, rights and privileges. Of course all this was given the appearance of holy zeal and said to be done in the name of religion as well as of the majesty and service of the king, but in reality it was greatly to the disservice of God, the king and the country. It was to this end that so many strange innovations, cruel persecutions, bloody edicts, an unbearable inquisition, the supersession of the bishops, the capture of the abbeys,[3] the proclamation of the regulations of the council,[4] cruel executions of the Christians and more unheard of inventions against the freedom of the country and the will of the people were proposed and executed.

We and other seigniors and brethren who sought and are seeking only to serve God, the king and the country well and continually and to further the freedom and prosperity of subjects and inhabitants, protested several times and showed how wrong all this was. We have always said that it is better to act with gentleness than with severity and we think that it is better and more reasonable to keep promises than to break them and to violate oaths. For these reasons the cardinal and his adherents and those who collaborated with him in Spain not only conceived a great hatred and unjustified envy for us, but also contrived to obscure and to distort the truth with false and deceitful practices and denunciations so that the gracious king, ill-informed about all these matters, thought that our loyal advice, actions and services originated from ambition and that his good loyal subjects were rebellious, disobedient and refractory (though this was quite untrue). Thus they succeeded in being allowed to proceed at discretion, which was what they had desired for so long.

It is clear that the inquisitions, executions, mandates, persecutions, innovations and proposals of the cardinal and his men (usurping on the powers not only of the governess but also of the king) damaged and harmed the country very much and alarmed, drove away, robbed and killed a very large number of the inhabitants. At the same time they impaired and hindered the old customary freedom. Nevertheless we see

[3] See Document 6, note 9. Abbeys were incorporated into the new bishoprics in order to ensure the latter sufficient revenues.
[4] The decrees of the Council of Trent.

nowadays with great heart-ache, and it is to be feared that if God does not help us – what we trust He will do and what we are preparing ourselves for to the utmost of our ability – we may see on an even larger scale, how greatly and grievously all the afore-mentioned innovations, proposals, oppressions, inquisitions, persecutions, murders, seizures, executions and tyrannies have increased and multiplied, and how totally inhuman they have become since the duke (in name of the king and shielding himself with the king's authority) arrived here with his Spanish soldiers.[5] And we also see how these countries have fallen from the greatest prosperity into the utmost misery, how the worthy inhabitants who enjoyed freedom in former times have been brought into unbearable slavery and how piteously the privileges and rights of the country together with the religion of God are lying there oppressed and destroyed.

[5] The duke of Alva arrived at Brussels on 22 August 1567.

12

Faithful exhortation to the inhabitants of the Netherlands against the vain and false hopes their oppressors hold out to them, 1568[1]

This is the prince of Orange's reaction to the duke of Alva's edict of 11 November 1568 against the many pamphlets appearing at the time. The prince had already been forced to withdraw his troops from the Netherlands after the failure of the year's campaign.

Awake therefore and do not allow yourselves to be further deceived by those totally false and vain promises which your oppressors and the common enemies put about in order to win a richer booty later. Do not allow your minds to be bewildered any longer by the beautiful titles to which they refer in that edict[2] and generally in relation to all their activities, trying to justify their iniquities, acts of violence, massacres and rapines by the authority of the king, the charge of the governor, the name of justice, the respect of sovereignty, the title of edicts, the pretext of religion, the hope of pardon, the feigning of clemency, the assurance of

[1] *Fidelle exhortation aux inhabitans du pais bas, contre les vains et faux espoirs dont leurs oppresseurs les font amuser* (Knuttel, no. 171).
[2] The edict of 11 November 1568.

gentleness, the promise of grace, and so many other sweet and beautiful attributes with which the prologue of that edict has been embellished. Do not be blinded henceforth by the unjust strictures which our common enemies pass on the virtuous acts of our liberators[3] in order to hoodwink your trustful minds, calling them in that edict rebellious, guilty of the crime of *lèse-majesté* (divine and human), seditious, mutinous, wretched forgers, enemies and disturbers of the public welfare, rabble-rousers, distributors of notorious pamphlets, publishers of booklets, seditious, malicious, turbulent, impudent people, accusing them of so many other vices and trying most unjustly to defame them. Open your eyes and consider the present situation more closely. If you sift out all the deeds and acts of one party and the other, you shall undoubtedly find the truth to be that all the vices with which those tyrants attempt to slander and traverse the holy, reasonable and necessary enterprises of those who for the true service of God, the king and the fatherland and the deliverance of you all, courageously endanger their lives, property and wealth, are in fact their own vices. It is they who must be blamed for deeds by which they openly disgrace themselves. You well know that by the king's own proper consent you are free and released from the oath and obedience you owe him, if he or others in his name infringe the promises and conditions on which you have accepted and received him, until finally every right has been restored.[4] I also remind you that according to your privileges you are permitted to close the gates of your towns and to resist by force not only the servants of your prince but also the prince himself, in person, whenever he attempts to proceed by force of arms.

You may also be assured that when later the king knows the truth, His Majesty will rightly be most angry that you did not resist those tyrants more vigorously in order to preserve his highly prosperous countries from extreme ruin, poverty and depopulation, or from the tyrant's efforts to establish their domination and satisfy their avarice. So nobody, neither you nor your liberators, may properly be accused of rebellion, disloyalty or other crimes if in fulfilling the duties, obligations and oaths which you all must observe, you do all you can to obviate and resist such manifest violent infringements of your privileges, such suppression of your liberties, such massacre of yourselves and ravishing of your possessions,

---

[3] The prince of Orange and his supporters.

[4] At his inauguration in 1549 Philip II had sworn to the *Joyeuse Entrée*, a Brabant privilege of 1356, to which this passage refers. Cf. Ria van Bragt, *De Blijde Inkomst van de hertogen van Brabant Johanna en Wenceslas (3 Januari 1356)* (Louvain, 1956), p. 106.

and exert yourselves to the utmost to chase away those foreign and tyrannical invaders, true rebels and common enemies of God, the king, the
fatherland and all the inhabitants living here at present as well as those
who have gone away. Look at the argumentation and conclusion of that
edict and you will see that if they should be in a position to rule the
Netherlands, you who have stayed in this country, have no hope of being
better treated than the refugees who might fall into their power. Do they
not declare in that edict that there are among you a great multitude of
people guilty of *lèse-majesté* and that they have only proceeded against
those who are most culpable? Do they not call you the accomplices of the
others, though you have dissimulated up till now? Do they not suggest
you are daily piling up new crimes one upon another? Do they not suspect
you of mutiny, rebellion and revolt, as they wrongly call the duty which
they know you are entitled to perform? Do they not command such a
pitiless inquisition against you all that there will hardly be one whom they
may not in some way or another judge guilty if they so wish? Do they not
force you either to become accusers and betrayers of all the good virtuous
men who love the fatherland and your liberty or to suffer death or other
heavy punishment according to the rules of their blood-thirsty cruelty?
Do they not want to force you, by putting a rope round your neck, for
ever to stop speaking not only about your salvation but also about your
liberty, rights and customs? Do you not see how they put you at the
mercy of officers, provosts and fiscals by confounding all order and justice? Do you still expect any grace, pardon or impunity, when it is so
widely known that they have had so many good inhabitants apprehended
and killed in divers places simply for having attended sermons, which they
say are new, although they were tolerated and permitted by the regent and
the magistrates?[5] Therefore, my seigniors, brethren and companions, put
aside these vain expectations, cease breaking your oaths, recognise the
truth, take a firm stand for the maintenance of your own welfare, resist
your oppressors with all your might, help by all means those who exert
themselves to pull you out of this miserable servitude.

[5] By the accord of 23 August 1566 Margaret of Parma had allowed Protestant
services in those places where they had been held so far.

13

Direction for the deliverance of the Netherlands from the Spaniards. To William of Nassau, prince of Orange, 1571[1]

Henry Geldorp (1522–85), the author of this rare pamphlet, written in rather complicated Latin, had been headmaster of schools at Sneek, Leeuwarden and Delft, but as an evangelical he emigrated in 1558 and became headmaster at Duisburg. The manuscript of this booklet was submitted to the prince of Orange through the intermediary of Wesenbeke in April 1571, but was not printed until October 1574. See R. Fruin, *Verspreide Geschriften*, II (The Hague, 1900), pp. 170ff.

Away with this caution and the paralysing hesitations which impede and even kill the bravery, heedless of danger, that is needed now. The gods help the brave, and people who trust them only if (to put it that way) they guarantee success in a duly signed contract, annoy, offend and estrange them. Our affair itself bids fair to succeed, because it is in accordance with the divine will, proceeds from the Word of Almighty God and is approved of by everyone for its justice, reasonableness and devotion except by people who, having once offended the gods, religion, heaven and hell, have been ruled ever after by pernicious stubbornness and execrable blasphemy. Not every hesitation signifies caution; often it is mere cowardice; and not every gentleness is a virtue, for often it represents a willingness to tolerate faults, and a refusal to inflict upon the godless the extreme punishment they deserve. Unless we desire to be moles, we should realise that the approbation of the Christian nations, who though not involved applaud us and abhor the tyrant, as well as the support we find in this country, the tyrant's indolence, the small number of mercenaries[2] and the fact that the whole fatherland is embittered by the execrable torments we suffer because of the blood lust and immorality of the enemy, by requisitioning and pillage, incite us to take revenge and clearly show us that we should not faintheartedly delay to seek the help God is willing to render us. As He exposes the enemy to us so defenceless

---

[1] *Belgicae liberandae ab Hispanis Hypodeixis, ad P.P.D. Gulielmum Nassavium, principem Aurantium* (Knuttel, no. 189).

[2] Alva had about 20,000 soldiers at his disposal in the Netherlands.

that his soldiers are like dirty rag-tag dragging on, why indeed do we tremble as though he were armoured with the whole of Lemnos?[3]

He who has always lifted up the pious and struck down the godless, calls us to put our faith in His armour. Why then do we despair if all the stables of the Poles and all the arsenals of the Germans are not put to our use? We are asked by various towns to give them the little support they need to make it possible for them to take our side and to help them afterwards against possible sudden assaults prepared by those among their population who leave the towns because of this. But why do we then waste our energy with philosophising about such pompous matters as camps, provisions, baggage and war equipment? We are invited by friends to come and help them. But why do we then represent them as Anak's children,[4] as the Jews once represented their enemies after forty years' wandering, when their hope of ever reaching their ancestors' dwelling-places had died away? He who is anxious and ponders too much, will never perform great feats; what the gods propose, should not be debated but taken in hand. Through hesitation the opportunity slips through one's fingers. Those for whom God's voice is as the trumpet of war, should fight, not deliberate. But where will be our operational base, you say, where shall we encamp, where shall we arrest the enemy, from where will our armies march out, whither shall we retreat, who will open the gates for us, who will take us in? Either those very people, I tell you, who could not open the town gates for you two years ago, because your army did not pass through their area,[5] or those who could have done so but preferred a form of slavery which left them some freedom to the total freedom that they thought too dangerous to seek, hoping that the tyrant would not repress them further. Now at last they have learned that their possessions, their homes, their lives are at stake, now they are being severely punished for their haughtiness towards you, now they honour you as their redeemer and invoke your help. They have atoned for their negligence with so much suffering. And if these wrongs had not been inflicted upon them by our enemy, that cruel monster, their unjust opinion of your cause would never have been obliterated and it would not have been transformed by the fatal disasters they have endured since they refused your help, into the greatest benevolence towards you and an

[3] The island of Lemnos was reputed to be one of the abodes of the Greek god Vulcan.

[4] Giants, Book of Numbers ch. 13:33.

[5] In October 1568 the prince of Orange had undertaken his expedition across the Maas to Brabant.

irrevocable hatred for the tyrant. Why then is it necessary to waste time by asking the towns to surrender to your troops? This is dangerous for those who take your side, because they cannot approach people either individually or collectively without often betraying themselves and are therefore forced to waste much time in waiting for good opportunities to advocate your cause. No, another policy should rather be followed, a policy by which surrender is safely effected by those who have been raised from despair or struck down by terror. What is the use of devious ways, when a short road lies in view?...

Do not think the present writer is just another heretic who has left his hiding-place to approach you with his advice, one of those heretics who loudly proclaim that the clattering of arms does not accord with the Gospel (justifying in this way both their greed and their cowardice), but send their people unarmed into the battle. No, such is not the advice put forward here. You may safely conclude treaties and call in the aid of your relations but God's help should come first for God will never tolerate the glory due to Him for overthrowing that tyranny being taken from Him. You should put into the field as little cavalry as possible, for it is expensive and unsuitable for a long campaign...You should choose your main military base in Holland. There you must take a place whence you can interrupt the traffic between Friesland, Overijssel and Amsterdam but protect the ships sailing from the Rhine to the Ocean through the mouths of the IJssel and the Zuyder Zee.[6] No war is necessary to disconnect these areas which are dependent on each other for their daily needs. And it will be easy enough to take a few badly defended towns on the coast of Guelders, and Holland. These will serve as refuges and markets for your men-of-war,[7] so that they need not look for harbours abroad where the inhabitants, not so much out of bad faith but because of the tyrant's terror or something else, might either upset our plans entirely or at any rate make them uncertain and thwart them. When you have a secure hold on these places the tyrant will no longer be able to make contact with his adherents, separated as they will be from each other by many rivers and water courses. Moreover, it will not be long before the adherents of the enemy will have enough of the dearth and the wrongs inflicted upon them.

And then, whilst one town after another will take your side, you will be

[6] The author may have had in mind a town like Enkhuizen on the Zuyder Zee, which figured prominently in the plans in 1568 as well as in 1570 and 1572.

[7] The fleet of the Sea Beggars, which had been formed on the authority of the prince and which used to find shelter particularly in English harbours.

able to make the German merchants and other inhabitants of the Ocean coast come to your new staple-towns to congratulate you. After organising your state, your happiness, your religion and your trade will perhaps inspire Brabant and Flanders and give them too the courage to choose liberty. If, however, they keep their eyes closed and stubbornly continue their way to destruction, you can (living in wealth yourselves) leisurely make war on the inhabitants of the other provinces whenever you want; or, if that is not the method you choose, you may harass them mercilessly even for ten years (as the Greeks did with Troy) by cutting them off from all trade and keeping them totally isolated and deprived of everything. It is true that such a strategy has fallen into oblivion after the difficulties which arose in France. But now peace is restored there[8] and only one enemy is left. This makes it possible to adopt again the opinion of those who, when your troops invaded Brabant,[9] thought that if the chances were against wiping out the enemy in one or two battles, one should look for an operational base from where one could, gradually gaining in strength, with a few expenses and as little risk as possible, try to exhaust the enemy slowly and skilfully, since one single fast attack would certainly not get him down. To make those who promised to support your sacred attempts wholeheartedly, firmly believe that you shall achieve all this under a lucky star, you must first assemble your scattered and often dis-united fleet in an orderly organisation and put it under military discip-line.[10] The leaders of the fleet should then efface the blemish of their many ignominious deeds by acting from now on with wisdom, justice, authority and severity. When their reputation is cleared they must without any delay come to the support of the towns most important to us and further their prosperity and freedom in such a way that it is clear to every one that, although till now the towns which chose our side indeed fared badly, the situation has now changed completely. And if this does not happen, father of the fatherland,[11] the Netherlands will fall into utter despair...This tyranny can only be destroyed by your bravery and trust in God. May God, the eternal revenger of all tyrants, grant to you and to all the oppressed the courage and insight to opt for the only correct strategy. Amen. 17 April 1571.

Yours most affectionately, N.N.

[8] The peace of St Germain of August 1570 with the Huguenots.
[9] See note 5.   [10] See note 7.
[11] This is the first time the prince of Orange is called 'father of the fatherland'.

14

Remonstrance of William of Nassau, prince of Orange etc., redeemer of the freedom of the Netherlands, to the States and the people, 1572[1]

This pamphlet in Latin, dated 16 June 1572, was of course intended by William of Orange as propaganda material during the early stages of the revolt in Holland and Zeeland. It was not drafted by Wesenbeke who was no longer in favour because without waiting for the prince's permission he had published a pamphlet in April 1572. Bor who printed the present document in a Dutch version wrongly identified it with Wesenbeke's pamphlet.

To prevent the venomous cuttle from hiding under its black ink, and contaminating and deceiving you in its flight, you must prove that we were wrong to accuse you of complicity in all the cruel deeds recently carried out. We are prepared to receive you back into favour but you must not take such risks again if you wish us to take you under our protection when to the common weal of the fatherland you surrender your towns to us and drive out the tyrant.[2] The finest towns, harbours, rivers and their mouths have, as you may see, set an example by throwing off their yoke with unprecedented courage and accepting my fleet and garrison,[3] so that I am now in a position to defend their newly won liberty. I am ready with well equipped auxiliaries and bear no grudge at all for the ingratitude I received in the past and I assure you that up till the final battle I shall fulfil the duty of loyalty, which I owe to the fatherland, to the hereditary countries and especially to those, over whom the king has given me authority, from which I have never been dismissed up till now.[4] These examples, I say, should remind you of your oath which places you under an obligation in particular to your burghers and – some of you – also to me. Indeed, the tyrant has never produced an official and written notice of

[1] Pieter Bor, *Oorsprongk, begin ende aenvang der Nederlantscher oorlogen*, 1 (Amsterdam, 1679), Appendix, pp. 138ff.
[2] The duke of Alva.
[3] Brill, Flushing and Enkhuizen had declared for the Prince in April–May 1572 and opened their gates to the Sea Beggars.
[4] The prince of Orange was stadholder of Holland, Zeeland and Utrecht until April 1567 and was then, after his departure for Germany, replaced by Count Bossu.

dismissal as is required in our law, nor has he so far proved the legitimacy of his power, as he should. Yet he has made and remade decrees to the disadvantage of the people of the Netherlands, making it appear that they were framed by the Spanish court although in reality they are the work of his personal agents there.

Consider, I pray you, whom you will more rightly follow, him who as you remember was solemnly entrusted with the care of all the king's provinces here about six years ago,[5] and who possesses, as you know, many fine estates of his own and of his children in your country[6] and whose hereditary right it is to protect the freedom of Brabant and the marquisate of Antwerp, or that barbarian upstart who leaves nothing to you, his enemies. It is therefore absolutely necessary that you renounce that effeminate Sardanapalus, that cruel Phalaris,[7] that tyrant, hated by God and mankind alike, who long ago was unanimously condemned by the decrees of the imperial court[8] so that you need have no fear. In fact he has never been able to impose his will except on people who were weakened by discord or who surrendered spontaneously. Soon he will undoubtedly succumb to his fate for he is obviously possessed by insane fury and madness. He even tortured his own servants, who carried out his measures (something which no tyrant in history has ever done before) and killed them as miserable examples. No one who knows the nature of tyrants can doubt that he has the same fate in store for you, unless, that is, you decide to save yourselves of your own free will through the blessed opportunity now offered rather than to be lost through your enormous stubbornness. You see how confident of victory he feels: he does not rely at all on military might, he has scattered some small groups of musketeers in a few towns,[9] and wallows in sensuality and stupid pleasures, unwilling despite sound advice to mend his ways. He knew well enough of course how

---

[5] In July 1566, in their second petition, the confederate nobles asked the regent Margaret of Parma, to entrust the government of the country to Orange, Egmont and Hoorne.

[6] The barony of Breda was part of the Nassau family possessions in the Netherlands. Through his first marriage Orange had acquired the county of Buren to which his eldest son Philip William was entitled.

[7] Sardanapalus, king of Assyria, ca. 650 B.C.; Phalaris, a tyrant of Agrigentum on Sicily (sixth century B.C.).

[8] The emperor, Maximilian II, as well as the German princes had shown their disapproval of Alva's activities in the Netherlands which were formally part of the empire.

[9] In 1572 Alva concentrated the approximately 20,000 scattered soldiers he had at his disposal, entirely in the Southern Netherlands.

people would react to his decision to enlist new troops and to his amassing such wealth through plunder and robbery over so many years. Everyone in Germany saw that he ignominiously dismissed Megen's army in its entirety, sent away part of Aremberg's without pay[10] and decimated the German army, beheading, hanging and quartering many noble, aged, capable officers well versed in all kinds of military service who were in possession of official discharge-papers and had been called to new functions. From now on people will be more on their guard.

As to the new Spanish troops with which he often threatens you in such a ridiculous manner, I assure you that this upstart, this child of unbelieving Jews (whose hatred of us is secretly inspired by his not being of Christian origin) has left more enemies behind among the families of the true old Spanish nobility than he has found or made here.[11] And this was why no pious soldier was prepared to join the army which with lies, artifices and threats he persuaded the poor king to raise against the wishes of the royal prince.[12] As a result he was unable to enlist an army in Spain itself until he brought together the most despicable disciples of African slaves. To these he added some rather thin garrisons which he succeeded in raising in Sicily, Apulia and Lombardy by dangling before their eyes the hope of planting colonies in our fatherland. On its way to the Netherlands this miserable crowd was joined by the refuse of Savoy, by Walloons and by people from the Alps, who have often deceived you, marching under the same banners as you and telling you in their barbaric tongue that they were Netherlanders. Chase him away, then, take your revenge, attack that monster, hated by Spaniards, Italians and Germans alike, see that this rogue of rogues, swollen with pride at his triumphs in Lower and Upper Germany,[13] does not escape you, this prototype of utter cruelty, who littered the gates, harbours, and streets of your fine towns with the corpses of your citizens, who spared neither sex, age nor rank, who slaughtered free-born men like cattle, who made children into orphans and accused innocent men, who plunged all your homes into mourning, who either laid out the slaughtered bodies on the wheel or would not allow them to be

[10] Aremberg was killed at the battle of Heiligerlee against Louis of Nassau in 1568. Megen who succeeded him as stadholder in the northern provinces, died at the beginning of 1572.

[11] The duke of Alva (Fernando Alvarez de Toledo) came of an old Spanish family. A dangerous enemy of his at the Spanish court was Ruy Gomez, prince of Eboli.

[12] Don Carlos, Philip II's eldest son, who died in prison in 1568.

[13] In 1547 at the battle of Mühlberg Alva defeated the princes of the Schmalkaldic league.

fetched for burial or at least made it impossible for you to give them a decent funeral.[14] I, on my part, will never desert you. He however is already so situated, as you can see, that if he tries to escape by sea, he will find himself surrounded by my fleet. If he wants to go to France he cannot fail to come up against strongly garrisoned towns[15] while if he goes back the way he came, he will find my army against him. Return at last to freedom, restore freedom to the state and return the state, restored in its old lustre and relieved from such sorrow, to the king, for if he had never gone away and, according to international law, had respected our deputies' safe conducts[16] (he was unable to do this because of the perfidy of his counsellors) all our possessions would not have been destroyed. In order to regain your former happiness you must, arms in hand, counter violence with violence. That the reasons for my advice may be known to every one I call God Almighty, who is my guide in my righteous attempt to protect you, to witness that I have only the following objectives in this war:

That with full respect for the king's sovereign power, all decrees contrary to conscience and to the laws, shall be annulled and that every one who so wishes, shall be free to adopt the teaching of the prophets, of Christ and the apostles which the Churches have taught until now and that those who reject these doctrines may do so without any injury to their goods as long as they are willing to behave peacefully and can show that they did so in the past.[17]

That the name of the inquisition shall be erased for ever.

That the activities of the sophists, the begging-friars and their adherents shall be kept in check.

That those who have no right at all to be in this country and, of course, are not allowed to oppress the souls of our humble people by force of arms, shall be banished.

That people be given back their houses, possessions, hereditary estates, their good name, their freedoms, privileges and laws, by which liberty is maintained.[18]

That state affairs shall be discussed in the States of the provinces in accordance with the custom of our ancestors.

[14] The so-called Council of Troubles, a special court established by Alva on his arrival in 1567, was the chief instrument of his reign of terror.

[15] Mons in Hainault had been held by Louis of Nassau since 24 May 1572.

[16] Montigny, Netherlands delegate to the king, was secretly put to death at Simancas in October 1570.

[17] This passage very clearly advocates freedom of religion.

[18] That is to say with annulment of the sentences of the Council of Troubles against the refugees.

That political matters will be dealt with by the king himself and by the States which are chosen in every province and not be dispatched secretly by hired foreigners through whose faithlessness and greed the present troubles have come about.

That those people be turned out of the magistracy, the army and the provinces, who according to the laws of the provinces and the agreements which princes make at their investiture have no right to be there.[19]

That he who has robbed the Netherlands of their freedoms without the king's warrant, shall be put on trial and plead his cause within the borders of our country in accordance with the sworn laws and customs of the Netherlands, and may give account of his deeds and await the verdict of the court.

But as the tyrant will not deviate from his course as long as he is not certain of being able to keep in his possession, to your utter ruin, all those rights and privileges of yours which he holds now as if they were withdrawn and obsolete, I pray you once again, because of the loyalty which you and I owe to our dearest fatherland, that with my help you rescue, take back and protect what you don't want to lose for ever. If you do not so, then I assert most solemnly that it will not be my fault if severer measures are taken. But if you take my admonition to heart (and I sincerely hope you will do this for your own sake) then swear allegiance firstly to Christ the only God our Saviour, next to the king who takes delight in the sworn laws, finally to me as patron of the fatherland and champion of freedom. You must keep your promises and help me to make peace in religious, legislative and judicial affairs, without wronging any class. You must propitiate God, you must see to it that the king is given back his authority and that peace is restored to the state. Then alone may you expect to regain that trade with free transit through Germany, England, France and Poland, which the tyrant, that inhuman destroyer, impeded, causing without any justification enormous damage to you, and to conduct it without being hindered by taxes, pillage and servitude. So much must I tell you, who still remain in the power of the tyrant, so that in future no one can plead ignorance in defence of his stubbornness. Delivered on 16 June 1572.

[19] The *Joyeuse Entrée* excluded foreigners from offices: Van Bragt, *Blijde Inkomst*, pp. 97, 105.

15

Instruction and advice for the Honourable Philip Marnix, lord of St Aldegonde etc., delegate of my gracious lord and prince, the prince of Orange, to go to the town of Dordrecht on behalf of His Highness and to address the assembly of the States as directed and charged by His Highness, 1572[1]

The meeting of the States of Holland on 19 July 1572 was convoked by the most ancient town of the province, Dordrecht. The stadholder was absent. Marnix of St Aldegonde, who had served the prince of Orange since early 1571 in various confidential capacities, attended as his deputy.

I. As the States and the deputies from the surrounding towns convened in the town of Dordrecht by 15 July, intend to discuss the common government of the country, His Highness's deputy will insist that they unanimously decide to recognise His Highness as governor-general and stadholder of the king over Holland, Zeeland, Friesland and the bishopric of Utrecht. This is the office to which he was lawfully and duly appointed by His Royal Majesty, and from which he was never dismissed in the manner required by the customs and rights of the country.

II. That they shall also determine how to reach an agreement in this matter with the other countries and provinces which have never had His Highness as their governor but should recognise him (who in his capacity of chief member of the States General of the country is responsible for protecting the country from foreign tyrants and oppressors according to its old rights and privileges) as their protector and in the absence of His Royal Majesty, as their head.[2]

III. That His Highness intends and desires that they shall recognise and accept the Honourable count van der Marck, lord of Lumey etc.,[3] as lieutenant-general and stadholder of the county of Holland, commissioned and invested by His Highness.

---

[1] R. C. Bakhuizen van den Brink, *Cartons voor de geschiedenis van den Nederlandschen Vrijheidsoorlog*, II (The Hague, 1898), pp. 190ff.

[2] Here too, Orange claims the general government for himself (cf. Document 14, note 5) in virtue of his position in the Brussels government before 1567.

[3] Lumey van der Marck was the commander of the Sea Beggars who took Brill on 1 April 1572.

IV. On condition, however, that the count van der Marck conform to the contents of the commission, which His Highness has sent to him for this purpose;

V. And that his lieutenancy shall not detract from the authority of other governors who have received from His Highness special commissions as governors of various towns.[4]

VI. The assembled States and deputies of the towns shall also debate and ordain the best and most suitable measures to take with regard to His Highness's warships, so that good and lawful order be established and maintained aboard them and over their commissioned officers; and similarly over the governors, captains, commanders and other commissioned officers. And also over the soldiery and others ashore, who hold any command or commission from His Highness within the county of Holland or are in some other way at his service, good and commendable order must be established and maintained for the protection of the country, with the least possible burden to the inhabitants so that all classes may be united in mutual harmony.

VII. And to this end all governors, lieutenants and commanders, general as well as particular, shall maintain good relations with each other and so likewise the towns with each other.

VIII. They shall further discuss and ordain the best and most suitable means of restoring and re-establishing in their old form and full vigour all the old privileges, rights and usages of the towns, which may have been suppressed and taken away by Alva's tyranny or otherwise, in accordance with the privileges and rights the king has sworn to maintain. Moreover the afore-mentioned delegate shall inform the assembly that His Highness has no other purpose than to restore, under the lawful and worthy reign of the king of Spain, as duke of Brabant, Lorraine[5] and Limburg, count of Flanders, Holland, Zeeland etc., the power, authority and reputation of the States to their former condition in accordance with the privileges and rights which the king has sworn to maintain. And without the States His Highness shall not endeavour to do or command anything that concerns the provinces or that may be harmful to them.

IX. On the other hand His Highness hopes that the States assembled there shall bind themselves – and shall also ask the other provinces to do so – not to enter into any accord, compact or agreement, either with the king himself or with any one who might or could pretend to have received an

---

[4] Sonoy was deputy of the prince of Orange at Enkhuizen and other places in the northern part of the province of Holland.

[5] The dukes of Brabant had been titular dukes of Lorraine since 1106.

order or commission from His Majesty, nor to do or to decide anything else concerning the whole of the country, without having His Highness's advice and consent and without consulting His Highness if he thinks this right.

x. His Highness on his part shall also bind himself not to undertake nor to command anything without the advice and consent of the States or at least the majority of them, and without consulting these States and countries, if and when they desire this.

xi. To this end the States assembled there and the delegates of the towns shall swear to His Highness between the hands of the delegate from His Highness, to be faithful to him forever and not to desert him, but to assist and help him in every possible way and faithfully to keep to these conditions in every respect. The afore-mentioned delegate from His Highness shall also promise by oath to protect them in every way and to keep to the said conditions, so far as they concern His Highness.

xii. Moreover, the afore-mentioned delegate from His Highness shall inform the States and deputies assembled there in detail of the position and circumstances of His Highness, and also of the conditions on which he has come to an agreement with the commanders and stewards.

xiii. And thereupon he shall request the town of Dordrecht together with the other deputies, every one for his own town, to stand security for three months' pay or at least to use their influence with the towns that this be done with all diligence and speed.

xiv. And meanwhile they shall raise as much money as possible with all speed and diligence, each town its due share, as His Highness needs to start paying his soldiers.

xv. It is understood that His Highness pledges on behalf of the towns, which will stand security, all the money which can be raised at Flushing, at Mons in Hainault[6] and elsewhere, either by laying a tribute on the enemy or in any other way, until they shall have got back their money; and that all the money His Highness shall take from such income and use for paying his soldiers, shall be deducted from the sum they have been asked to provide.

xvi. That in order to make it possible for him to pay his soldiers they shall do all they can to raise money on bonds issued by His Highness, and covered by cash expected to come in from elsewhere or by some goods and merchandise which His Highness may sell somewhere else.

xvii. The afore-mentioned delegate shall also ask them, on behalf of His

[6] Cf. Document 14, note 15.

Highness, to establish good relations with the other towns situated in Brabant, Flanders, Hainault, and in Gelderland, Overijssel, Friesland etc., and other provinces.

XVIII. And he shall adjure them with letters and other suitable means and vehemently insist that they attend to the freedom and the prosperity of the fatherland and join the common alliance and accord and, abandoning the cause of the Spaniards, determine to obey the king and to accept the protection of His Highness in accordance with their old rights and privileges.

XIX. He will make them see the firm unbreakable bond and the benefit which their union will give to the whole country.

XX. And will discuss with them the best and most suitable means of inducing other towns like Utrecht, Amsterdam, Rotterdam etc., to join.[7]

XXI. And will discuss with them the nomination of magistrates and governors of the towns of Holland, asking their advice and that they submit the names of capable nobles for consideration and nominate such as are with His Highness.

XXII. And will consider the best way to bring from Amsterdam the ships which are at anchor there.

XXIII. (crossed out)

XXIV. Will also discuss with them the best and fittest means of dealing with the clergy and others who have declared themselves in public adverse to this cause, and what must happen to their possessions as well as themselves.[8]

By His Highness at Aldekercken[9] in the district of Guelders on 13 July 1572.

[7] In July 1572 Rotterdam joined the revolt. Amsterdam remained on the side of the Spaniards until 1578.

[8] In his further explanation of 20 July 1572 Marnix said that it was the prince's intention that there should be freedom of religion for the Reformed as well as for the Roman Catholic Church, pending other provisions by the States General. This did not apply to clergy who sided with the enemy.

[9] Kaldenkirchen near Venlo.

16

Missive from the knights, nobles and towns of Holland to the States of the country, 12 September 1573[1]

In this document the States of Holland addressed themselves to the States General of the loyal provinces convoked by the duke of Alva in September 1573.

Nevertheless, dear brethren, considering how matters stand at present, you may see that the Lord reaches out His hand and will not let us become objects of plunder or of disgrace. Why do you not gird yourselves up with manly courage and join us at last in shaking off this unjust and unbearable yoke from our necks in concerted action? For if the duke has been able to accomplish so little up till now, although we were set against each other and the greater part of the country helped him, what will he be able to accomplish if in perfect harmony and due obedience to his Royal Majesty, our gracious lord, we co-operate in chasing these foreign tyrants and rulers out of the country and in good earnest together protect our old rights and privileges? And if he has not been able to subdue the small country of Holland with part of Zeeland over such a long time and with all the forces he has raised in Italy, Spain, Germany, France as well as in the Netherlands, what will he be able to accomplish, when Brabant, Flanders, Gelderland, Friesland, Overijssel, Artois, Hainault, Luxemburg and other provinces of the Netherlands or part of them, join Holland and Zeeland and together offer him resistance? We are indeed in no doubt that with the help of God we should soon be masters of the situation and shall restore our oppressed fatherland to its former prosperity. For all things considered, if you would only withdraw your help from him and even if you would never draw your swords against him yourselves, what would he be able to do? For it is clear that his whole activity consists of frightening you by vain threats and icy pride. And by his false and idle pretexts or the subtle intrigues of his instruments or assistants he gets you to hand over your power to him and this allows him to establish his despotism and tyranny, against your advice and undoubtedly also contrary to the king's good intentions. What he propounded to all of you in

[1] *Sendtbrief der ridderschap, edelen ende steden van Hollandt aen die Staten van den lande van herwaerts overe* (Knuttel, no. 210).

the States in August last year may still be fresh in your memory. His Royal Majesty, he declared, had sent the sum of ten hundred thousand guilders from Spain, and that was the utmost that he could expect from Spain. On the strength of this he made you believe that he had raised 12 regiments of German soldiers, 50 companies of Spaniards, 150 regiments of Walloons and Netherlanders and besides those 10,000 German horsemen and 3,000 horses of the troops[2] and 2,000 light horses, besides a large number of men of war and the usual garrisons. He made so bold as to promise you positively that he would drive all his enemies from these Netherlands within six weeks or at latest within two months, only asking you to collect money to pay the soldiers afterwards so that they would not stay on indefinitely and eat up and ruin the whole country.[3] Whereupon the duke of Medinaceli, who was seated on his left hand side, promised you that for his part he would do all he could to assist the duke of Alva with life and property in order to fulfil his promises etc.[4]

Now you may judge for yourselves whether he has accomplished all that, or if he has ever been able to raise anything like such a number of soldiers. It is clear that not only six weeks but two months have long passed by; in fact, it is more than a year ago that he made this declaration and still he is as far as ever from making good his calculations. From this we can conclude that he is bent only upon extorting money from your people with false pretexts and arguments to drag on the war. Meanwhile he deceives the king completely and puts His Majesty to great expense in waging a harmful and unnecessary war against his own subjects. Yet it is obvious enough that the money he receives is not used at all for paying his soldiers for he owes the Spaniards more than twenty-eight and his German soldiers more than thirteen and fourteen months' pay. So his declaration, at the afore-mentioned meeting of the States, that the king had told him he could not expect any more money from Spain than those ten hundred thousand guilders (which he then said he had received) was not without foundation. And since he is without any help from elsewhere, he sees that you are his last recourse and he has thus ordered you to assemble

[2] Troops of ordinance, see Document 6, n. 11.
[3] At the meeting of the States General in August 1572 Alva asked for a yearly supply of 2,000,000 florins instead of the tenth penny, which had met with much opposition in 1569 and again in the autumn of 1571 when deputations were sent to the king from the provinces.
[4] The duke of Medina Celi had been appointed as Alva's successor in 1571. He had indeed arrived in the Netherlands but in the circumstances never entered upon his duties.

now to impose on you the sum of 2,000,000 guilders a year, besides all the innumerable and unbearable expenses with which he has taxed the country so far and has squeezed it to the bones nay to the marrow of the bones.[5]

But, dear brethren, be mindful of what you have to do. Consider that one day His Majesty and his Council of Spain or the heirs and descendants of His Majesty will want to thrash out the whole affair and hear a true account of it and will no longer be satisfied with the veiled statements which they now receive from the duke and his followers. And when they then find that this war does not only cost the king and the countries enormous sums of money – at least 20,000,000 guilders so far – but also causes irrevocable damage and great losses of people, towns, villages and hamlets loyal to His Majesty, simply because of the duke's despotic aim to oppress all the king's faithful subjects entirely against all right and reason, do not doubt that this will grieve the king very much and that he will wreak vengeance on the men responsible for the damage done to his hereditary countries or who have supported this policy. If you continue to conspire with the Spanish tyrant against your own compatriots and your own country and to help him with money and other means, one of three things is sure to happen: either this war will remain undecided for a time, as it has now been for more than a year and a half, or God will give us total victory over our enemies, or finally they will gain the victory over us. But in all three cases the war will necessarily ruin and destroy the country.

If things remain as they are now and the grim war continues, business will be ruined, sea-borne trade will be stopped, industry will have to close down. As a result the entire country will become so impoverished and disorderly that famine and dearth will inevitably follow and then we can expect revolts and rebellions, severe diseases and plagues, which will completely destroy the country. Furthermore the provinces of Holland and Zeeland and all surrounding countries will be overrun meanwhile by soldiers and completely ruined. Because of this people in Brabant and Flanders, provinces that have also been squeezed by the troopers and soldiers, will no longer be able to get any butter or cheese or other staple food or salt and will necessarily fall into utter distress and misery. As an aftermath of the domestic war all kinds of plunder and robbery will be committed; even towns, villages and hamlets loyal to His Majesty will be burned down. And the worst danger is that during this war the dykes in

---

[5] The same demand therefore as in August 1572.

Zeeland or Holland may burst by storms or thunderstorms, or one of the parties may pierce them out of desperation so as not to fall into the enemies' hands.[6] Many thousands and thousands of men and cattle will then die a miserable death, the country will be irreparably damaged and His Royal Majesty and all his descendants will suffer irredeemable losses.

But in the second case, if God gives us victory over our enemies, this will be accompanied by frightful massacres of innumerable good inhabitants used by the duke of Alva for his purposes, for as long as he can get money and men, he will certainly not stop trying to extirpate and ruin us completely. So that it will not be possible to overthrow him without horrible bloodshed being added to all the other disasters, which, as we have told you, will befall the country during the war.

But if he gets the upper hand (which God in His mercy forbid) then all you can expect is eternal and ignominious slavery as he will consider all of you and all towns to be rebellious and refractory because of your refusal of the tenpenny tax,[7] which was the principal reason, he believes, for the recent war. He will therefore undoubtedly think that all who refused it, even if they did not openly take up arms against him, are nevertheless his open enemies and rebels responsible for his difficulties. He will therefore punish them with the sword and the stake just as he will punish those of us, who openly resisted him with arms, convinced that the others would have done the same if they had had the courage or the opportunity or the power. We hope, though, that things will not go as smoothly for him as he supposes, for we are firmly resolved, one town after another, to fight to the last man before we surrender to this foreign and cruel tyrant, so that he will never attain his aims without bringing on the country the disasters we have described before.

This clearly shows that if you help him any longer in this war and assist him with money, and do not stop him and do not openly resist his intentions, our poor fatherland cannot escape utter ruin and destruction. If you want to know what he is planning and how he intends to deal with the king's lands and with all of us, you must read his explicit threats in his letters of

---

[6] This actually happened in West Friesland during the siege of Alkmaar early in October 1573.

[7] In 1569, when for the first time Alva proposed the tenth penny and other taxes, the towns of the Netherlands in particular offered vigorous resistance to it. The governor was finally satisfied with a yearly supply of 2,000,000 guilders until 1571.

pardon.[8] In these he tells us that if we refuse to obey him, he will ruin and destroy this country so that no traces survive, and that what is still intact will be utterly destroyed root and branch, and that he will people this country, so far as any country remains, with foreigners. By these and similar menaces he shows openly that his ultimate purpose is to ruin and raze this country to the ground.

[8] These were issued in July 1573, some days after the fall of Haarlem which had been under siege for seven months.

17

A missive in the form of a supplication to His Royal Majesty of Spain, on behalf of the prince of Orange, the States of Holland and Zeeland, etc., 1573[1]

This missive was drafted at about the same time as the previous document (September 1573). Alva was still in office; he was dismissed by the king in October and left in December.

Therefore we can hardly imagine that if he knew the truth Your Majesty would permit such gross injustice, great outrages and wilful wantonness. For has there ever been a king or potentate who treated his subjects so improperly? Your Majesty's forefathers, very blessed be their memory, displayed such gentleness, clemency and regal moderation towards their subjects that they set a laudable example of these virtues not only to their descendants but to all the kings and potentates of Christendom. When any misunderstanding arose between His Majesty and his subjects, and even if the subjects openly took up arms because of some misdemeanour on the part of officers or for a similar reason and were again reduced to obedience by their lords and princes, your predecessors were so far from wishing to commit such examples of cruelty and wilfulness that they assiduously took care in all capitulations to specify expressly in every article that all the privileges and freedoms of the subjects should be kept and observed inviolate. So that we should indeed do too gross an injustice and outrage to Your Royal Majesty if we allowed ourselves to be persuaded that Your Majesty had deviated so far from the laudable example of your forefathers and from the bounden duty of all pious kings and princes that,

[1] *Sendbrief in forme van supplicatie aen die Conincklicke Maiesteyt van Spaengien, van wegen des Princen van Orangien, der Staten van Hollandt ende Zeelandt* (Knuttel, no. 213).

instead of doing justice to his faithful subjects and giving audience to them, listening graciously to their pitiful complaints, he should send a tyrant to them who would cruelly slaughter and ruin them all, and reduce them to perpetual distress, slavery and servitude.

If we accepted the pardons[2] the duke so often proposes to us now, as if, on behalf of Your Majesty the king, he graciously wishes to forgive us our former misdemeanour or rebellion (as he calls it), we would therefore injure Your Majesty's high authority too much. For we know for certain that Your Majesty will not accuse or condemn us of any misdemeanour or rebellion before he has heard us and has learned the truth about our cause. Now who has ever given Your Majesty any information about this? Or when has Your Majesty listened to any one who was not our avowed adversary and enemy? It is indeed well-known that both sides should be heard before sentence is passed. The chronicles highly praise Alexander the Great who, when examining one party, always shut and stopped one ear by resting his head on his arm and being asked why he did this, answered: to give the other side as good a hearing as the first. This has been known to all nations and peoples as right and just and quite in accordance with natural law. So that no criminal will be condemned, even if he had committed the worst imaginable offences, without his defence being heard.

Now, most gracious king, we go down on our knees to you and pray you in all humility to lend an ear to us and to weigh our cause on the scales of justice. So far Your Majesty has received by post letters and notes from the duke of Alva and his adherents and has been informed only by them of the state of affairs in this country. So far our mouths have been gagged, our tongues pierced by glowing iron, our lips shut by burning tongs so that we should not make our distress known, so far the roads have been blocked, that neither our letters nor our moans might reach Your Majesty's ears.

How could Your Majesty in such circumstances accuse and condemn us of any misdeed, let alone of rebellion and refractoriness (things we have abhorred as long as we live)? If the duke again produces his letters of pardon and tries to subdue us by such means because he sees that he cannot have his way by force (thanks to God's miraculous mercy and clemency), why should we be in the least impressed or recognise that they are addressed to us, who have never let ourselves be tempted to swerve from the obedience we owe Your Majesty? Unless, that is, we wished to

2 See Document 16, note 8.

accept and recognise the duke of Alva instead of our king. For it is him we have opposed and not Your Majesty, whom we shall faithfully serve with our lives and possessions under God unto death. We therefore have no interest at all in his pardon, which is only addressed to the towns which have allowed themselves to abandon the obedience due to the king. However we understand his intention well enough. He would like to set himself up as our king and hopes that by accepting his cunning pardons we will confess to having sinned and will thus condemn ourselves. For if we accept his pardon, then do we indeed declare ourselves guilty of rebellion and resistance against our king, of revolt and sedition, of heresy and apostasy of the Christian faith, of derogating from God's and the king's majesty. By accepting his feigned and false pardons he wants us to seal and sign this with our own signature so that afterwards he can justify his policies before Your Majesty and other kings and potentates and conceal his horrible tyranny, saying that if we had not committed misdeeds deserving such cruel punishments and torments, we would never have accepted pardons and forgiveness.

We call God, who knows all hearts, and Your Royal Majesty to witness that if we committed the misdeeds of which we are accused in these letters of pardon, we do not desire any pardon but would like to pay for them with our lives as the most wicked and evil creatures on earth. None of us, most gracious king, will refuse to have his limbs racked with the most diabolical torments, if he is found to have committed such atrocious misdeeds. Nay we pray the duke of Alva (if he allows himself to be affected by any prayer) to specify a proper, just and merciless punishment for all who come to him for pardon and confess that they have committed the afore-mentioned crimes. We also give him leave to break his word or faith, for why should he keep faith with people so unfaithful to God and their king that they did not scruple to treat secular and divine authority so scandalously and disdainfully?

However, never, to all eternity shall it be shown that this idea occurred to us, far less that we ever carried it into effect. From the beginning we have always shown our king all due obedience and regard and we have also tried to serve God Almighty, Father of Jesus Christ, in spirit and in truth in accordance with His commandment and His Word, as far as our frail powers have permitted and we wish to go on doing so to the last drop of our blood. But we saw that instead of administering right and justice and listening to our complaints and objections and fulfilling Your Royal Majesty's promises the duke of Alva wanted to oppress us in a horrible and unprecedented tyrannical way against all right and reason, against all our privileges and freedoms, and to ruin the whole country and to treat us more cruelly than the Turks or Jews have ever treated their vanquished enemies; and that before Your Majesty and all Christian potentates and nations he falsely accused us of apostasy, rebellion and heresy and that we were unable to obtain audience or receive any comfort and consolation in the whole world. Then we were compelled to take up arms and to try in every possible way to free our poor oppressed fatherland from such atrocious tyranny. We would rather die one after the other than surrender to such a tyrant. This is still our intention, if Your Majesty is unwilling to graciously listen to our complaints, to administer right and justice to us against such violence. For we are not so ill-informed of God's Word, thank God, but that we know quite well that our lives and deaths are in God's care and that the death which no one in the world escapes, is only a passage to eternal life.

If therefore our death would please and help some people, we would rather die an honest death for the freedom and prosperity of our fatherland than be reduced to slavery and be trampled on by wanton foreigners, who have always displayed hatred and displeasure towards us. We should then indeed hand on to our descendants the honestly reaped glory that their forefathers refused to be slaves of the Spanish inquisitors and did not hesitate to redeem a shameful life by an honest death.

We fight for freedom of conscience,[3] for the freedom of our wives and children, of our lives and possessions; the point is whether the duke of Alva and his adherents will be our tyrannical lord and the arbitrary master of all we cherish or whether we shall unto death preserve and protect our liberties with our sword in the service of God our Lord and Your Majesty our most gracious king.

[3] The religious problem and the freedom of conscience are specifically mentioned here, in contrast to Document 16, pp. 102ff.

18

The prince of Orange to Philip Marnix, Delft, 28 November 1573[1]

Marnix of St Aldegonde had fallen into the hands of the Spanish officer Julian Romero near Maaslandsluis (to the west of Rotterdam)

[1] Gachard, *Correspondance de Guillaume le Taciturne*, III, pp. 88ff.

on 4 November 1573. He was detained first at The Hague, afterwards at Utrecht. The Beggars for their part had taken the Spanish stadholder Bossu captive in the battle at the Zuyder Zee on 11 October. So there was the possibility of exchanging prisoners.

Monsieur Marnix, I have received your two letters, the first of the 7th and the second of the 21st day of this month. In these you dealt chiefly with two points, first of all telling me what happened at the time of your arrest. As to the apologies you offer, you may rest assured that I and the States are completely satisfied with the way you have carried out your duties. Your mind may be easy on that matter and you may rest assured that we will always support you and your affairs. I very much hope that Monsieur Noircarmes[2] and Seignior Francis Valdez will treat you as Seignior Julian Romero[3] treated you. If they do otherwise, I will be forced to do the same to those whom we keep in captivity. I will be very pleased to hear what they think about exchanging prisoners, as I have written to Seignior Francis Valdez, but so far I have not had his answer to a note under cover of my letter in which I mentioned the persons to be exchanged in the first place; you were among them.

As to the other point I think that in order to deliver this people from this miserable war, you would like to induce and persuade me to enter into some treaty and prejudicial accord, which would ruin rather than save the country. I will not conceal from you the fact that I have communicated the contents of your letters to the States of these provinces and to other honest men of rank in order to get their advice on your proposals, and to hear their opinion. I did not wish to act on my own authority, in contravention of the oath and obligation I have towards them, or unknown to them, to undertake something on my own initiative. Rather, I wish to act in the same way as I do in other affairs concerning the well-being of the country, as every one knows. After mature deliberation on this matter with the other persons mentioned and after weighing all the circumstances properly, the States unanimously declared that they know, as I do too, that all men, and especially Christians, have been expressly commanded by God to pursue peace and that besides the duty which obliges them to render Him obedience, their natural inclination incites them to desire

---

[2] Philip of St Aldegonde, lord of Noircarmes, the conqueror of the town of Valenciennes in March 1567 replaced Bossu as stadholder. He resided at Utrecht and died in March 1574.

[3] Francis Valdez was the commander of the Spanish troops which had laid siege to Leiden. Romero was an old campaigner of Charles V and Alva.

union, concord and peace. You know very well that from the beginning and ever afterwards, we have desired nothing so much as the tranquillity and prosperity of the country based on a good and sure peace and this is what we still desire. The innumerable cruelties, unjust decisions, brutalities, and other outrages perpetrated contrary to all divine and human rights, which caused these troubles and forced us all, each according to his place and rank, to take up arms, always distressed us deeply and still do so.

As you know, we do not fight His Majesty but must protect ourselves and avoid being finally overwhelmed and ruined completely and placed forever in intolerable servitude, and made slaves of a master who tyrannises over our bodies, possessions and consciences. Such tyranny will inevitably cause horrible desolation, because the greater part of the inhabitants of the country will flee to the woods and forests with their wives and children, and be in an even more calamitous and miserable condition than troubles and wars waged with a clear conscience before God could bring about. Wars always cause endless suffering and disasters. There is therefore nothing the States and I desire more fervently than to see the miseries and desolation mentioned above brought to a conclusion, so that we may live in happy prosperity and in complete obedience to His Majesty, and we feel ourselves obliged before God and moved in our hearts to pursue and embrace such a great good. If the issue is whether we should make an accord or peace causing more misfortune, misery and still greater injury to the glory of God, which we are bound to pursue above all things, as well as to the fatherland, we feel obliged rather to endure all the misfortune, calamities and discomfort of the war than for some relief, for some imaginary tranquillity and an ill-assured and therefore short-lived peace willingly and knowingly to rush headlong into the enormous and horrible evils we have in our own time seen arising from such accords. For you will remember that the only result of the accord concluded in the year 1566 with so much pomp and circumstance at the command of madame the duchess of Parma herself,[4] regent at the time, and her councillors, was the extirpation of the true religion according to the Word of God, the slaughter of many thousands of God's children and the execution and banishment of seigniors, nobles, burghers and many other persons of all walks of life and both sexes, who, relying upon similar pardons and treaties, were miserably deceived, and lost their lives and possessions. Memory of the massacre in France too, which happened in

---

[4] The accord of 23 August 1566 concluded by order of the governess with the confederate nobles (see Document 7, note 2).

spite of a peace so solemnly sworn,[5] cannot be effaced from our hearts and teaches us where to place our trust. We cannot forget that it took place a long time after the war, in time of peace and even during a wedding-feast. We should truly consider what would in all probability be in store for us, with our country still full of soldiers and especially Spanish soldiers.

[5] The massacre of St Bartholomew's Eve, 24 August 1572.

19

The prince of Orange to Count John of Nassau, Dordrecht, 7 May 1574[1]

This letter from the prince of Orange to his brother John was intercepted; only in 1593 did it fall into the hands of John's son William Louis, who sent it to prince Maurice. John of Nassau (born 1536), the prince's eldest brother, left the army to fetch money from Cologne some days before it was crushed in the battle of Mook on 14 April 1574.

Monsieur my brother, the last day of last month I received your letters of the 25th inst. and was very sad to hear that, despite your great diligence, you have not succeeded in getting reliable information about the lot of His Highness duke Christopher or of my brothers.[2] In truth great injustice is done to you as well as to me, if their death is being concealed from us – if indeed the Lord God decided to let them die. I wish to assure you that this secrecy has done more harm than good to our cause and I personally have been much blamed for it, because all those who ask me about it, think that I conceal the truth from them because I feel uneasy about the future and, suspecting that this is the reason, every one talks of it as they list, and the greater number of them think that the situation is entirely hopeless because their death is kept a secret. I confess to you that

[1] Groen van Prinsterer ed., *Archives ou Correspondance inédite de la Maison d'Orange-Nassau*, le série, IV, pp. 385ff.
[2] Christopher, son of the Elector Palatine Frederick III, Louis of Nassau (born 1538) and Henry of Nassau (born 1550) were all three killed in the battle of Mook, where Sancho d'Avila with his Spanish troops was victorious. The Spaniards had been forced temporarily to raise the siege of Leyden to counter the invasion by Louis of Nassau and his men.

I could regret nothing more, though it is true that we always have to conform to the will of God and respect His divine providence and trust, that He who spilled the blood of His only son to maintain His church, will do only what will redound to the progress of His glory and maintenance of His church, though it seems impossible. And even if all of us should die, and all poor people should be massacred and pursued, we must be assured that God will never forsake His flock. We now see a most memorable example of that in France. After so many seigniors, nobles and other persons of various condition, age and sex were massacred[3] that every one thought that was the end and that all those of the religion and the religion itself would be entirely extirpated, we see that nevertheless they now hold their heads higher than ever, and that the king[4] is involved in more troubles and unpleasant difficulties than before. We must hope that the Lord God whose arm stretches far, may use His power and pity on us.

Now, to change the subject and to let you know the state of affairs here since the recent defeat. You may rest assured that all the people of these provinces have been very much frightened by it. They see that our enemies have taken such heart, that they intend to invade this country with all their forces – which they can easily and, humanly speaking, without endangering themselves, use for this purpose. They are not at all mistaken about this, for no nation in the world rejoices more at good tidings or is more dejected by some mishap. They are so bewildered now that they do not know what to do, or where to begin. They think that all is completely lost and that no help whatever is available. Moreover, it unfortunately so happened that the new governor had, as I understood, issued a very ample pardon pardoning everyone with only fourteen or fifteen exceptions.[5] You may imagine that because of such perplexing events and set-backs there will be many here who will go so far as to accept this pardon or at least will be more unwilling to do what is necessary to put matters right. To prevent all difficulties, we need to think of some suitable means of comforting them. You may rest assured that I for my part will do my duty to the utmost of my ability, as I have done so far, foreseeing clearly that, if this country should one day be lost and brought back under the yoke and the tyranny of the Spaniards, the true religion will be gravely endangered in all other countries and may even humanly speaking be uprooted for ever leaving not the least vestige. In time the Germans will realise what damage has been done, as will the English who,

3 St Bartholomew's Eve 24 August 1572. 4 Charles IX (died 30 May 1574).
5 The new governor, Requesens (since November 1573) issued this pardon on 6 June 1574. About 300 persons were excluded from it.

awaiting the outcome of events in our country, have always wanted to proceed with what they consider great caution,[6] and the poor French, who have so readily taken up arms again for the sake of religion will find themselves in even greater perplexity, for if this country is lost (which God forbid) it is to be feared that the king of France will conclude a new alliance with the king of Spain, in order to extirpate this religion at one blow if they can. For my part I am of the opinion that the kings of France and of Poland pretended to favour and help us,[7] because they feared that Duke Christopher and my brothers would join those of the religion in France, rather than because they felt well-disposed towards us. But however this may be, we have to find some way of getting assistance, the more so as in the long run we cannot hold out nor bear such great expenses. This makes me beg you with all the affection I have for you, to apply all your wits to finding some suitable remedy. In my opinion the best thing would be for the princes of Germany to advance a considerable sum of money to enlist sufficient foot as well as horse and to negotiate meanwhile with the king of France on this basis: His Majesty should come to a firm accord with his subjects, permitting them free exercise of their religion in all security: He should then turn his forces, with those of the king of Poland and those of the Protestants, against the king of Spain; the troops raised in Germany will also come to his aid and assistance. This can be done safely because the king of Spain would not suspect that such a levy was to be raised against him to further the objectives of the king of France. To encourage the king of France, the princes of Germany may promise him that, when he grants his subjects the right to exercise their religion freely, they will form a league with him to help and defend him against all those who may outrage and attack him for this reason. On the other hand it seems to me this country might well be induced to put itself entirely under the protection, institutions and ordinances of the Holy Empire, contributing as many as three electors[8] and forming a league with the Hanseatic towns if that is thought useful; or maybe you know some other solution. For I must confess to you frankly that I am so perplexed by such a great multitude of affairs and by grief and melancholy too, because

---

[6] Queen Elizabeth had since 1572 stood aloof from the revolt in the Netherlands.

[7] Henry of Anjou was chosen king of Poland in 1573. Shortly afterwards he succeeded his brother Charles, king of France, who died in May 1574.

[8] When the Netherlands were united in the Burgundian circle by the emperor, Charles V, in 1548, it was stipulated that they should contribute as much to the ordinary taxes of the empire as two electors but in case of war with the Turks as much as three. Such a contribution amounted to a share of three per cent.

of the loss of His Highness Duke Christopher and my brothers, whom I firmly believe to be dead, that I hardly know what I do, and yet since this has been the will of God, we have to bear it patiently...

As to money, the States now assembled, have granted me the sum of 150,000 guilders a month, for six months or for as long as necessary. This is truly a good and considerable sum and I am surprised that after so many sackings and losses, the country can still scrape it up. But notwithstanding this, when I weigh the expenses against it, I think we still have far too little. The ordinary expenses which we have to bear if we want to defend the country are so enormous that I see very little chance of providing for extraordinary wants, if we don't find some one to come to our aid. In this connection I recollect that I told you some time ago, that we could defend this country against all the forces of the king of Spain for two years, but that then we would inevitably need help, unless God can defend the country without any help, as He has done so far. But I speak in human terms. As the two years will soon have expired, it is high time that some princes and potentates offered to assist us, and if there is no one willing and if for lack of help we are lost, in the name of God, so be it! It will always be said to our honour that we have done what no other nation has done before us, to wit, we have defended and maintained ourselves in such a small country against the great and horrible assaults of mighty enemies without any help. And if the poor inhabitants here, foresaken by every one, persevere despite everything, as they have done till now, and as I hope they continue to do, and if God does not wish to punish and ruin us entirely, it will cost the Spaniards half of Spain in goods as well as in men, before they have finished with us.

20

A kind admonition to the States of Brabant, Flanders etc. on their supplication handed to Don Luis de Requesens, 1574[1]

This is a reaction from the States of Holland and Zeeland to a remonstrance that the States General at Brussels addressed to

---

[1] *Vriendelicke vermaninghe aen de Staten van Brabandt, Vlaenderen, etc. op de supplicatie by hen aen Don Loys de Requesens onlangs overghegheven* (Knuttel, no. 220).

Governor Requesens in June 1574. Requesens had brought his financial demands to the notice of the States General, whereupon the latter formulated a series of political desires.

If you do not help Don Louis to obtain 6 or 7,000,000 pounds of gold,[2] you will fall out of favour with him. But what troubles will he be able to cause you? Who is he? Would he be able to mention his grandfather? Where does he come from? Is he not a foreigner, who has not a foot of ground and neither friends nor relations in these provinces? It is not in keeping with our laws and ancient traditions that he should want to be regarded as stadholder, governor and captain-general of these provinces. For though he can show His Majesty's authorisation to prove this, yet he has not been legally accepted as such in these provinces. And besides, what power has he? Are not the soldiers, upon whom he chiefly relies, wandering foreign scoundrels, who would serve the devil for money? What will they do, if they don't get any money from him? Undoubtedly every one will go his own way. There would be no way of preventing them sacking towns or the country. On the other hand, who are Your Honours? Are you not lords of this country as well as honest powerful people? And are not the provinces full of your friends, relations and other well-wishers? And are you not the States, the supporters and protectors of this country? Is it not true that because of this all provinces and towns adhere to you? And would not the soldiers born in these provinces be on your side in time of need? Even the foreign soldiers, the Germans as well as the Swiss, would go over to you, if only you offered them money. The Spaniards and Italians could send Don Louis back to his convent to don his cowl once again,[3] if he escaped his deserved punishment with them.

And if you think it would be too dangerous to do this alone, would the inhabitants of Holland and Zeeland and their associates not be willing to help you to carry it into effect? They would surely not fail you. They have eagerly taken up arms against the common enemy when he was having his will in everything and was at the height of his power and triumph, and are they not still eagerly waging this protracted war against him? It is to be expected that they will eagerly defeat and exterminate him with your help

[2] In his proposition to the States General of 7 June 1574 Requesens demanded a yearly sum of 2,000,000 guilders instead of the tenth penny, in conformity with the arrangement proposed by Alva in 1569 for six years. According to his calculation there remained 6 or 7,000,000 out of the 12,000,000 guilders to be paid.

[3] Don Luis de Requesens y Zuniga was Grand Commander of Castile and knight of the Order of Santiago.

or your connivance. They cannot forget the old friendship they have had with you and hope the same from you. And it would be wretched if two neighbours should become hostile to each other because of a foreign power which, having crushed the one with the help of the other, would also destroy the other in due time.

And do you wish a nobler, more powerful, better known and more willing leader than the one who is offering his service to you of his own accord through deep affection to the dear fatherland? This is His most Serene Highness the prince of Orange. Is he not of imperial descent[4] and has he not so many fine estates in these provinces that simply because of this he is the most powerful man next to the king in these provinces? Who does not know of his estates in Germany, in the two Burgundies[5] and his principality of Orange? Is he not burggrave of Antwerp?[6] And is he not the principal and first member of the Council of State which with the legitimate governors is charged with the government of all these provinces together?[7] And is he not stadholder and captain of Holland, Zeeland, West Friesland and Utrecht? And was he not brought up mainly at the Court of Brussels? And has he not rendered the provinces many a service under the emperor, Charles, and the king? And has he not, with two enormous armies from Germany, defied the common enemies in their own lair,[8] when those to whom the highest government had been entrusted by His Majesty, who was absent in Spain, would no longer listen to any advice and treated the provinces villainously and tyrannically? And has he not jeopardised all his possessions and his life to free these provinces from the most villainous Spanish slavery? Have not all his brothers done the same? And does he not belong to those who have shaken off the Spanish yoke to live and die for the dear fatherland and to keep it prosperous and united?

But Your Honours do not want to do anything against the king. But can it be that such an honest hero and prince is then plotting against the king? Far be it from such noble blood. Are the people of Holland and Zeeland and their associates plotting against the king? Far be it from such brave and excellent souls. But this is interpreted differently. By whom? By the Spaniards, the papists, the monks and their adherents. But all these are sworn enemies of the king. Do the Spaniards know the king

---

[4] Adolph of Nassau had been elected king of the Romans in 1292.
[5] The duchy of Burgundy and the Franche Comté.
[6] See Document 14.
[7] See Document 14, note 5 and Document 15, note 2.
[8] The campaigns of 1568 and 1572 against Alva.

otherwise than as one dominated by the inquisitors? Do the papists and monks know the king otherwise than as a vassal and slave of the pope? How do the inquisitors treat the king? Do they leave anything more to him than the mere title? Don't they usurp the entire government? Is the king allowed to do anything but what pleases them? If this were otherwise, undoubtedly he would have visited these fine provinces of his a long time ago to stave off the present misery.[9] Has the duke of Alva done anything that has been to the honour or credit of His Majesty? Behold the triumphant statue in the castle at Antwerp.[10] Remember the triumphant pomp with which he had the pardon proclaimed at Antwerp in 1570.[11] Remember the words: everything is mine and I am king. It would take too long to demonstrate in detail that the duke of Alva has not been the king's friend. You say that the case of Don Louis is different? What is different about a hypocritical and dissimulating monk? There seems to be this difference, that Don Louis conducts his affairs with more adroitness and deceit. The inquisitors, perceiving these arts in him, have thought him a fitting replacement for Alva. Moreover, he is an inquisitor himself and more inclined to promote the grandeur, power and profit of the college of the inquisition than was Alva.

But is it necessary to dwell upon this any longer? It is clear to all the world that what has been done in these provinces these eight years on behalf of the king, and is still being done, is not the work of the king, but of the inquisitors and the pope. Those who protect the dear fatherland from the despotism and tyranny of foreign lords, cannot be the enemies of their legitimate and true lord and of their dear fatherland. But those who aid and adhere to the foreign lords are indeed enemies and traitors of both. The inquisitors have the king with them in person, and we have the king with us by his oath. The oath remains the same and does not change and is not subject to accident; quite the contrary is the case with the person of the king. And as the person of the king is all but imprisoned by the inquisition and as he cannot act according to his own will, it is his oath that gives us the right to use the name of the king in our struggle for the protection of his honour and of the dear fatherland. It is certainly wrong for the common enemies to use the king's name so boastfully, because they

---

[9] In their supplication the States General also demanded that the king visit the Netherlands.

[10] The statue was cast from the guns seized in the battle of Jemmingen in 1568 and bore the inscription *regis optimi fidelissimo ministro*.

[11] After much delay he promulgated this pardon with many exceptions in July 1570.

do so neither with the king's unqualified consent nor by virtue of his promises and his oath.

But if we suppose that this present government exists with the king's full consent, or even that he himself governs us in this way, is it then true that the provinces have accepted him as their sovereign on such conditions that he should govern without laws and rules at his own pleasure? Our ancestors were too experienced and wise to accept sovereigns in this way. And in the opinion of the Spaniards Your Honours yourselves committed *crimen laesae majestatis* in the year 1549[12] because you refused their request to change the old way of inauguration. Our ancestors have left us laws of investiture which specify that if the king, being here in person, perseveres in the present sort of government, he would no longer rightly be sovereign, and the subjects would be absolved from their duties and their oath, until he would give up this method of government as unreasonable and wholly contrary to his promises, and be willing to reign reasonably and in accordance with his promises. And our ancestors displayed exceptional prudence when as a condition for his solemn recognition they made the sovereign agree to being refused service and submission in the event of bad government. It was also very prudent of them to insert in the conditions for recognition a clause obliging all officers entering upon their duties, to swear to maintain the laws and not to oppose or break them in any way, by word or deed. As Your Honours swore this oath too, in the present case you should act not so much prudently as bravely to avoid being accused of perjury.

[12] When Philip was recognised as their future lord by the States of the Netherlands, cf. Document 12, note 4.

21

Discourse of John Junius de Jonghe, 1574[1]

This discourse was written by Doctor Junius de Jonghe of Brabant. He had been in the service of the Elector Palatine Frederick III since 1565 and was appointed governor of Veere by the prince of Orange in 1573. He went to Utrecht as a hostage in July 1574 to replace Marnix of St Aldegonde, who was then allowed to go to Holland to

[1] *Discours van Johannes Junius de Jonghe op den brief van den heere van Champagny* (Knuttel, no. 224).

take part in peace negotiations. The Discourse is Junius's answer to a letter of 13 August 1574 from the governor of Antwerp Frederick Perrenot, lord of Champagny (brother of Cardinal Granvelle), who conducted these peace negotiations on the Spanish side.

If you tell us that it is surprising that the subjects force the sovereign to convene the States [the States of Holland and Zeeland] are greatly astonished, for they are sure that you know perfectly well that the king in his goodness committed himself to allow this because he realised it was the basis and support of his authority and his entire royal power. In a good political and civil government the States are the leaders and the most important men of the people and represent the masses. What other men than the States of the land could so naturally be united with a good king who wishes to be a father and shepherd to his people? As there is nothing that accords better with the head of a human body than those members in which the force of life resides, because they are the principal instruments through which the life creating spirit, coming from the brain, is spread through the complicated system of nerves and veins in the entire body and keeps each separate member in natural community with the general body, so a good king spreads through the States to the entire body of the commonalty not only the benevolence, grace and privileges, thanks to which he keeps them united, but also the goodness, laws and ordinances by which the people are kept in good discipline and unity...

You say that only as a special favour did our king's ancestors allow the States General to assemble for matters of the highest moment. Even if this were true, it would indeed be most offensive to pretend that the king is less well-disposed towards these provinces than were his ancestors. This would mean that he has, in your view, a conception of authority and a method of government totally different from that which they had. If this were true the fruits to be expected from his rule would be the opposite of what his ancestors enjoyed: the hatred of the subjects instead of love, tyranny instead of lawful government and finally total ruin instead of prosperity.

But I cannot think that you are so ignorant of history or that your knowledge of the states of these Netherlands has grown so dim that you do not know that after the time of Charlemagne this country and these provinces were united into one body with many other neighbouring provinces under the name of Austrasia or – after Lothario,[2] one of

---

[2] In 855 Lothario II became king of a realm extending from Burgundy to the North Sea, afterwards called Lorraine.

Charlemagne's descendants, to whom the country was given – Lorraine. And though Lorraine was later divided between various successors, the parts nearly always had some union of friendship and mutual alliance or confederation with each other until duke Philip the Good *quasi iure postliminii*[3] again joined them into one inseparable body and tied them together by very many fine ordinances, laws and privileges, given to the whole. Philip assembled all the States as often as was necessary,[4] showing himself to all alike as a father of their country and a shepherd of the nation. The emperor and pope then even offered him the chance of making a kingdom of these Netherlands,[5] but he would never permit this because he was averse to ambition and because he would not degrade the provinces and towns by such an innovation or do anything contrary to the oath he had sworn to them.

If you argue that our king possesses some provinces at present which then had nothing in common with them, I answer that the said duke at that time possessed other provinces in much the same state, which were afterwards separated from the provinces which remained in his possession. Thus, after he had gained possession of Holland and Zeeland, Philip the Good left these provinces united into one state to his son and only heir Charles the Bold.[6] Charles was more ambitious and openly tried to make a kingdom of the Netherlands and might have succeeded had he not been prevented by the States of the country, which opposed this plan, as well as by the envy of Frederick III, emperor at the time.[7] However this may be, nevertheless he left to his only daughter[8] the whole of the Netherlands as a united body, joined together by many strong indissoluble ties. Her husband Maximilian, who became emperor afterwards, and after him his son Archduke Philip obtained them in the same way;[9] and the emperor,

[3] The right of returning to the old legal position. Cf. *Corp. Iur. Just.*, 1, 6 pr. D. 1, 8.

[4] This was done for the first time in 1465.

[5] Emperor Frederick III was willing to elevate the duchy of Brabant to a kingdom within the Holy Roman Empire, but refused to detach the Burgundian Netherlands from the Empire in order to allow the creation of a kingdom of Burgundy.

[6] Holland and Zeeland actually came into Philip's possession in 1433 (after Jemina of Bavaria's abdication). The conveyance of his provinces to Charles the Bold took place in 1465 (Philip died in 1467).

[7] This passage refers to the negotiations at Treves in 1473 and the Emperor's sudden departure which ruined Charles's expectations of a royal title.

[8] Mary, 1477–82.

[9] Maximilian, Holy Roman Emperor from 1493, acted as regent for his son Philip the Fair from 1482 till 1494.

Charles V, too, the father of our king, sacred be his memory, left them as an inheritance to his son.[10] Charles V, not satisfied with the junction and union mentioned before and clearly expecting that afterwards attempts would be made to set the provinces against each other in hatred and quarrels under the pretext that they had nothing in common with each other, abolished and removed all the differences which existed in their legal systems (for some were legally dependent on the crown of France, some on the empire and some were organised in yet another way). At a general diet in Germany[11] he united all the provinces into one body with the consent of all princes and estates of the empire, ordaining that henceforward all these provinces inseparably united should be held in fief from the empire; to this end they should contribute to the ordinary imperial taxes as much as two princes of the empire. This was held inviolate by His Imperial Highness, sacred be his memory, as well as by our king, so that His Majesty sent the count of Hoogstraten, sacred be his memory,[12] to Germany to emphasise that the said provinces are one body or one circle of the empire.

As they have always been recognised as such I was very surprised to hear you say that these provinces are so different in the matter of sovereignty and jurisdiction and that they have nothing in common with each other but their geographical location. Why do they assemble together in the matter of taxes and requests[13] and why are the taxes afterwards divided and levied according to the individual power of every province? Do you really want the provinces to be but one body over tax matters but when steps are needed to stop the total destruction of the whole country each province to deal with the matter independently without taking measures in common with the others? This is in my poor opinion not only beyond all reason but also has some semblance of tyranny and injustice. But I would ask you this: when His Majesty reminded the States of the distress of the French war in the year 1557, how could they then have taken that heavy burden upon themselves unless unitedly? And how

---

[10] Maximilian once again acted as regent after Philip's death (1506) until his grandson Charles V assumed personal power in 1515.

[11] At Augsburg in 1548 (see Document 19, n. 8). The feudal ties between the provinces of Flanders and Artois and France were severed in 1529.

[12] Anthony Lalaing, count of Hoogstraten, Knight of the Golden Fleece and supporter of Orange in his struggle with Granvelle, made this journey to Vienna before April 1566. He was wounded during Orange's campaign in 1568, and died shortly after.

[13] At least the so-called patrimonial provinces, that is, the provinces which had been part of the Burgundian possessions since the time of Philip the Good.

could they have succeeded in carrying it but thanks to their exceptional loyalty to the lord of their country and the admirable harmony with which, to the highest praise and honour of His Royal Majesty, they raised the nine years' subsidy?[14] So it seems that in order to wage war against a foreign potentate, the provinces of the Netherlands as well as their States are considered to be one single body, whereas in this disastrous domestic war which brings total ruin upon them, they have to be considered separate from each other and not entitled to assemble the States General to remedy the common disease by means of a common medicine.

For who does not know that the provinces of these Netherlands have always derived the greatest advantage from being united with each other? Has this union not been the origin of the old custom they have always observed, of assembling towns and provinces for the meeting of the archers and crossbowmen and bearers of other old-fashioned arms, which they call the *landjuweel*? Why else have the towns and provinces always met for public repasts and plays by order of the authorities unless it were to demonstrate the great unity of these provinces, as Greece showed her unity in the meeting of the Olympic Games? Is not the name of Netherlanders, or Flemish, as the Spaniards call us nowadays, common to all the Netherlands? Though two languages are spoken in the Netherlands, these are so familiar throughout these provinces that in many towns both languages are almost equally spoken. Are not nearly all the provincial High Courts subordinate to the Great Council of Mechlin[15] and have the ecclesiastical jurisdictions not traditionally been subject to Cologne or Mentz?[16] What further evidence do you wish to hear beyond that which I have produced, that all these provinces are only one circle or province of the empire?

How could you think it strange that a circle of the empire assembles its states simultaneously? In fact, if one province is allowed to assemble without the other such a circle might be considered a monstrosity...

And even if the fact that the king and the emperor, Charles, sacred be his memory, issued their edicts and placards about religion in all the provinces in general, should be the only evidence, does not this in itself refute your statement that these provinces of the Netherlands have

---

[14] The States General had been allowed to supervise the way in which the nine years' subsidy was spent.

[15] The Great Council of Mechlin was the supreme court of justice, created by Charles the Bold in 1473.

[16] Not Cologne and Mainz but Cologne, Rheims and Treves were the archbishoprics to which the Netherlands belonged before 1559.

nothing in common with each other? And is the request of the people of Holland and Zeeland[17] not wholly justified by the rule *Quod omnes attingit, ab omnibus probari debet*,[18] that is, what concerns all in common, must be decided upon by all? For as the great rigour of the edicts issued in all the provinces of these Netherlands in general has brought about a general rising of the people, why should the General States of all the provinces not assemble together?

[17] This request of the States of Holland and Zeeland to the king was handed to Marnix in July 1574. He delivered it to Champagny who in his turn sent it back as unacceptable with a covering letter to Junius dated 13 August 1574.
[18] This famous formula is first to be found in the Constitution of Justinian of 531. It was cited throughout the Middle Ages. Cf. *Corp. Iur. Can.*, c. 101, I, n.2.

22

Brief and true account of what happened at the peace negotiation of Breda, 20 March 1575[1]

This pamphlet contains documents about the Breda peace negotiation, begun in February 1575 between delegates from governor Requesens and from the States of Holland and Zeeland. The following extract is taken from a declaration by the prince of Orange and the States of 20 March.

His princely Highness and the States are considered rebels and open enemies of His Majesty. Yet it should be understood that they have not offended His Majesty nor deprived him of his authority. On the contrary, it was for the benefit of His Majesty that they defended the provinces and towns, their lives and their possessions, their houses, wives and children against the tyranny of the duke of Alva and his adherents which was inevitably leading to the eternal destruction of the provinces; and it was to help the king that they used all possible means and exerted themselves to the utmost to drive their adversaries out of their country. His princely Highness and the States have always declared openly that their intention was by no means to arm themselves against His Majesty or to desert him or to be alienated or separated from him, but to keep themselves united

[1] *Cort ende warachtich verhael van het gene dat op de handelinge van den vrede . . . tot Breda gheschiet is* (Knuttel, no. 239).

with other countries under His Majesty. Nor was it ever their intention to take or withhold or seize goods from spiritual or temporal persons who did not assist their adversaries. Thus His Highness and the States cannot think that any good will come from what is now being proposed. They are particularly distressed by a number of conditions put by the other party which stipulate that the Roman Catholic religion should be observed, that people should live according to the Roman Catholic rules or depart from the country etc.[2] These suggest that the present religion is a heresy and those who observe it heretics. In reality, however, no other religion is being observed here than the catholic and apostolic religion, corresponding to the Holy Gospel and God's teaching, in which every one finds comfort and security. It is only the grave glaring abuses especially disagreeable to God Almighty that have been eliminated in order to render unto Caesar the things which are Caesar's and unto God the things which are God's.

With all respect and frankness His princely Highness and the said States with their associates,[3] do not think it in any way advisable to accept the aforementioned proposals under these conditions and restrictions. They cannot forget the horrible fate that befell the counts of Egmont and Hoorne, the lord of Montigny,[4] and many others, nobles as well as other persons of high rank, and they are impressed by the numerous accounts of cases of contracts and promises being broken.

Indeed it is not at all feasible to expel from these countries and their dear fatherland so many people rich and poor, young and old, who have embraced the reformed evangelical religion thanks to the enlightenment and renewal of the Holy Ghost and the grace of God. And indeed, to force so many good faithful subjects of His Majesty to wander in foreign countries and look for new dwelling-places with great loss of and damage to their possessions which they could only sell at low prices (if there were enough buyers, which does not seem very probable), is a much stranger and more cruel act than to dismiss from these countries 3 or 4,000 Spaniards, who have eaten their fill, and to send them back to their own fatherland or to their usual garrison-town, where they might render service to His Majesty. The departure of the former from the provinces of

[2] The conditions made by the delegates from Requesens.
[3] The Guelders town of Bommel and the county of Buren had by 1574 already entered into an alliance with Holland.
[4] Montigny, who was sent to Spain on an official mission in 1566 (see Document 6, note 2) was imprisoned and finally executed in secret at Simancas in October 1570.

Holland and Zeeland would cause great depopulation and loss of trade and craft, industry and navigation, on which the whole prosperity of the Netherlands depends. These would all be transferred to other countries to the indescribable harm and reduction of His Majesty's revenues. This has happened to a certain degree, as is generally known, during the last few years because of the rigorous edicts and horrible executions and the introduction of the Spanish inquisition.

23

Pacification of Ghent, 8 November 1576[1]

The Pacification was signed at Ghent on 8 November 1576, four days after the mutiny of the Spanish soldiers had culminated in the Spanish fury at Antwerp.

Greetings to all those who will see these papers or hear them read. These countries have fallen into great misery and distress through civil war, haughty and harsh government, wilfulness, robberies and other disturbances committed by the Spaniards and their adherents during these nine or ten years. In order to take measures against these evils and to prevent further troubles, oppressions and poverty in the country by means of a lasting peace and pacification, commissioners of His Majesty and of the prince of Orange, the States of Holland, Zeeland and their associates met at Breda in the month of February in the year 1575, and put forward several measures by which such a pacification could be furthered. But the proposals did not bear the fruits which had been expected;[2] on the contrary, instead of the relief and compassion which it was hoped His Majesty would give us, the Spaniards continued every day to oppress and ruin the poor subjects and to reduce them to eternal slavery. Several times they themselves rose in mutiny, threatening lords and towns and taking many places by force, robbing them and burning them down.[3] This is why the councillors entrusted with the government of

---

[1] A. S. de Blécourt and N. Japikse, *Klein Plakkaatboek van Nederland* (The Hague, 1919), pp. 113ff.

[2] See Document 22, pp. 124ff.

[3] The mutiny started when the Spaniards captured Zierikzee at the end of May 1576. The rebel troops then gathered at Alost in Flanders.

the countries[4] declared them to be enemies of His Majesty and the common weal and why the States have been forced, with the permission of the aforementioned councillors, to take up arms. In order that total ruin be staved off, that the inhabitants of all these Netherlands united in a lasting peace and agreement may jointly force the Spaniards and their adherents who are a public plague, to depart and that they be given back their old privileges, customs and freedoms, by which trade and prosperity could return there, now, with the consent of the councillors entrusted with the government of the countries and as a consequence of the peace negotiation started at Breda, for the glory of God and the service of His Majesty, this present treaty has been drafted between the prelates, nobles, towns and members of Brabant, Flanders, Artois, Hainault, Valenciennes, Lille, Douai, Orchies, Namur, Tournay, Utrecht and Mechlin, representing the States of those countries, and the prince of Orange, the States of Holland, Zeeland, and their associates, through commissioners deputed on both sides respectively . . .[5]

This eternal, lasting peace, alliance and union is concluded under the terms and conditions following hereafter.

I. All offences, injuries, unlawful acts and damage done during the disturbances between the inhabitants of such provinces, as are involved in the present treaty, wherever and however they have been committed, shall be forgiven, forgotten and regarded as not having occurred so that no one may mention them or may be sued for them.

II. In consequence the said States of Brabant, Flanders, Hainault etc. as well as the Prince, the States of Holland and Zeeland with their associates promise sincerely and honestly to keep, and oblige all inhabitants of the provinces to maintain, from now on a lasting and unbreakable friendship and peace and to assist each other at all times and in all events by words and deeds, with their lives and property, and to drive and keep out of the provinces the Spanish soldiers and other foreigners who have tried, without any recourse to law, to put to death lords and nobles, to usurp the wealth of the provinces, and to reduce the commonalty to

---

[4] In the absence of a governor after Requesens' death in March 1576 the Council of State condemned the mutineers as enemies of the country in edicts of 26 July and 22 September. The latter edict was issued after the councillors at Brussels had been imprisoned for a time by supporters of the prince of Orange led by William of Heze, commander of the troops recruited by the States of Brabant.

[5] The meeting of the States General started at Brussels on 25 September, when delegates from Brabant, Flanders and Hainault alone were present. On 19 October negotiations started at Ghent between delegates from both sides.

perpetual enslavement. In order to furnish whatever will be necessary to resist those who might thwart them in this, the said allies also promise to be willing and prepared to pay all necessary and reasonable contributions and taxes.

III. Moreover it has been agreed that immediately after the departure of the Spaniards and their adherents and after law and order has been restored, the two parties will be bound to do their utmost to convoke an assembly of the States General composed in the same manner as the meeting in which the late emperor Charles, blessed be his memory, transferred these hereditary Netherlands to His Royal Majesty, our most gracious lord.[6] The assembly must settle the affairs of the provinces in general and in detail, not only the matter and exercise of religion in Holland, Zeeland, Bommel and associated places and the restitution of the strongholds, artillery, ships and other things belonging to the king, which during the said disturbances were taken by Hollanders and Zeelanders, but everything that furthers the service of His Majesty and the prosperity and union of the provinces. This will be done without contradiction or impediment, delay or postponement from either side, either with regard to the ordinances, statements and resolutions which will be passed there, or with regard to their application. To this both parties shall submit entirely and in good faith.

IV. Henceforth the inhabitants and subjects on both sides, no matter which province they come from or what their status, quality and condition, will be allowed to move freely, to come and to go, to live and to travel everywhere for commercial and other purposes, in all freedom and security. However those of Holland, Zeeland or others of whatsoever province, condition and quality they may be, shall not be allowed to disturb the common peace and quiet outside the provinces of Holland, Zeeland and associated places, or in particular to attack the Roman Catholic religion and practice, nor to slander any one or cause scandal by word or deed because of his Catholic faith, on penalty of being punished as disturbers of the common peace and of serving as an example to others.

V. In the meantime no one may be lightly accused, arrested or endangered; all edicts about heresy formerly made and promulgated, as well as the criminal ordinance made by the duke of Alva,[7] shall be suspended and shall not be put into operation, until the States General shall ordain otherwise, provided that no scandals occur.

[6] At Brussels on 25 October 1555.
[7] In July 1570, when his power in the Netherlands seemed to be firmly established.

VI. The prince shall remain admiral general of the fleet[8] and stadholder of His Majesty for Holland and Zeeland, Bommel and other associated places and be in command there as he is at present, with the same officers, judges and magistrates, without any change or innovation unless with his consent and will. His Excellency shall also be in command of the towns and places, which he now holds, until the States General ordain otherwise after the departure of the Spaniards.

VII. But as regards the towns and places included in his commission from His Royal Majesty which are at present not under the authority of His Excellency,[9] this point will remain in abeyance until these towns and places have joined the other States in this union and settlement, and His Excellency has given them satisfaction on those matters which are of importance to them when they come under his government, either with regard to the exercise of religion or otherwise, so that the provinces be not torn asunder and to avoid all dispute and discord.

VIII. And meanwhile no edicts, mandates, provisions or writs shall be valid in the provinces and towns governed by the said Prince, except those which have been approved or issued by His Excellency and by the council, the magistrates and other officers in those places without prejudice to the jurisdiction of the Great Council of His Majesty in future.

IX. It has also been agreed that all prisoners taken during the recent disturbances shall be released, in particular the count of Bossu,[10] without payment of ransom – unless the ransoms have been fixed and agreed upon before this treaty was made – but that they should pay the prison expenses.

X. It has also been agreed that the said prince and all other lords, knights, nobles, private persons and subjects, of whatever status, quality or condition, and also their widows, dowagers, children and heirs on both sides shall be rehabilitated and allowed to take possession of all their seignories, estates, prerogatives, shares, credits which have not been sold or alienated, in the condition in which these possessions are at present. For this purpose

[8] When the Prince of Orange was appointed stadholder of Holland, Zeeland and Utrecht in 1559, he had already laid claim to the title of admiral general of the province of Holland.

[9] In 1577 treaties of satisfaction were concluded with the towns of Haarlem, Schoonhoven and Oudewater in Holland, Goes, Tholen and Zierikzee in Zeeland and in 1578 with Amsterdam. Maintenance of the Roman Catholic religion was guaranteed for the time being. Utrecht again accepted the prince as stadholder in 1577.

[10] Maximilian Hennin, count of Bossu (See Document 14, note 4), was taken captive by the Beggars at the Zuyder Zee in October 1573.

all writs of default and contumacy, all arrests, sentences, seizures and executions performed since the beginning of the disturbances in the year 1566, both because of religion and because of the taking up of arms and what has happened since, shall be annulled, revoked and declared null and void. Equally all documents of lawsuits, acts and actions relating to this shall be destroyed and struck off the registers, without any necessity to obtain any other verdict or provision than this present treaty, notwithstanding any laws, rights, customs, privileges, prescripts, official, conventional, customary or local regulations, nor any other exception to the contrary, which will be suspended and cease to be operative in these and in all other matters concerning the said disturbances. To this effect these regulations are now suspended as far as necessary with the proviso that there is no general derogation without previous specification.

XI. It must be understood that among those who will profit by this settlement will be my gracious lady the wife of His Serene Highness the elector of the Rhine, formerly the widow of Lord Brederode,[11] concerning Vianen as well as other properties to which Her Serene Highness or her deputy may lay claim.

XII. Also the count of Buren[12] will be included as regards the town, the castle and the estate of Buren, to be used by the said count as his own property after the departure of the garrison.

XIII. And the pillars, trophies, inscriptions and effigies erected by the duke of Alva to the shame and disgrace of the afore-said and all others, shall be destroyed and demolished.

XIV. As to the yields of the said seignories and estates, the arrears of dowers, usufructs, rents, and interests recoverable from the king, the country, towns and all others which were due before now and have not been paid, nor received by His Majesty or his deputies, each shall receive his due.

XV. It should be understood that all yields of the afore-mentioned estates, interests and other properties that have fallen due since last Midsummerday 1576, shall remain to the profit of those who are entitled to them, but that part of the yields have already been received by the collector of the confiscations or others of which in such cases no restitution shall be made.

---

[11] Amelia, countess of Neuenahr, married the Elector Palatine Frederick III in 1569. Her first husband Henry Brederode, lord of Vianen, died in exile in 1568.

[12] Orange's eldest son, Philip William, born in 1554 of the marriage with Anne, heiress of Buren (d. 1558) was kidnapped when a student at Louvain by Alva and sent to Spain. The town of Buren which had remained loyal to the Prince, fell into Spanish hands in 1575.

XVI. But if during some years the afore-said real burdens, interests or other income have been seized and received in the name of the king by way of confiscation every one shall for the same period be kept free and exempt from all rents due from his lands and properties from which he could not profit because of the recent disturbances; the duration of this exemption shall be related to the length of the period during which the goods could not be normally exploited. And as to the household effects and other movable property which have been lost, sold or otherwise alienated on either side, there shall be no redress for anyone.

XVII. As to the real estates, houses and rents which have been sold or alienated by way of confiscation, the States General shall in each province appoint commissioners to inquire into the difficulties if such shall arise and to make reasonable recompense to the former proprietors and also to the purchasers and new owners of the properties and rights for their redress and eviction respectively.

XVIII. The settlement of personal annuities and liabilities and all other claims, complaints and grievances which the interested parties on both sides bring forward and advance afterwards as resulting from the disturbances, howsoever they may do so, shall be dealt with in the same way.

XIX. All prelates and other ecclesiastical persons, whose abbeys, bishoprics, foundations and residences are situated outside Holland and Zeeland and who nevertheless possess property within these provinces, shall come again into the possession and enjoyment of their properties in the same manner as has been ordained for secular persons.

XX. But regarding the conventuals and other ecclesiastics who are professed or have their prebends within these two provinces and their associates but left them because the greater part of their properties was alienated, they shall henceforth be reasonably provided for along with those who have stayed, or if the States so prefer, the use of their goods shall be given back to them. All this however is provisional and awaits a decision by the States General on their further claims.

XXI. Moreover it has been agreed that all bequests, statements of disinheritance and other deeds, drawn up *inter vivos vel causa mortis* by private persons, by which the legitimate heirs are deprived of their legitimate inheritance and disinherited or received only a small portion by reason of the said disturbances or of religion, shall be held null and void by virtue of this agreement.

XXII. And as the States of Holland and Zeeland in order better to cover the expenses of the war have increased the value of all specie of gold and silver, which they cannot spend in other provinces without a great loss, it has been agreed that the deputies of the States General shall consider accepting the same standard as soon as possible so that the rate of the said coins may be fixed as uniformly as possible, in support of this union and its trade.

XXIII. As to the opinion put forward by the deputies of Holland and Zeeland, that the States General of all the Netherlands should take over all debts incurred by the Prince for his two expeditions and large armies[13] for which the States of Holland and Zeeland as well as those provinces and towns which surrendered during the last campaign,[14] stand surety, as they declared, this matter is left to the discretion of the States General. When general peace has been restored, a report or remonstrance shall be submitted to them so that they may take appropriate action in this matter.

XXIV. The provinces, seignories and towns on the opposite side,[15] shall not be included in this common accord and pacification or able to enjoy its benefits until they have actually joined this confederacy. But they are free to do this whenever they see fit.

After the report, agreement and assent of the councillors entrusted with the government of the provinces as well as of the States of these provinces on the one hand, and of the prince, the States of Holland, Zeeland and their associates on the other, the said members of the Council of State and the representatives of the States General have promised and sworn by virtue of their powers and commission and promise and swear now to observe and to keep this treaty of peace in all the said points and clauses and also in all that will be defined and ordained by the said States General in regard to it; and to have it ratified, sworn to, signed and sealed on both sides by the prelates, nobles, towns and other members of the said provinces, and especially by the said prince, in general and in detail, within a month, to everybody's satisfaction. And acquainted with the foregoing the said deputies signed this in the town-hall of the town of Ghent on 8 November 1576.

[13] In 1568 and 1572.
[14] This refers to the towns of Tienen, Diest and Mechlin, Dendermonde and Oudenaarde, which fell into the hands of the prince during his campaign of 1572.
[15] Luxemburg in particular kept aloof.

24

First Union of Brussels, 9 January 1577[1]

Don John of Austria, the king's half-brother and Requesens' successor as governor of the Netherlands, was reluctant to subscribe to the Pacification of Ghent and found support among members of the aristocracy at Brussels. The prince of Orange sought to counteract loyalist tendencies by making the States General re-affirm in a solemn declaration the main points contained in the Pacification. The delegates of Holland and Zeeland signed this declaration – called the First Union of Brussels – although they had reservations about the passages on religion which they thought were not quite in accordance with the Ghent treaty.

We the undersigned, prelates, clergymen, seigniors, nobles, judges, magistrates of the towns and rural districts and others who constitute and represent the States General of the Netherlands now assembled in this town of Brussels, and others who owe obedience to the most exalted, powerful and illustrious prince, King Philip, our sovereign lord and natural prince etc., inform every one now and for the future that as we saw our common fatherland being oppressed by the Spaniards in a most barbarous and tyrannical way, we were moved, urged and compelled to unite and join together and to help each other with arms, advice, men and money against the said Spaniards and their allies, declared to be rebels to His Majesty and to be our enemies.[2] And we declare that this union and association has since been ratified by the Pacification recently concluded on the authority and with the approval of the Council of State entrusted by His Majesty with the general government of these provinces. The aim of this union is total loyalty and firmness and mutual fidelity for ever and we do not wish any misunderstandings to give rise among us to feelings of suspicion or fear of evil intentions. On the contrary we desire the work of this union to be undertaken, expedited and executed with total sincerity, loyalty and diligence, so that none of the subjects or inhabitants of these provinces can reasonably be discontented or entertain doubts regarding us. For these reasons and in order that nothing is done to the detriment of

[1] De Blécourt-Japikse, Klein Plakkaatboek, pp. 117ff.
[2] See Document 23, note 4.

our common fatherland and its righteous defence, and nothing required for our righteous defence, now and in future, is left undone through negligence or connivance, we have promised and promise, by virtue of our power and commission and on behalf of ourselves as well as our successors, upon the word of Christians, honest men and true compatriots, inviolably and forever to keep and entertain this union and association, without any of us being permitted to disengage himself or break away by oblique ways, secret understanding or otherwise. We do this to conserve our holy faith and the Catholic Apostolic Roman religion, to accomplish the Pacification, to drive out the Spaniards and their allies and duly to obey His Majesty; we do it for the prosperity and peace of our fatherland, for the maintenance of all our privileges, rights, franchises, statutes, customs and old usages. To this we shall devote all available means, money, men, advice, as well as property, even our lives, if necessary. No one of us may give any private advice, counsel or consent, or be in secret communication with people who do not belong to this union, nor inform them in any way of what is or will be discussed, advised or decided in our assembly for all of us will conform in everything to the purport of our general and unanimous resolution. And if any province, state, country, town, castle or house be besieged, attacked, invaded, overwhelmed or oppressed, or if any of us or any other man who has exerted himself for the fatherland and its common defence against the Spaniards, or rendered other services connected with this, should be pursued, imprisoned, held to ransom, hurt, molested or harassed personally or in his property, honour, rank or otherwise, we promise to help them by all the said means. We also promise to bring about, either by force or otherwise, the deliverance of the prisoners. And if we break our pledge we shall be deprived of our nobility, name, arms and honour, be taken for perjurers and disloyal enemies of our fatherland before God and mankind and incur the taint of infamy and cowardice forever. And to validate this our holy union and association, we have signed this in our own hands and put our signature, 9 January 1577.

25

Advice and answer of the prince of Orange and the States of Holland and Zeeland to some articles concluded in the form of a Perpetual Edict, 19 February 1577[1]

Notwithstanding the First Union of Brussels the States General continued negotiations with Don John. These resulted in an agreement issued by the governor in the form of a Perpetual Edict (12 February 1577). Don John declared his acceptance of the Ghent treaty which was interpreted to mean that the Roman Catholic religion was to be maintained in all provinces. Of course this was done without Orange's collaboration. The delegates of Holland and Zeeland further refused to attend the meetings of the States General.

[The prince of Orange and the States of Holland and Zeeland considered many articles in the Perpetual Edict unacceptable and intended to write their objections down and to send them] to the States General and to explain to them at the same time that it was now the right time to request, to insist on and to obtain, after the example of our ancestors, an extension and an augmentation of the privileges, rights and freedoms they have handed down to us, because we now have such a good opportunity to make sure that we should not relapse into the same unpleasant situation. But when they were engaged on drawing up and writing down these points and articles, they were given a copy of the missive which the said gentlemen of the States had written to Don John,[2] from which they gathered that the States promised to come to an agreement with Don John without waiting for an answer to the said articles and asked him to sign these articles with the promise to have them published and to receive him in the country. This has come as a great surprise to the prince and the States of Holland and Zeeland. They noticed that the attitude of the States General had greatly changed and that the date of the said missive which was handed to them, was almost the same as that at which the lord of Willer-

[1] *Advis ende andtwoorde des Prince van Oraenge ende der Staten van Hollant ende Zeelant op sekere artijculen besloten by maniere van een eeuwich Edict* (Knuttel, no. 297).
[2] Dated 8 February 1577.

val[3] had come to them. But even apart from the apparent inconsistency they feel that this important affair upon which the total prosperity or ruin of all these Netherlands depends is rushed through with unreasonable haste. Nevertheless they think and firmly believe this was done with the intention of freeing the provinces from the Spaniards and other foreign oppressors of the fatherland more speedily. Therefore they cannot but desire (as they do with all their heart) and pray to the Lord God that the end will be what all true patriots are hoping for.

As it would now be useless to raise objections or to discuss or refute what has been done, they promise and assure the States that they shall so far as they are concerned observe the peace of Ghent in every way. They hope that the said gentlemen of the States are of the same opinion, and pray them always to show this in their actions, as they are always willing to do themselves. Moreover, they wish to prove by their acts that they desire nothing else but to expedite the departure of the Spaniards and other foreigners and the confirmation of peace and tranquillity as well as of the old privileges, rights and freedoms of the provinces. Consequently they are prepared to approve and to sign the said articles, on condition that first of all the said States shall decide firmly and irrevocably (and confirm this in an official deed drafted in due form and properly signed by the States, governors of the provinces, commanders and colonels) that if the Spaniards do not actually leave the provinces within the time fixed and agreed upon with Don John,[4] the gentlemen of the States General shall put an end once for all to all these pretexts and these lengthy proceedings that have been so harmful to us so far, and cut off all further communication with Don John and use force to compel the Spaniards to depart without lending themselves to any negotiation or conference of whatever kind. And they are asked to make a second deed and contract in which they promise that if they have to use force to make the Spaniards depart, neither they nor the governors, commanders and colonels shall receive, admit or recognise Don John or any one else as governor of the country, before he has redressed and entirely made good all points which are in any way contrary to the privileges, rights and freedoms of the country, or in any way detrimental to the Pacification of Ghent (according to which everybody will again be put in possession of all that belongs to them, in

[3] Adrian d'Oignies, lord of Willerval was sent by the States General to bring the message to the prince.

[4] In the Perpetual Edict the governor bound himself to withdraw the Spanish troops within twenty days; the States were to raise the money to pay them off; after this the withdrawal of the other foreign troops would be discussed.

Burgundy[5] as well as in the Netherlands). All the said privileges and freedoms shall be confirmed, ratified and affirmed, as the States solemnly promised when writing to their deputies at the time of the peace-negotiations at Ghent on 28 October 1576.[6]

Middelburg, 19 February 1577.

[5] Mainly in Franche Comté, where the prince of Orange owned valuable landed property.
[6] At this date the delegates had come to an agreement at Ghent on the treaty of Pacification.

26

Letters written by His Highness to the States, prelates, nobles, towns and some private persons of the provinces of the Netherlands, 14 August 1577[1]

These letters were published by the governor Don John at Namur on 14 August 1577 in order to justify his attack of 24 July on the citadel of this town.

Now see that there are some peace-breakers and malcontents who have too much influence with these States. Some of them all ill-affected towards our Catholic religion or prompted by distrust caused by their bad conscience, others want to profit by the war, as they did the last time. They try in all possible ways to involve you in a new civil war, without knowing what purpose it would serve or how the country can derive profit from it – for, as you know, it is only deep misery, terrible disasters and total ruin which it can produce. We are surprised that such a small number of ill-advised evil-minded people have acquired so much credit and authority that they could get so many honest men, prelates, churchmen, seigniors, nobles, wise men, notabilities and good subjects, even though Catholics, to arm themselves against their own religion, their legitimate prince, their parents, friends, their fatherland and themselves, their flesh and blood.

If one examines the matter carefully, it is obvious that the war they want you to wage (for we will not begin it and we will wage it only de-

[1] *Lettres escriptes par son Altesse aux Estatz, prelatz, nobles, villes et aucuns particuliers des provinces du pays bas* (Knuttel, no. 318).

fensively, if we are forced to do so) is inevitably directed against the Catholic religion or against the king our sovereign seignior and legitimate prince or against ourselves. And it must be concluded that you want to change either your religion or your prince or your governor, or all three of them. If you oppose the religion, of what use is the promise of all the States, repeated so many times,[2] that they do not want to change it for anything in the world? In that case you fight God, His ordinances, His doctrine, the holy tradition of our holy mother church in which you have been born, baptised, instructed and bred, your own salvation; and you support the sectarians, the heretics, your sworn enemies who have brought about your destruction and ruin and will always do so. And if you intend to wreck the true religion (which we shall never believe), you may rest assured that His Majesty will avail himself of all means God has given him, to keep you from doing so and to maintain the Catholic religion of which he rightly calls himself the protector and defender. If it is against your king and sovereign prince, that you intend to make war and if you want to change your lawful seignior (which we cannot imagine either), consider first of all if human and divine law permit this and what just and legitimate reasons you have. Consider what His Majesty has done against you and your country, especially after the recent accord[3] and consider too whether you will be better off with another when you have forsaken your lawful seignior and what profit you will derive from this change. And if you do want to fight the king, you can take it that His Majesty will not tolerate it and that you cannot attempt it without incurring the opprobrium of rebellion and of *lèse-majesté*, with which, I believe, you would not like to be charged, nor to be everywhere defamed.

If you fight us, you must explain in what respect we have contravened the accord, and whether we have not done all that we have promised. We sent the Spaniards home, returned the fortresses to the inhabitants, restored the privileges, and we have shown the utmost patience. We have even tolerated insults and indignities for which we had no redress at law as the legal system is totally undermined by the audacity of the people, and we wanted to avoid new riots.[4] If we are told of instances where we broke the accord we are willing to seek an appropriate solution. But if all the good things we have done for the country, first in Spain where we

---

[2] The first Union of Brussels and the Perpetual Edict expressly intended to maintain the prevailing Roman Catholic religion.

[3] The Perpetual Edict of February 1577.

[4] Don John no longer felt safe in Brussels and Mechlin and consequently left these towns.

spoke and acted on your behalf before our arrival here[5] and then in the Netherlands where we drew up and scrupulously carried into effect the treaties and accords ratified by His Majesty – if all this does not satisfy the States and if they think that another governor will be more beneficial for them, then God forbid that our person should be the cause of another war.

[5] The governor arrived at Luxemburg at the beginning of November 1576 after staying in Spain for some months.

27

A short account of the true causes and reasons which have forced the States General of the Netherlands to take measures for their protection against Don John of Austria, 1577[1]

Marnix of St Aldegonde wrote this justification by order of the States General in the autumn of 1577. Some letters from Don John and his secretary Juan de Escovedo to the king, which were intercepted and handed to the prince of Orange, were also published by him in this pamphlet.

It is common knowledge that Don John intends, as he has always done, to set the country ablaze with war; and, as Escovedo says, to remedy matters by fire and bloodshed. Indeed, the States could not avoid or escape such a pressing need to act as they did, unless they wished to commit treachery and to break the oath by which they swore to protect their fatherland. For they have been called by God and men to be the protectors of the privileges, rights and freedoms of the common people, whom they represent in the three estates of clergy, nobles and towns. Not only does their oath bind them to protect the common people; they have also received in their hands the oath of the king[2] along with that of His Highness so that they must see to it that this is kept. Moreover they are bound and united by the alliance and union they have concluded, of

[1] *Cort verhael van de rechte oorsaecken ende redenen, die de Generale Staten der Nederlanden ghedwonghen hebben hen te versiene tot hunder beschermenisse teghen den heere Don Jehan van Oostenrijck* (Knuttel, no. 310).
[2] Sworn in 1549.

which His Highness has himself approved,[3] on penalty of being for-swearers and devoid of all honour.

The sovereign may not wage or declare war on another prince or foreign nation without the consent of the States because the privileges of the country prohibit this. If the prince should abuse his power and break the privileges and wrong the common people contrary to all reason and justice, they are bound to oppose this by force. In that case they may refuse him obedience and choose a governor to rule them until the mistakes committed be corrected. This appears conclusively from the privileges of the country and the examples set by our forefathers in con-formity with written law.[4] Who can deny that the States are duty-bound to resist with weapons a stadholder of the prince, who before being accepted as governor by all provinces[5] and even before carrying out the principal points and conditions on which he ought to have been accepted in conformity with the Perpetual Edict, already takes up arms against the country and like an enemy captures its strongholds,[6] with the intention of destroying everything by fire and sword? Not only does he attempt to get free of the unbreakable obligations already entered into by oath and mutual contract; he also intends to oppress and to trample on the privi-leges, rights and freedoms of the fatherland.

For it is so well known that His Highness did not carry out the condi-tions to which he bound himself when he was accepted, that no proof is needed. We have already seen that contrary to the said accord he invoked the help of foreigners[7] and held councils and private councils with people who are sworn and public enemies of the common peace and prosperity of the country and entirely suspect to good patriots. And we know that instead of punishing the soldiers, Spaniards as well as Germans, who brought about the ruin and piteous desolation of these provinces, for their misdeeds, in conformity with the seventh article of the said edict,[8] he has not only approved them and considered them his best servants, but he has asked them to help him in the current affairs of state and has favoured them and recommended them seriously to His Majesty.

[3] At the beginning of May 1577 Don John was received by the States General within the city-walls of Brussels and accepted the Union concluded by the provinces of the Netherlands.   [4] See Document 47.
[5] The States General and the governor held fruitless discussions with the pro-vinces of Holland and Zeeland at Geertruidenberg in May 1577.
[6] On 24 July 1577 Don John took the citadel of Namur by surprise but an attack on that of Antwerp failed.
[7] Especially the secretary Escovedo.
[8] The Perpetual Edict of 12 February 1577.

28

___

Articles by which Archduke Matthias was accepted as governor and captain-general of the provinces in the Netherlands, 1577[1]

This document contains the conditions on which Matthias of Austria was accepted as governor by the States General on 8 December 1577, after they had declared Don John to be an enemy of the country.

I. The archduke as lieutenant of the king and governor of these countries shall take the oath to His Majesty the king as the supreme lord and legitimate prince of the Netherlands and also to the States General, to the welfare of the Netherlands.

II. Similarly all other governors of provinces as well as of towns (where there may be governors, and usually were, in accordance with the privileges) and all colonels, captains, soldiers and officers shall take the oath to the king their lord and legitimate prince, under the governor general in the name of the king, and at the same time to the States General, to the welfare of the provinces.

III. They, and the governor too, shall be bound to observe all the following articles, and especially to maintain each and all of the privileges, rights, usages and customs of the country and to restore, preserve and keep them inviolate.

IV. The governor shall govern the country with a Council of State, nominated by the States General, made up of men born in the country, capable and qualified, true to the country, without greed and ambition, detached, no longer driven by the passions raised in the party conflicts of recent years, wise and expert in the matter of policy as well as of war.

V. All matters which will be deliberated upon by the said council, shall be decided on and decreed by a majority of votes; the governor is not allowed to conclude matters within other private or secret councils.[2]

VI. If it should be revealed that some member of the said council or someone else who holds an important post in the gift of the king, does not carry out his duty as he should, appropriate measures shall be taken at the request of the States General.

[1] Bor, *Oorsprongk*, I, pp. 927ff.
[2] A reminder of Don John's practices (see Document 27).

VII. The king shall continue to make appointments to offices he has always been competent to make appointments to, but he shall be humbly requested to appoint capable and qualified persons who meet the requirements of article IV. All other remonstrances concerning these offices shall be remitted to the forthcoming assembly of the States General required by the Pacification of Ghent.[3]

VIII. The said governor and councillors shall not come to any decision on important matters concerning public affairs such as requests for and levying of money, declaration of war or conclusion of peace, alliances and confederacies with foreign princes or countries and other such matters, without the permission and approval of the States General. Nor shall they issue any important edicts or decrees, or introduce any new customs or general usages, without the prior advice and agreement of the States legally assembled in each province according to the rules and, if required, even of the States General.

IX. The governor is obliged to communicate to the council all letters received which in any way concern the state of the provinces, in order that they be advised and resolved upon properly by means of a vote.

X. In the same council nothing shall be dealt with unless the greater part of the councillors are present.

XI. All deeds and despatches drawn up by the said council shall be initialed by one of the councillors.

XII. The governor shall restore according to the Pacification of Ghent and the Perpetual Edict all ancient privileges, usages and customs which can be proved to have been encroached on, violated or forcibly taken away or abolished.

XIII. The deputies of the States shall be allowed to assemble for as long as they think necessary for settling the affairs of the country, and the States General shall be allowed to assemble as often as they wish.

XIV. On an important matter which requires a general or common assembly, at the request of any one of the provinces, the other provinces may, nay must, also assemble without awaiting the governor's command, authorisation or permission.[4]

XV. In the same way the States of each province may assemble whenever they think it advisable.

XVI. The Pacification of Ghent shall be maintained in all its points and

[3] See Document 23.

[4] In 1477 Mary of Burgundy was forced by circumstances to grant the so-called Great Privilege which, contrary to precedent, authorised the States to meet on their own initiative. This however was withdrawn in 1494.

articles without being encroached on or violated under any pretext whatsoever.

XVII. The governor shall have his ordinary guard of archers and halberdiers from the Netherlands, as other princes of the blood and governors of these Netherlands have had, and if he wants to increase their number for some exceptional purpose, it shall be done with the approval and advice of the States.

XVIII. The governor and the members of his council shall on the advice of the States appoint the general of the army by sea and land, the admiral or general of the horse, the field-marshal and colonels and all of equal rank.

XIX. He shall not raise any additional foot-soldiers or cavalry, nor garrison the towns, except with the consent both of the States and of the towns where the garrisons are to be sent, according to the privileges of the said towns, except in case of emergency.

XX. He shall not appoint a governor in any province without the advice and agreement of the province. The governor shall, if possible, be resident in that province or have estate and revenue there or at least his appointment shall be approved by the province.

XXI. In war time he shall take all important decisions in the Council of State enlarged with a Council of War. Only people acceptable to the States General shall be appointed to the said Council of War.

XXII. All revenues of the States shall be administered by the States and their commissioners. The demesne and finances of the king will continue to be administered in the usual way so that the royal authority will in no way be injured. If it appears that other measures are needed, this can be indicated now or in the forthcoming meeting of the States required by the Pacification of Ghent.

XXIII. The States may accept the proposals made by the neighbouring kingdoms and princes and the surrounding provinces and towns in case of need, notably if war has been declared. The governor shall uphold and maintain what the States have already accepted or will accept.[5]

XXIV. Those who took up arms against the States and the fatherland and sided with Don John during the recent disturbances, will be prosecuted by law. These lawsuits must not be prevented or delayed, so that from now on no one will dare to disturb the public peace and welfare. Only those are excepted who have asked to return or who can prove that they were deceived or forced by Don John against their will to support him.

[5] Both Queen Elizabeth of England and the duke of Anjou (Henri III's brother) had offered their assistance to the States General.

Their cases shall be judged by the said States General, provided they return within the time fixed and determined by the States General.

xxv. The castles which it was agreed should be demolished but which are still intact shall really be dismantled now. Decisions will be taken about the other castles or soldiers, who it is feared may serve to oppress the provinces, on the advice of the forthcoming meeting of the States General required by the Pacification of Ghent.

xxvi. In general nothing done in the past or in connection with the recent disturbances shall be investigated or made cause for reproof. All those matters fall under the first article of the Pacification of Ghent where they are said to be forgiven, forgotten and regarded as not having occurred,[6] with the exception, however, of what is contained in the twenty-fifth article of the present treaty.

xxvii. His Highness shall maintain as good resolutions, without opposing them in any way, all that has been done, ordained or decreed by the States General since the departure of the said lord Don John to the castle of Namur,[7] and the king shall be requested to be pleased to do likewise.

xxviii. The archduke shall also use all his influence with His Imperial Majesty, the electors and other princes of the Holy Empire that, to establish more tranquillity in these provinces, they induce by all means the king our sovereign lord to expedite the departure of the said lord Don John of Austria and all his retinue, and the reunion and restitution of the towns and places held at present by the said lord Don John. This the German princes are bound to do, for this country, together with the county of Burgundy,[8] forms a circle of the Holy Roman Empire, and is thus under the protection of His Imperial Majesty as well as of the Empire.

xxix. Further, whilst His Highness is governor-general, he shall take no one into his service who is not a native of this country with the exception of the foreigners whom he has brought with him or whom he wants for his personal service if the States allow this. But neither they nor those who are already with him shall have anything to do with the political affairs of these provinces, nor aspire to any commission to office or interfere in public affairs or administration.

And if the said archduke after accepting the government on the said conditions comes to infringe any of these conditions, the States declare beforehand that they have the right to admonish him and, if he should not correct the infringement, to take up arms for their lawful protection against the lord archduke or others.

[6] See Document 23. [7] On 24 July 1577. [8] See Document 19 note 8.

29

Second Union of Brussels, 10 December 1577[1]

The Second Union of Brussels was concluded by the States General when they entrusted Archduke Matthias with the governorship. The unity of all the provinces of the Netherlands in their fight against Don John appeared to be restored.

We the undersigned, prelates, clergymen, seigniors, noblemen, judges, magistrates of the towns and rural districts and others who constitute and represent the States of the Netherlands now assembled in this town of Brussels, and others who owe obedience to the most exalted, powerful and illustrious prince, Philip, king of Spain, our prince and lord, make the following known to every one now and for the future.

We declare that we have never wished anything more ardently than the restoration in these Netherlands of unity, lasting peace and quiet after so much distress and calamities of war. After the conclusion and acceptance of the Pacification of Ghent a concord, alliance and union was conceived and ratified to confirm and corroborate the Pacification yet further and to join the hearts of the inhabitants in so close a union and alliance,[2] that there should no longer be any room for any suspicion that new discord should arise. To forestall possible calumnies on the part of our adversaries and of malevolent people who try to make all the world accuse and denigrate us as if our Pacification proceeded from a desire to change our state and religion as well as our prince, we stated in that alliance that it was our intention to maintain the Roman Catholic religion as well as the obedience due to the king our lord, all this in accordance with the terms of the Pacification of Ghent, which His Majesty himself has since sanctioned and ratified.[3]

However, much to our regret it came about that some people, ill-disposed towards their own fatherland and wishing to aggrandise themselves at the expense and to the detriment of the poor people,[4] instead of

---

[1] De Blécourt-Japikse, *Klein Plakkaatboek*, pp. 118ff.

[2] The First Union of 9 January 1577, Document 24.

[3] Philip had ratified the Perpetual Edict concluded by Don John and thus accepted the Pacification.

[4] Don John's supporters after his action at Namur of 24 July (Berlaymont and his son were among them).

taking our intention and declaration in good part and uniting with us, as they had solemnly bound themselves, to drive out the common enemy, have tried to conceal their malevolence under cover of these two points: the Roman Catholic religion and the obedience due to the king. To give some semblance of reason to their iniquitous pretensions and greed they laid their own crime at our door and accused us most unjustly of having been the first to violate our promise. They did not content themselves with taking up arms against their own fatherland; they also tried and are still trying everyday to lead astray the most zealous patriots, together with devoted adherents of the Roman Catholic religion and other ill-informed people. They hide behind these two points, saying that the States allow these points to be infringed in defiance of the terms of the Pacification of Ghent and the ensuing Union. Their purpose is to induce them by these false imputations to side with them and to sow new dissension and discord among these provinces. Thus they hope to get the better of the people and at the price of total ruin to be able to give free rein to their iniquitous greed.

When it was seen that both the ill-informed inhabitants and those who turned out to have little difficulty in finding a show of reason and plausibility to conceal their own schemes, were approached with such arguments, several even among people most devoted to the well-being and peace of the country have become somewhat suspicious and distrustful although they themselves could not be enforced to adhere to the Roman Catholic religion because this was explicitly forbidden by the Pacification of Ghent.[5] They thought that the said First Union of Brussels might in fact have been intended to deceive them and to hamper them with a network of obligations contrary to the Pacification of Ghent. As a result of this, several persons shrank back from this first Union and alliance, which therefore did not have the effect and the fruits that we had wished and hoped for. This is why we now want to make it clear to every one that our intention has always been and is still to maintain, observe and confirm the Pacification of Ghent in all sincerity in each of its points and, according to the terms contained in it, to defend, to guarantee and to maintain the Roman Catholic religion, together with the obedience and loyalty legitimately due to our prince and lord the king of Spain. For the sake of greater assurance and to dispel all feelings of distrust, we decided to make this declaration and to make known to all that our intention has never been nor is at present to infringe, violate or diminish in any way the Pacification of Ghent or to oppress, hurt or damage contrary to it those

[5] The provinces of Holland and Zeeland.

who, having abandoned the Roman Catholic religion, have joined us and united with us in the Pacification. For their part the adherents of the new religion declare that it has not been nor is their intention to violate, oppress or damage the adherents of the Roman Catholic religion or violently to prevent or to disturb its exercise. All of us want to live in friendship and union with each other according to the terms of the Pacification, and unanimously and with the same zeal we wish to use all our means and powers, even at the risk of our lives, to resist the efforts of the enemies of our common fatherland and to cut across the projects of all those who, under whatever colour and pretext, unreasonably and iniquitously take up arms to oppress and violate our ancient privileges, rights and liberties and to bring us under the yoke of foreign enslavement.

To this end we swear and promise each other, calling the sovereign God to witness, to enforce and to observe what we have declared above and to see to it that it is also observed by others, in total fidelity and sincere loyalty without deceit and malignity, and to maintain, to guarantee and to defend each other to the best of our ability in this righteous and holy strife. We who adhere to the Roman Catholic religion therefore promise and swear that we shall not permit or suffer any plots or attempts to be made against those, who have abandoned the Roman Catholic religion and are united with us in this Pacification, of whatever rank, condition or province they may be. Nor shall we allow them to be injured, molested or disturbed in any way because of their religion. Rather we shall permit them to live in peace under the Pacification of Ghent.[6] We shall take them under our care and protection according to the most generous possible interpretation of the Pacification, without fraud or malignity or chicanery or similar subterfuges or deceit. Reciprocally we who have abandoned the Roman Catholic religion promise and solemnly swear, that we shall make no attempts against the Roman Catholic religion and its exercise, nor shall we injure or disturb any one in any way because of it in word or deed nor scandalise them. We shall ensure that no one shall hinder, or order others to hinder, or disturb in any way, or molest or annoy Roman Catholics or obstruct the exercise of their religion, their services and ceremonies. All of us will be bound to defend and guarantee to clergy as well as laymen their Roman Catholic religion and its exercise and their estates, dignities, honours, privileges and possessions, without suffering any wrong, injury or disturbance to be laid upon them in any manner whatsoever. In general we shall to the best of our ability maintain the ancient

6 See the treaty of the Pacification, Document 23.

privileges and customs, rights and usages of our common fatherland, its provinces and private inhabitants. And everyone of us shall re-establish and restore, maintain and make people maintain and restore, to the best of our ability all the privileges, both the general and the special ones, which can with perfect justice and right be proved to be valid irrespective of whether they were taken away by force or violence or lost through misfortune. And in order to confirm and maintain this with greater certainty and efficiency and to avoid in future all discord and division, which might arise in default of a commander-in-chief, we promise and swear to accept provisionally, until otherwise ordained by His Majesty and the States General, the archduke, Matthias, of Austria as lieutenant-governor and captain-general for His Majesty in these Netherlands. We shall obey him in accordance with the conditions and articles which the States will put before him and about which we shall come to an agreement together.[7] He will ratify these by solemn oath and at the same time swear and promise to maintain, ratify and approve of this association and union and to keep it firm and stable, and he will swear and promise not to infringe or violate it in any way either in general or in any of its points and articles.

Thus concluded and resolved upon in the assembly of the States General at Brussels, 10 December 1577.

[7] See Document 28.

30

Answer to a pamphlet entitled 'Declaration of the opinion of lord Don John of Austria', 1578[1]

This is a reaction to the declaration published by Don John on 25 January 1578, shortly before he beat the army of the States General in the battle of Gembloux. It was written by Marnix of St Aldegonde, who sat on the new Council of State, under governor Matthias. It was published on 18 March 1578 by the famous Antwerp printer Plantin.

Don John says that he desires two things only: the conservation of the

[1] *Antwoorde op een cleyn boecxken . . . ghenoemt de Declaratie van de meyninge van heer Don Jan van Oostenrijck* (Knuttel, no. 343).

Roman Catholic religion and the re-establishment of the king's authority. However, as religion is a gift of God and cannot be implanted or impressed on people's minds by force of arms, how can one reasonably say that Don John wanted to preserve the Roman Catholic religion or to maintain it by taking up arms? For how will he do this? Will he put to death all those who will not recognise this religion? If he takes this course then we shall again find ourselves in the hell of civil wars. For there are many people and towns who would rather be cut into pieces than await the fury of these executions. The results clearly show how little the late emperor Charles, blessed be his memory, achieved in Germany by taking up arms for the same reason. And already three kings in France[2] and the duke of Alva and the commander of Castile[3] in Holland and Zeeland have to our great harm made us wiser by experience. Shall we always be tripped up by the same stone, trying to eradicate by force what is hidden in the depths of our souls and can be reshaped by God alone? Perhaps. However, this much is certain: the inquisition will be re-established, the old edicts will be re-newed, scaffolds and gallows will be set up again and everywhere in the country great multitudes of poor people will be burned to death and hanged and robbed: people, who wish to be loyal subjects to His Majesty and to perform their duties to their fellow-creatures, as long as they may serve God in accordance with their conscience. But what kind of peace and quiet will there be? Shall we not see that the country will thus be sub-mitted to a greater tyranny than ever before? Nevertheless, if by such means the Roman Catholic religion could be preserved, then there might be some justification for these policies; in reality, however, they will totally destroy it. For experience proves convincingly that nothing is more harmful to its conservation than force of arms and violent persecution. Nothing makes the clergy more hated and consequently brings them into greater danger than their public refusal to side with the rest of the popula-tion. This was manifest in Holland and Zeeland where the expulsion of the clergy was (as the inhabitants declare) caused by the fact that the clergy, in violation of the alliance they had concluded, refused to join the others. They had daily secret dealings with the Spaniards and this for reasons of security led the States of the province to deliver the country from them completely.[4] And if despite the conclusion of the Pacification of Ghent and

---

[2] The brothers Francis II, Charles IX and Henri III, who succeeded each other on the throne of France after 1559.
[3] The Spanish governor, Requesens.
[4] This passage refers to the treatment of the Roman Catholic clergy in the provinces of Holland and Zeeland after the revolt of the year 1572.

its ratification by a firm union, this weed of discord and dispute is again sown here among the common people and if one wants to exterminate either the one or the other party contrary to the promises made in the Pacification, it is greatly to be feared that discord will again burst into the flames of civil war and bring about the ruin of the country in general, and of the clergy in particular, for the clergy, being rich and free from many taxes, is much exposed to hatred.

This brings me to suppose that Don John appears so stubborn on the point of religion because he hopes to use it as a means to sow dissension in the country and, as his councillor Escovedo says, to set the inhabitants by the ears.[5] For Don John knows of course that the real way to conserve the Roman Catholic religion is through solid unity and firm mutual solidarity, without partiality over religion. The example of Germany clearly proves this.[6] There the adherents of both religions daily associate with each other; nevertheless there is no country in the world where the clergy are more respected or richer or more powerful.

This is why the bishops and universities in the Netherlands were quite right in holding that the Pacification of Ghent was conducive to the conservation of the Roman Catholic religion and did not tend to harm or ruin it as Don John himself made people think.[7] If Don John wants to preserve the Roman Catholic religion in the way prescribed by the Pacification, then there is no need to take up arms. For all on whom he is waging war, whichever religion they profess, support the Pacification, as they have often made clear especially in their recent declaration in the States General and as they have also proved by their deeds.[8] But if he intends to preserve religion by raising new disturbances, murders and civil wars, which ruin the country and its honest inhabitants by arson and bloodshed, then we must assume that religion is only a pretext to cover his malevolence towards these countries, which he desires to destroy even if this also causes the fall of the Roman Catholic religion. For it is certain that since the conclusion of the Pacification of Ghent, the adherents of the religion called 'reformed' have behaved with greater discipline and discretion than under the duke of Alva or any of the other previous governors: they have not introduced any innovation or made any change or alteration however small. On the contrary in obstinately taking up arms under

[5] See Document 27.   [6] Since the religious peace of Augsburg of 1555.
[7] This declaration by the bishops in the Netherlands and by the theological and juridical faculties of the university of Louvain was inserted into the text of the Perpetual Edict.
[8] At the Second Union of Brussels of December 1577.

cover of maintaining the Roman Catholic religion Don John runs a great risk bringing us into great disorder and confusion.

31

Answer from the States General of the Netherlands to a proposition from His Imperial Majesty, 1578[1]

This reply by the States General to the mediatory proposals of the emperor, Rudolph II, transmitted by the ambassador Otho Henry count of Schwartzenberg in January 1578, was published at Plantin's on the same day as the previous document. Marnix may also have been the author of this document.

Thus it is clear that His Majesty, who is far away from these provinces and ill-informed, ordained (or rather it was ordained in his name) and presented to the States conditions which cannot be fulfilled without harming the interests of His Majesty or bringing about the destruction of the whole country, and which are moreover totally contrary to the king's declaration and promise.[2] And yet Don John does not cease proclaiming these conditions everywhere, and using the pretext of religion and of the obedience due to the king – such peaceful and beautiful matters – to sow discord and dissension among the inhabitants of the country and to set them by the ears so that they will ruin each other (as Escovedo explicitly writes to the king of Spain).[3] That is why the States, putting an end to the extravagantly subtle and dangerous religious disputes, are forced to unite more strongly and to ask for the help and assistance of other nations, even to ally themselves with foreign princes.[4]

As the king decided to ruin the men who so far rendered him allegiance, obedience and gallant service and still are doing so and promise to do so in future and as he deprives them of their hope of a peaceful settlement, what remains to these poor people but to have recourse to what both divine and secular right allows in such matters, what nature commands,

[1] *Antwoorde van de generale Staten van de Nederlanden op de propositie ghedaen van weghen de Keyserlijcke Maiesteyt* . . . (Knutttel, no. 347).
[2] When he accepted the Pacification in 1577.
[3] See Document 27.
[4] Queen Elizabeth and the duke of Anjou.

THE REVOLT OF THE NETHERLANDS

what reason prescribes and law permits, that is, to taking up arms and providing for their prosperity and safety by all means that present themselves and staving off the great dangers which threaten them? As long as they breathe they will try to shake off the yoke of this miserable foreign enslavement and to secure their possessions from pillage, their wives and children from rape, themselves from the senseless cruelty of the most cruel enemies in the world. What else can they do as they see that the duke of Alva and all other authors and perpetrators of these wretched manoeuvres have great influence in the king's high and secret council[5] and that Don John follows almost exclusively the advice of people whom he solemnly swore to punish as an example to others? His advisers are the men who set fire to the most beautiful and famous towns in the country and stole their treasures, who destroyed the king's provinces and whose hands are stained with the blood of his most faithful and best subjects. It is they whom Don John holds in the greatest respect and who settle things to their liking. This is an outrage to all well-disposed people. What hope can they entertain when they see that all decisions are being taken by the most cruel murderers who are appointed as judges of their lives and inherited possessions? They have seen such deceptions for so many years and so many shocking examples of hypocrisy and dissimulation that they know they cannot now seek the protection of Don John's government unless they should wish willingly and knowingly to strike a rock and be shipwrecked ten times and cause all nations in the world to mock at their deplorable and foolish credulity.

[5] After his return to Spain in 1573 Alva remained one of Philip II's chief counsellors.

32

A letter containing an advice concerning the state of affairs in the Netherlands, 1 June 1578[1]

This pamphlet in the form of a letter to Marnix of St Aldegonde contains arguments in favour of making the duke of Anjou sovereign of the Netherlands. The author poses as a German nobleman in

[1] *Lettre contenant un avis de l'estat auquel sont les affaires des Païs-Bas* . . . (Knuttel, no. 358).

Cologne who, thanks to a long stay in France, is able to write in French. In 1578 the States General were negotiating with Anjou; this resulted in the conclusion of a treaty in August.

Seeing that supplications and remonstrances have for so long now been vain and dangerous, you have in your extremity had recourse to extreme remedies, that is, to arms and war, and thus you have made clear in a straightforward manner that you refused any longer to accept the tyrant or his accomplices, or any one who bears the name of his country. If this does not mean deposing as unworthy a king from his kingship by public authority I do not know how otherwise to define it.[2] And matters standing thus I cannot see why you should be in fear of what you have already done, and how you can have forgotten so soon that you actually wished to do what you are still doing every day not because you like it, but because you are driven by the impulse that naturally drives men to seek their self-preservation. Indeed, your safety and salvation are at stake, for as you know, the places have already been appointed where the greater part of those people who are still alive after the civil war will be transported and the towns where new inhabitants from abroad will be sent.[3] One of your main privileges, I am sure, allows you to declare that the tyrant is no longer your seignior and you are no longer his subjects. What remains to be established is, whether you are entitled and willing to change the form of your government and may refuse to live under the protection of a good and righteous master.

It really would be doing you an injustice to call this in question. For if hatred of the seigniory and not of the bad seignior has caused you to take up arms, then you are rebels indeed and no prince could help or favour you for fear of setting his own country a pernicious and dangerous example of rebellion.[4] But you show clearly that this is not at all what you want. You are so accustomed to living under seigniors, that even when you condemned your prince of the crime of tyranny and waged war on him, you claimed to do so in his name and under the authority of a man who was his lieutenant and near relation.[5] It is much to be doubted if your States acted well and wisely in this matter; I shall soon give you my opinion about this when I discuss our archduke. But I see that the wisest among you already repent of this policy and recognise that they have tried to reconcile two opposite policies, namely to expel a king and at the same time to establish a lieutenant who must represent him. This may be a good joke

[2] Philip II himself appears here as a tyrant.   [3] Cf. Document 16.
[4] Cf. Document 26.   [5] Philip's cousin, Archduke Matthias of Austria.

but this is not the time for jokes. I conclude that you want to have a prince and that you know it is not possible for you to be saved without having one. Whether this is so, because you are perplexed by the chaos around you or rather because of the discord amongst your seigniors, nearly all of whom consider themselves as equal,[6] is unimportant. What matters is that you must ascertain who will be the most useful and legitimate seignior.

As to usefulness, I have already told you that Monsieur[7] would be a better choice than all the other neighbours, not only because you need his help but also because your greatest happiness consists in having a seignior who is weak rather than violent, and who will be too busy establishing a modicum of authority to try and subdue you. I do not know anybody else but Monsieur in whom the qualities you need are so well united with each other. He has a natural gentleness as well as very little power and when he arrives in your country everything will be strange to him and he will need a long time to familiarise himself with conditions here. As to the justice of the nomination, there are good arguments to prove it. On the one hand the rights of sovereignty that the house of France has always had in Flanders and Artois, until the treaty of Madrid,[8] suffice to allow Monsieur to claim that his honour obliges him to revenge the wrong the Spaniard has done his house. On the other hand it is quite natural for you, after rejecting the Spaniard, to call on a prince who is a lineal descendant of the house of Burgundy and who is only one degree less near to the succession than Philip II.[9] And finally it is your own free will expressed through so many embassies that makes him your just and legitimate seignior. In consequence you need not be afraid of being blamed when you take steps to achieve a happier life and to free yourselves from that monstrous power that has rendered you wretched and miserable. You need fear neither the desires nor the designs of Monsieur Anjou who would never have conceived of becoming your lord had you not asked him first, and who, employing all his means to free you from a great evil, can have no other power than that which is conferred upon him by respect for him personally and by your laws.

[6] An allusion to the rivalry among great nobles such as Orange, Aerschot and Lalaing.

[7] Francis of Alençon, duke of Anjou, well-known leader of the political centre-party in the French religious wars.

[8] The peace concluded between Charles V and Francis I in 1526.

[9] Philip II was lineally descended from the Burgundian dukes, the duke of Anjou from the French king, Charles V, brother to the Burgundian duke, Philip the Bold (d. 1404)

33

A supplication to His Highness and to members of the Council of State handed in by the inhabitants of these Netherlands, who protest that they desire to live according to the reformation of the Gospel, 22 June 1578[1]

> This supplication was drafted during the national synod of the reformed church held at Dordrecht in June 1578. Peter Loyseleur de Villiers, the prince of Orange's court-chaplain, is held to be the author.

The Protestants cannot immediately make generally known their great wish to live peacefully and quietly with their fellow-citizens and compatriots but they hope to produce a very convincing proof of this in course of time when suspicion and distrust has been removed, and they promise before God to do so. Meanwhile they pray your Highness[2] and you, gentlemen, very humbly that you may be pleased to propose such measures for their security as you may think suitable and they will be willing to conform to your good counsels and obey you in everything to the best of their ability. They hope that they will find some princes, great lords and friends of these provinces,[3] who will do them the honour of vouching for the truth and constancy of their promise.

And all things considered, the said Protestants pray very humbly with all their hearts and in all submissiveness that Your Highness and you gentlemen, to whom this state has been entrusted, and for which you are obliged to account to God and men, may be pleased to take away all reasons for suspicion and distrust among the poor inhabitants of these Netherlands who raise their eyes to you. They ask you to devise and to deliberate upon means by which with good will and to every one's satisfaction the exercise of the one and the other religion may be permitted to the same extent until God will be pleased (conquering by His mercy our manifold sins, which are the only reason of so much evil and misfortune)

---

[1] *Supplicatie aen sijn Hoocheyt ende heeren des Raets van State overgegeven door de inwoonders deser Nederlanden, welcke protesteren, dat sy begeren te leven nae de Reformatie des Evangeliums* (Knuttel, no. 363).

[2] The Archduke Matthias.

[3] These must be either the queen of England, the elector Palatine or the duke of Anjou.

to conciliate the contradictory opinions prevalent in these provinces in the matter of religion by means of a good, sacred and free or at least national council.[4] They hope that by your wise counsel and prudence you may prevent the disasters and misfortunes which have befallen our neighbours[5] who may hardly take breath so far and that by your prudence you may stop the outrages of the enemy who under the pretext of our dissent tries to plunge us into an abysss of disorder. They hope that by your mature deliberation you may give satisfaction to the poor inhabitants who feel and know the illness but who expect from you, their chosen physician, the medicine beneficial to their health and hope that they will be led by you, whom they have raised to be their rulers, to a safe haven. May you be pleased to attend to the examples of our neighbours and others, some of whom have prevented the threatening disaster by their wise prudence,[6] others (grown wise by their distress and misery) have preferred to apply a remedy even when the long-lasting illness was in an advanced state rather than, doubtful of their prosperity and health, to bring utter ruin upon themselves.[7]

Have pity upon those who have put themselves under your protection and apart from God can expect no relief but from you. Therefore see to it that by a sacred law of pardon and oblivion all things done by both parties be totally forgotten so that in the future none shall be examined or molested because of any matter that may arise from the religious difference. In such a manner the Protestants shall promise to subject themselves to all reasonable conditions and to keep inviolate and to confirm as well as possible all conditions it may please Your Highness to propose. And though the said Protestants are ready to sacrifice themselves, their lives and possessions to the fatherland, yet they very humbly pray you to remember that for many years they have suffered greatly for their fatherland and that since the union of the provinces their loyalty and obedience has been great.[8] And if any of them has done anything which was not universally approved,[9] then appropriate counter-measures can be taken.

[4] According to the Pacification of Ghent the States General were to decide on a religious settlement; here it is proposed that a church-meeting should perform this task.

[5] In France in particular during the wars of religion.

[6] The Empire since the religious peace of Augsburg of 1555.

[7] In France religious edicts of 1576 and 1577 had created better conditions for the Huguenots.

[8] Since the Pacification of Ghent of 1576.

[9] This passage may refer to the actions of the Calvinists at Ghent, which were a matter of great concern to the prince of Orange.

Those mistakes are not mortal sins such as those commit who, feigning zeal for the common good, go openly over to the enemy. And if any wrong should be done to the Protestants (which is not to be hoped) then by the grace of God they are not the less intent upon persevering in what they know they owe to the fatherland.

34

Cry of the watchman. A warning to all lovers of the glory of God, the fatherland and its privileges and freedoms, 1578[1]

This pamphlet was written before 1 October 1578, the day of Don John's death. Peter Dathenus, the Calvinist minister officiating since September 1578 at Ghent, is the author of the Dutch translation. In this fragment the leading nobles of the Netherlands are attacked for being unreliable in the fight with the Spaniards.

You know the men who have helped to introduce, establish and execute the duke of Alva's tyranny and who have to the best of their ability supported and strengthened the authority and the violence of the cruel and haughty Spaniards. You know the men who in every one's opinion have brought the ensuing misery and calamities upon you but nevertheless you let them administer your most secret and important affairs. Are you really so simple as to think that they have so quickly turned from wolves into sheep, from tyrants into reasonable and humble rulers, from traitors to the fatherland and enemies to its freedoms into protectors and lovers of the country and its freedoms? Can a fountain give fresh and salt water at the same time? Do you not believe rather, what is the truth too, that they have turned their coats inside out and changed their speech but have kept the same duplicity and malevolence? Do you not see that some of these people who have done much harm and damage to the fatherland have been recently exposed? You may rest assured that there are still many around who await their opportunity for playing their game. Do not think that they would have taken part in your affairs to such an extent

---

[1] *Wachtgheschrey, allen liefhebbers der eeren Gods, des vaderlandts ende der privilegien ende vrijheden des selven, tot waerschouwinghe ghestelt* (Knuttel, no. 379).

if they had not been previously assured that they would be given a warm welcome and be well provided for by the Spaniards after surrendering to them some fortresses or towns through treachery or otherwise or rendering some other important service. You deceive yourselves if you think that either the time or the honour you give them will soften or change their hearts and their wickedness, for in this way you make them the bolder, nay you hand over to them the knife with which to cut your throats. You know those who favour Don John and are able to help him and who secretly further his cause by preventing and restraining what is necessary for the deliverance, peace and prosperity of the fatherland. You know too those who keep clear of the Spanish tyranny but try to bring you under another one which is as insufferable and unbearable.[2] And on the other hand you have come to know by their deeds those who truly love the fatherland. Why do you not open your mouths so that the bad may be expelled and worthy, capable people take their places, not only in the States and the Council of State but also in the treasury and in all towns where the same measures are required and especially in the Council of War?

For humanly speaking, your ultimate hope lies in improving the command over your army and soldiers in whom you will otherwise be deeply disappointed. For it is precisely the men who are in command there who have always been servants, friends and companions of the Spaniards.[3] To mend and adjust this, what more is required than a firm and irrevocable stand on your part? Do not give in to the delusion that time will blunt the sharp edge and that you must adapt yourselves to circumstances and dissimulate.[4] Such words are used by men who are satisfied with the present situation and who have gained their ends or by men who want to betray you. Have you not seen that in France the men who fought against tyranny as champions of a good cause, were almost entirely ruined when they wanted to manoeuvre, to dissimulate and to adapt themselves to circumstances? Have you not witnessed the horrid slaughter in which perished not only those who adapted themselves (as they thought) to the times but also the poor people?[5] Thus Almighty God has shown how much such proceedings displease Him, for to want to adapt oneself means to

[2] Apparently an allusion to the arrangements then made with the duke of Anjou.
[3] The author may have had in mind here Emanuel Philibert Lalaing, baron of Montigny, who was the commander of the Walloon troops of the States General.
[4] These passages seem to explicitly criticise Orange's attitude.
[5] A reference to the events of St Bartholomew's Eve 1572.

dissimulate, which is nothing but a lie and duplicity which God cannot leave unpunished.

Therefore make up your mind, come to a decision, set seriously to work, discard the wrong, material, human considerations, so that at last you may attain liberty and be free from these torments. Do you think that those whom you have set over you as States will ever seriously endeavour to improve your condition unless you start yourselves? For where did your deliverance begin and who began it? Was it begun by the council of the great and by distinguished men? Did it not rather start through you? Would you not still be in the old enslavement if you had not taken the matter in hand yourselves? Therefore, as God has given His blessing to your initial actions, do not doubt that the end result will be good and blissful too, if you carry on on the same lines. But if you deviate from this course, then I foresee that with your eyes open you wish to ruin yourselves and to lose all the advantages you have gained. For you can see the misfortunes and the danger very clearly before your eyes and yet do not use or apply the medicine and means which are at hand. Therefore you must restore your system of government to its traditional form and fashion, that is, according to your privileges and freedoms. Of what use will these be to you if they are kept only written on parchment and not put in practice? Why have you borne your arms for so long, suffered such heavy losses and spent so much money? Is it not in order to establish a free, well-ordered and safe state and government? Do you think it possible to attain this end as long as you have at the helm of the ship men who instead of navigating it into the port try to head for the rocks? Do you not see that by such suffering you might easily perish? Who will grieve at the news of your ruin? You despise the means which are sure to bring about your deliverance and do not take advantage of the opportunities God vouchsafes to you.

35

The true patriot to the good patriots, 1578[1]

This pamphlet is ascribed to Peter Beutterich, chief counsellor of Count John Casimir of the Palatinate who in October 1578 arrived in Ghent with his troops paid for by Queen Elizabeth. It contains an

[1] Le vray patriot aux bons patriots (Knuttel, no. 392).

apology by the Ghent Calvinists, directed against the duke of Anjou rather than the prince of Orange, who is hardly mentioned. It was written after 1 October 1578, when the capture of Menin in South Flanders by the malcontent Walloon soldiers of Montigny, which is mentioned in it, took place.

We must discover what is hidden under the cloak of the one and only Roman Catholic religion considered to be guaranteed by the Pacification of Ghent. The Pacification is held in such esteem that some of the most patriotic-minded and the greater part of the simple, honest people are blinded by the subterfuges and pretexts based on it. Their zeal for the common liberty subsides and comes completely to an end, and they dare not undertake anything against the tyranny for fear of burdening their conscience by harming the Roman Catholic religion in however small degree. This scruple, though small, these champions of the one and only Roman Catholic religion put on a par with the highest mountains.[2]

Maintaining the one and only Roman Catholic religion in this country and maintaining tyranny there, comes to the same thing. I say that maintaining the one and only Roman Catholic religion in this country and maintaining a tyranny greater than that which prevails among the Barbarians and Turks, is one and the same thing. The Turks tyrannise over the body, and leave the conscience free, the champions of the one and only Roman Catholic religion want to tyrannise over both body and mind.

To maintain the one and only Roman Catholic religion means the reintroduction of the penalty of banishment and confiscation, the re-kindling of the stakes, the re-erection of the gallows in all parts of these provinces, the reintroduction of the inquisition and finally the resurrection from hell of those horrible and cursed edicts, at the remembrance of which all good patriots are filled with horror and abomination, when they call to mind the shedding of Belgian blood spilled by so many different martyrs on account of this sole pretext: the one and only Roman Catholic religion.

In this way it would be in vain and to your cost, patriots, to have taken so much trouble, to have undergone such exertions, to have incurred such expenses, to have exhausted your means, and, as it were, to have taken the bread out of your own and your children's mouths. In vain have you overcome so many dangers, surmounted so many difficulties, and been

[2] Some Roman Catholic provinces, especially Hainault, objected from the outset to the introduction of a religious peace, when this came up for discussion in the States General in July 1578.

shipwrecked so many times to attain full liberty. In this way you would turn yourselves into the most miserable, contemptible, even abominable beings who have ever lived on earth.

Will the world always be so blind? Is it possible that the Netherlands should once again be so mad and frantic as to bring even greater ruin on itself in order to maintain the Roman Catholic superstition? To establish the Roman Antichrist? Will parents, friends, confederates and allies, fellow citizens, fathers, mothers, children, brothers, sisters, discard patriotism and love to maintain the one and only Roman whore? Have not all disasters in Christianity, all wars and all that is connected with them, been planned by and taken their source in Rome, to be spread everywhere through the most flourishing kingdoms and provinces, all this to maintain the one and only Roman Catholic religion?

The poor world has been so blinded that to establish the reign of the Roman Antichrist it has tried to ruin the reign of Jesus Christ. Let us be Christians, let us be good patriots and fellow-citizens, let us be good parents, friends and allies to each other. Let us establish our liberty by such means as God has given us in hand. Let us leave to the Pope and to his helpers elsewhere the care of establishing his Roman religion in Rome. This however should not be done at our expense nor should it ruin us and our offspring.

True liberty and the maintenance of the one and only Roman Catholic religion are incompatible. Maintenance of the Roman Catholic religion and restoration of the Spanish tyranny amounts to the same thing. There is no difference between the aim of the Roman Catholics and the Spaniards. The latter want the establishment of the one and only Roman Catholic religion, and so do the former. The latter want people to render the king his due obedience, and so do the former. We do not deny that due obedience must be rendered to the king and sovereign lord, we avow it in our hearts and say it publicly. But there is a great difference between the obedience we owe to our sovereign and that which those champions of the one and only Roman Catholic religion require from us. In their view rendering the sovereign due obedience does not mean obeying him according to law, justice and equity, and to the privileges and old customs; in their opinion it amounts to doing everything the tyrant commands, without uttering a word, without challenging it, without resisting; properly speaking, it amounts to being a serf and slave.

This is the end which these petty tyrants, the champions of the one and only Roman Catholic religion, have in view; this has been the aim of the Spaniards. How much have Holland and Zeeland suffered because they would not submit to the yoke of the Roman Catholic religion! What hardships they have endured! We[3] who have achieved some degree of liberty thanks to the constancy and courage of Holland and Zeeland, but since the Pacification have not yet greatly exerted ourselves, do we shrink back, do we bow to the mere bragging of these Roman Catholics? . . .

As to the other point, that the Flemish and particularly the inhabitants of Ghent want to organise themselves in the manner of Swiss cantons, it is clear that some of those who talk about leagues and Swiss cantonments, do not know that Ralph of Habsburg,[4] from whom the whole present house of Austria is descended, was the protector and defender of the liberty of the Swiss, when they established it against the tyranny of their seigniors, as history bears witness. But not to enlarge upon this, if these calumniators think that holding one's own and protecting oneself from the tyranny and violence of the Spaniards and their adherents and the like, implies entering into an alliance in the Swiss way, we will concede that they are indeed concluding an alliance in the Swiss way. If they mean that allying themselves in the Swiss way implies that the towns and provinces promise to help each other and to oppose by all possible means those who want to introduce the same tyranny as that of the Spaniards, under whatever pretext, is it not something commendable, worthy of all good patriots, not only to ally themselves in the Swiss way but even to wish to do all they can to ensure that all the provinces and towns in this country join? This would be the only true antidote to the Spanish poison and those who bestow this boon on the fatherland would merit perpetual praise from posterity. But if allying themselves in the Swiss way is thought to imply the abolition of all obedience, all duties, all respect due to the magistrates, who will be able to prove that they have ever felt inclined to ally themselves in the Swiss way? They know that the Word of God admonishes, exhorts and commands obedience to the laws, decrees and ordinances of the sovereign magistrate, paying him tributes, taxes and other duties and bearing with a good grace the yoke of subjection, even if the sovereign should be an infidel, provided that the sovereign authority is kept inviolate and that the conscience of the inhabitants is not subject to tyranny. For in that case, one should follow St Peter's rule, that one should rather obey God than men.[5] It is not necessary to embark upon a discussion of the duty of the subject to his sovereign magistrate, for this is not only a somewhat delicate matter but it carries us too far. It would also

[3] The other provinces of the Netherlands (Flanders, Brabant, etc.).
[4] King Rudolph of Habsburg (1273–91).
[5] Acts of the Apostles V:29.

take the good patriots too long to reply to the calumnies and the fabricated lies of their enemies.

36

A discourse upon the permission of freedom of religion, called Religions-vrede *in the Netherlands, 1579*[1]

This discourse is ascribed to the well-known Huguenot Philip du Plessis Mornay, who stayed in the Netherlands in the autumn of 1578 and together with the court-chaplain Villiers and Marnix of St Aldegonde was one of Orange's chief counsellors. It was written before Don John's death (1 October 1578) but not published until 1579. The author claims to be a Roman Catholic supporter of religious liberty.

I ask those who do not want to admit the two religions in this country how they now intend to abolish one of them, I mean the religion which they think is the feeblest. It goes without saying that you cannot abolish any religious practice without using force and taking up arms, and going to war against each other instead of taking up arms in unison against Don John and his adherents and delivering us from the insupportable tyranny of the foreigners. If we intend to ruin the Protestants we will ruin ourselves, as the French did. The conclusion to be drawn from this is that it would be better to live in peace with them, rather than ruin ourselves by internal discord and carry on a hazardous, disastrous, long and difficult war or rather a perpetual and impossible one. Taking everything into consideration, we can choose between two things: we can either allow them to live in peace with us or we can all die together; we can either let them be or, desiring to destroy them, be ourselves destroyed by their ruin. To all appearances in truth in a very different case Samson set about it in the same way as we want to. He was assiduously pursued by the Philistines. These people, on the contrary, although struck down so many times, demand only quiet and freedom from pursuit. He was alone against many, and in his despair could only hope; we are many against one; we have sufficient means to save ourselves, and for us there is no reason why we should lightheartedly seek our own perdition . . .

[1] *Discours sur la permission de liberté de religion, dicte Religions-vrede, au Païs-Bas* (Knuttel, no. 425).

As we cannot forbid these people to practise their religion without starting a war and cannot destroy them by that war without being destroyed ourselves let us conclude that we must let them live in peace and grant them liberty according to the articles of the *Religions-Frid*,[2] or such others as may be proposed. For there is certainly a grave danger that if we examine their intentions more carefully those people who pontify at one time about conscience, and at another time about order, do not have any regard for the Church or the fatherland. They only want to profit at the expense of both Church and fatherland, fearing that if all were unanimous and allied together, they might be called to account for having consumed the people's means of support, and be relieved of the position and rank they hold unworthily and illegally. To avoid the evils which menace them, they can only think of keeping the two parties in dissension and discord and thus troubling everything...

Let us remember that all of us are men, Christians, people who love ourselves, the church and the fatherland, who believe in one God, profess one Jesus Christ, desire one reformation in this state. As men, let us love; as Christians, let us instruct and support each other. We ruin ourselves by war and internal discord. As lovers of ourselves and of what concerns us, let us demand peace and union. The Church ruins itself when war makes us, instead of Christians, people who despise all religion. Let us stop debating and fighting and in tears turn back to God, beseeching Him to re-establish religion among us to His glory. In this country there are now two religions. If both may not be professed freely, we will surely make war upon each other. If this should happen, the country will be laid waste and we will lose everything. Let us then live in peace with each other, let us help each other to drive away the Spaniards and their adherents and let us come so close to each other that nothing will ever divide us. Let all of us, seigniors, nobles, clergymen, merchants, peasants, agree to demand the promulgation of the *Religions-Frid* and its observance, for without it we can only expect confusion, desolation, and total ruin. I pray God Almighty who disposes of all things at His pleasure, that it may please Him in His mercy to grant that all inhabitants of these Netherlands live together in harmony and in unity.

[2] On 9 June 1578 a motion to this effect had been introduced in the States General by the prince of Orange and was afterwards seconded by petitions of the members of the Reformed Church of 22 June (see Document 33) and 7 July. The word *Religions-Frid* is German for religious peace and was used as a sort of technical term in the Netherlands.

37

Treaty of the Union, eternal alliance and confederation made in the town of Utrecht by the countries and their towns and members, 29 January 1579[1]

The treaty of the Union was signed on 23 January 1579 by Count John of Nassau as stadholder of Gelderland, and by delegates from the provinces of Holland, Zeeland, Utrecht and the Ommelanden of Groningen. Friesland, Overijssel and Drenthe held aloof for the time being and the towns of Flanders and Brabant did not accede until later (Ghent on 4 February 1579). The prince of Orange, to whom the idea of a general union was of paramount importance, did not join until 3 May 1579, when it was certain that the Walloon provinces united by the Union of Arras (6 January 1579) would soon make peace with the duke of Parma and the king.

It is clear that since the conclusion of the Pacification of Ghent, according to which nearly all the provinces of these Low Countries undertook to assist each other with their life and property in driving the Spaniards and other foreign nations and their followers from this country, the Spaniards as well as Don John of Austria and more of their leaders and captains have sought and are still seeking by all means in their power to bring these provinces wholly or partly into subjection under their tyrannical government and into slavery. Through force of arms as well as through trickery they are trying to divide and dismember them and to annul and subvert the Union set up at the Pacification so that the countries and provinces may ultimately be brought to ruin and destruction. Indeed they are known to have recently addressed themselves by letter to some towns and districts soliciting their collaboration, and to have attacked and surprised others, viz. in the duchy of Gelderland.[2] So those from the duchy of Gelderland and the county of Zutphen,[3] and those from the counties and regions of Holland, Zeeland, Utrecht and the Ommelanden between the

---

[1] 'Verhandelinge van de Unie, eeuwich Verbondt ende Eendracht, tusschen de Landen, Provintien, Steden ende Leden van dien hier nae benoemt. . . gesloten', C. Cau ed., *Groot Placaet-Boek*, 1 (The Hague, 1658), pp. 7ff.
[2] Parma threatened the Overkwartier of Gelderland (the district of Roermond in the present-day Dutch province of Limburg) in particular.
[3] The delegates of Gelderland did not sign the Union as early as 23 January. The district of Zutphen did not join until January 1580.

river Eems and the Sea of Lauwers have thought it advisable to ally and to unite more closely and particularly, not with the intention of withdrawing from the General Union set up at the Pacification of Ghent but rather to strengthen it and to protect themselves against all the difficulties that their enemy's practices, attacks or outrages might bring upon them, and finally, to make clear how in such cases the provinces must behave, and can defend themselves against hostilities, as well to avoid any further separation of the provinces and their particular members. For these reasons the deputies of the afore-said provinces, fully authorised by their principals, have drawn up and concluded the following points and articles. By so doing they do not desire to withdraw from the Holy Roman Empire.[4]

I. The afore-said provinces shall ally, confederate and unite – and are allying, confederating and uniting herewith – to hold together eternally in all ways and forms as if they were but one province, and shall not separate themselves from each other nor have themselves separated by testament, codicil, gift, cession, exchange, sale, treaties of peace and marriage or for any other reason, however it may come about. However, this is agreed without prejudice to the special and particular privileges, freedoms, exemptions, laws, statutes, laudable and traditional customs, usages and all other rights of each province and of each town, member and inhabitant of those provinces. Not only shall the provinces not hinder each other from exercising these rights nor impair nor prejudice them in any way, but they shall help each other by all proper and possible means, if necessary with their lives and their property, to maintain and strengthen them and they shall protect and defend them against all and every one – whoever he might be and in whatever capacity he might act – who may actually design to encroach upon them. It is understood, however, that the disputes which exist, or may arise in the future, between some of the provinces, members or towns who are party to this Union, concerning their particular and special privileges, freedoms, exemptions, laws, statutes, laudable and traditional customs, usages and other rights shall be decided by ordinary courts of justice, arbiters or amicable settlement, without interference by any of the other countries or provinces and their towns or members (as long as both parties submit themselves to judicial proceedings) unless it might please them to intervene with intent to bring about an agreement.

II. In accordance with and in fulfilment of the union and alliance, the

---

[4] The emperor and the electors were in that same year invited by the Netherlands to act as mediators at the Cologne peace conference.

provinces shall be bound to assist each other with their lives and property against all acts of violence which anyone might perpetrate against them on behalf of (or allegedly on behalf of) His Majesty the King or his servants. This applies when the Spaniards take action because of the Peace Treaty of Ghent (because the provinces then took up arms against Don John of Austria and accepted the archduke Matthias as their governor)[5] and all its present and future consequences, or only on the pretext of wanting to re-establish, restore or introduce the Roman Catholic religion by force of arms, or on account of some innovations or alterations which since 1558[6] have taken place in some of the provinces, their towns or members, or on account of this present Union and confederation or similar causes. The afore-said provinces shall be bound to assist each other both when violence is done to any one of them (or its states, towns or members) or when all together are attacked.

III. The provinces shall be bound to support and defend each other similarly against all foreign and indigenous lords, rulers or princes, countries, provinces or their towns and members who want to perpetrate acts of violence against all or any of them, to wrong them or to make war on them. The decision in this matter shall however rest with the confederation as a whole and shall be taken after an investigation of and in accordance with the situation.

IV. In order better to protect the provinces and their towns and members against all force, it has been decided that the frontier towns and other towns where this is thought necessary (whatever province they belong to) shall be fortified and strengthened on the advice and by command of these united provinces. These towns themselves and the provinces in which they are situated shall be liable for the cost but one half of it shall be paid back to them by the generality. If on the other hand the provinces find it advisable to build new fortresses or bulwarks in any of the provinces or to alter or abolish those that are there now, all the provinces are to share the necessary costs.

V. And in order to meet the expenses which must be incurred for the defence of the provinces in such cases as mentioned above, it is agreed that in all the united provinces there shall be imposed, levied and either publicly let out to the highest bidder (for periods of three months or any other convenient period) or collected, everywhere in the united provinces and their towns and members, uniformly and on the same footing, for the general defence of these provinces, certain duties on all sorts of wines,

---

[5] See Document 28.   [6] After the king had left these provinces.

foreign or domestic beers, the grinding of corn and cereals, on salt, gold, silver, silken and woollen clothes, on horned cattle and seeded fields, on slaughtered beasts, on the sale and exchange of oxen and horses, on goods brought to the weigh-houses and such other duties as may be agreed upon by common advice and consent, in accordance with the relevant decree that is to be drawn up and issued.[7] Moreover after deduction of liabilities the income of the estate of His Majesty the king shall be employed for the same purpose.

VI. These duties shall be raised or lowered by common consent according to circumstances and needs and they are intended for no other purpose than for the general defence and fulfilment of those financial obligations which the united provinces shall have to bear; they may never be expended for any other purpose.

VII. The frontier towns – and others if necessary – shall be bound to receive at any time all such garrisons as the united provinces may think good and, on the advice of the governor of the province where the garrison is to be billeted, may order them to receive. They have no right to refuse them. But the garrisons shall receive their pay from the united provinces, and the captains and soldiers shall swear fidelity not only to the united provinces as a whole but also to the particular town or towns and province to which they are sent, as shall be explained in the articles of their instruction. Also order and discipline are to be maintained amongst the soldiers lest the burghers and inhabitants of the towns and countryside (either clerical or secular) be unreasonably burdened or annoyed. Moreover the garrisons shall not be any further exempted from any duties or imposts than the burghers and inhabitants of the place to which they are sent; these burghers and inhabitants shall receive from the united provinces an allowance for lodging them as has hitherto been customary in Holland.

VIII. In order to make sure at any time of the assistance of all the inhabitants of the countries, all the residents of each of these united provinces, towns and rural districts shall be mustered within one month from now, that is to say, all those who are between eighteen and sixty years of age.[8] Once their number is known, the allies shall at their next meeting decide how best to promote the security and protection of these united provinces.

IX. No armistice or peace treaty shall be concluded nor any war started nor any duties or contributions pertaining to the generality of the united

---

[7] Article V was not carried out. Federal taxes were never levied.
[8] This article too remained a dead letter. The army was made up of mercenaries.

provinces demanded but by the unanimous advice and consent of the afore-said provinces. But in other matters concerning the conduct of this confederation and whatever depends on it or follows from it, all decisions shall be taken in accordance with the advice and opinion of the majority of the provinces of this alliance. The votes will be counted as is usual in the general assembly of States until it is decided otherwise by the confederates. But if it happens that the provinces cannot reach an agreement on matters of armistice, peace, war or contributions, their differences must provisionally be referred and submitted to the present stadholders of the provinces who will bring about a settlement or at their own discretion give their judgment on the differences. If, however, the stadholders cannot agree among themselves they will select and ask such impartial assessors and assistants as they themselves choose to consult. And the parties shall be bound to accept the decisions taken by the stadholders in the aforesaid manner.

x. None of these provinces or their towns or members shall conclude any confederation or alliance with any neighbouring lord or country without the consent of these united provinces and allies.

xi. It is therefore agreed that if any neighbouring princes, lords, countries or towns want to ally with these provinces and to partake in their confederation, they may be admitted by the common advice and consent of these provinces.

xii. Moreover the provinces shall be bound to agree on a common policy with regard to the coinage, that is to say, in the matter of currency exchange rates, in conformity with such decrees as shall be made thereupon at the first opportunity. None of the provinces shall have a right to change these without the consent of the others.

xiii. Concerning the matter of religion: Holland and Zeeland shall act at their own discretion whereas the other provinces of this Union may conform to the contents of the Religious Peace Treaty already drawn up by the archduke Matthias, governor and captain-general of these countries, in collaboration with his Council on the advice of the States General,[9] or else they may introduce (all together or each province independently), without being hindered or prevented from doing this by any other province, such regulations as they consider proper for the peace and welfare of the provinces, towns and their particular members and for the preservation of all people, either secular or clerical, their properties and rights, provided that in accordance with the Pacification

9 See Document 38, note 2.

of Ghent[10] each individual enjoys freedom of religion and no one is persecuted or questioned about his religion.

XIV. All those who live in convents and all the clergy shall, in conformity with the Pacification of Ghent, be entitled to their properties lying in any of these united provinces by reciprocity, that is to say, that if any clerical person from those provinces which during the war between the counties of Holland and Zeeland and the Spaniards were in Spanish hands, should have left any monastery or convent and settled in territory then in possession of Holland or Zeeland, he shall be given proper maintenance during his lifetime by his own convent or monastery as shall also be done in the case of those who have left Holland and Zeeland for some other province of this Union and are now residing there.[11]

XV. Moreover those who are living or did live in any monastery or college in these united countries and for religious or other acceptable reasons want to leave it or have left it already, shall be given as long as they live proper maintenance in accordance with the means of the monastery or college. But those who after the date of this Union go into any monastery and leave it again shall not be entitled to maintenance although they may take back for their own use what they brought in. Moreover all those who are now living in monasteries or colleges or enter them after this date, shall enjoy freedom and liberty of religion and also of clothing and dress; they shall obey the prior of the monastery in all other matters.

XVI. And if (which God forbid) some misunderstanding, quarrel or discordance arises among the provinces which they cannot resolve, this difference, if it concerns some of the provinces in particular, shall, after one of both parties in the dispute has asked for this, be dealt with and settled by the other provinces or those whom they delegate for that task. If it concerns all the provinces a decision shall be taken by the stadholders as is explained in the IXth article. They shall be bound to give judgment or to bring about a settlement within one month or less if the matter is very urgent. The decision of the other provinces or their delegates or the stadholders in the matter will be accepted and carried out and no further appeal or further action on the strength of any right, whatsoever that might be, of appeal, relief, revision or nullity will be allowed.

---

[10] See the Treaty of the Pacification, Document 23.

[11] This means that monks and nuns who had left the loyal provinces and gone to Holland or Zeeland were entitled to subsidies from their former monasteries or convents. Although in theory the same applied to Roman Catholics who had left Holland and Zeeland because they refused to submit to the new religion, it was hard for them to get their claims accepted as most of the church lands had long since been confiscated.

XVII. The provinces and their towns and members shall avoid provoking foreign princes, lords, countries or towns and, in order to avoid any provocation that might lead to a war, the provinces and their towns and members shall be bound to administer due law and justice to all foreigners and residents of the afore-said provinces. And if any of them fails to do so the other allies shall (by all proper ways and means) see to it that justice is done and that all abuses, which might prevent this and obstruct justice, shall be corrected and reformed in accordance with all men's rights and privileges, laudable and traditional customs.

XVIII. None of the united provinces or their towns or members shall introduce without general consent any imposts, convoy dues or other similar taxes, burdening and prejudicing the others, nor shall they impose higher taxes upon any of these allies than upon their own residents.

XIX. In order to meet all questions and difficulties that may arise, the allies, being convened by those who are authorised to do so, shall be bound to come to Utrecht on the day set. There the questions or difficulties (which should be stated, as far as possible, unless the matter should be kept secret, in the notice convening the meeting) shall be discussed and a decision be taken with the general advice and consent of the allies or by a majority vote in the way described above, even if some of the allies do not attend the meeting. In the latter case those who are present have the right to take such decisions as they consider best for these united provinces in general. These decisions shall also be binding on those who are absent except in very important matters on which some delay might be permitted. In such cases those who have not attended the meeting shall once more be summoned to a meeting at some later date on penalty of losing their vote for this occasion. The decision of those who are present at that meeting shall be binding and considered valid notwithstanding the absence of some of the other provinces. Those who are unable to attend shall be allowed to send their opinion in writing and this shall be taken into proper account when the votes are counted.

XX. For the same purpose all allies and each of them in particular shall be bound to notify those authorised to convene those meetings of all matters arising or occurring which they consider to be important for the general benefit or to the detriment of these united countries and allies; thereafter the other provinces shall be convened in the way described in article XIX.

XXI. And if there is anything obscure or doubtful in these articles which might lead to questions or disputes, the interpretation thereof shall be determined by the allies who shall with general advice and consent decree what they consider proper. If they cannot agree among themselves they shall ask for the intervention of the stadholders of the provinces in the manner described above.

XXII. If it is found necessary to make on some points or in some articles of this Union, confederation or alliance, any alteration or addition, this shall also be done with the common advice and consent of the afore-said allies and in no other way.

XXIII. The united provinces have promised and are promising herewith to keep and observe, and to ensure that others keep and observe, all these points and articles and each of them in particular and not to do anything contrary to them or to have anything done or to allow anything to be done either directly or indirectly in any way or manner. And they declare that if anybody does or tries to do anything to the contrary, this action shall henceforward be null, void and invalid; to this effect they pledge the lives and properties of themselves and all residents in their respective provinces and their towns and members; in case of contravention these may be arrested, held and charged anywhere by any lord, judge or court that can or is allowed to lay hands on them, for the sake of maintaining this union and everything contingent upon it. For that purpose the afore-said provinces renounce all exemptions, favours, privileges, reliefs and generally all other profits of rights which stipulate that no general renunciation may take place without a preceding particular renunciation.

XXIV. And to strengthen this union, the stadholders of the afore-said provinces who are now or will in the future be in office as well as all the magistrates and commanding officers of each province, its towns or members, shall swear an oath to keep and observe this union and confederation and each of its articles in particular and to ensure that they are kept and observed.[12]

XXV. All militia bands, fraternities and guilds that exist in any town or hamlet inside this union shall swear the same oath.[12]

XXVI. And letters shall be drawn up in due form containing the above-mentioned articles. They shall be sealed by the stadholders and those principal members and towns of the provinces who are specially demanded and requested to do so by other members and towns and they shall be signed by their respective secretaries.[12]

Explanation of the XIIIth article[13]

Since some seem to raise objections to the XIIIth article of the union made

[12] The articles XXIV, XXV and XXVI were not implemented.

[13] This additional article, dated 1 February 1579, appears to be a last attempt to avoid severing ties with the Walloon provinces.

on the 23rd of this month between the deputies of Gelderland, Zutphen, Holland, Zeeland, Utrecht and the Ommelanden between the river Eems and the Sea of Lauwers, thinking that the purpose and intention was not to accept anybody as a member of the same union except those for whom, on the advice of the States General, the Religious Peace Treaty was drawn up by the archduke of Austria and the Council of State, or at least only those who would tolerate both religions, viz. the Roman Catholic and the Reformed, the afore-mentioned deputies who are responsible for and have concluded this Union, have decided to declare herewith (to prevent all misunderstanding and distrust) that it has never been and is not now their purpose and intention to exclude from the union and alliance any towns or provinces which want to maintain the Roman Catholic religion exclusively and where the number of the residents belonging to the Reformed religion is too small to enable them to enjoy, by virtue of the Religious Peace, the right to exercise the Reformed religion. On the contrary they are willing to accept as members of the union such towns and provinces as wish to maintain the Roman religion exclusively if these want to subscribe to the other points and articles of the union and to act as good patriots. For it is not their opinion that one province or town should lay down the law to others in the matter of religion, as they want to further peace and unity amongst the provinces and to avoid and to take away the main occasion for quarrels and discord. Utrecht, 1 February 1579.

38

A discourse containing a true understanding of the Pacification of Ghent, of the Union of the States and other ensuing treaties in the matter of religion, 1579[1]

This authoritative plea for religious peace was published before the special session of the States General at Antwerp in March and April 1579, where the prince of Orange intended to raise this subject again.

[1] *Discours contenant le vray entendement de la Pacification de Gand, de l'union des Estats, et aultres traictez y ensuyviz, touchant le faict de la religion*, J. K. van der Wulp, *Catalogus van de tractaten, pamfletten, enz. over de geschiedenis van Nederland aanwezig in de bibliotheek van Isaac Meulman*, I, no. 412.

I think that we have elucidated well enough the true meaning of the Pacification of Ghent and the ensuing negotiations and shown that the States in no way violated the principles involved when they drafted the decree of religious peace.[2] The *Religions-Frid* is the only means of keeping peace and harmony among the inhabitants of these provinces; and the principal intention and aim of the Pacification and the Union was to establish peace.[3] Consequently all those who stir up discord or make war because of some points of detail and justify this by referring to the Pacification and the Union, should be considered violators of both because they contravene their principal intention. It is the general intention which must be taken as the rule to be applied to all ensuing cases. And should any difficulty on that subject arise, it must be solved not at the whim of some private persons but by the States who are the authors of the Pacification and Union. We shall develop this point somewhat further. Obviously contracts can never be concluded between men in so valid a way that there will never be need for revision. The acts of men are never perfect; man is far too ready to seek his own advantage and to surprise his partner by interpreting the contract concluded with him in a partial manner. It is this which is at the root of so many misunderstandings between men. The only way to overcome such difficulties is for the partners to make sure that they may negotiate further contracts to settle the differences which have arisen out of the original one. It is beyond doubt that the Pacification of Ghent and the Union, contracts concluded between men, are subject to partial interpretation. Don John in particular made this quite clear. When he wished to renew civil war in our country he interpreted these agreements in his own way and so found a pretext to start war. The States replied by putting forward the only correct interpretation, declaring that it was their intention never to go to war again, and they have carried their point. When Don John took the castle of Namur and other places[4] and justified all his deceptions by a false interpretation of the Pacification, Union and Perpetual Edict, the States repudiated this by developing their correct interpretation somewhat further in accordance with their good intentions,[5] as I have already fully explained. From this it appears that the intention of the States has been

---

[2] The States General resolved in their meeting of 12 July 1578 to submit the draft of the religious peace to the States of the provinces.

[3] The Union of Brussels of 9 January 1577.

[4] On 24 July 1577 Don John took the citadel of Namur, together with the fortresses of Charlemont and Philippeville by surprise.

[5] The second Union of Brussels of 10 December 1577.

from the outset to keep enough authority and power in their own hands to enable them to obviate all misunderstandings and intrigues by means of which these treaties might in future be used for any purpose other than the original.

It is in the nature of contracts that at their conclusion the aim is always to appease the parties in such a way that no discord will arise between them and that they will remain friends forever. This aim can never change, because contracts are concluded to end controversies. However, it is not possible to provide against particular problems that may arise and will mar the effect of the general purpose of the contract. If this happens, the contract must be renewed and reworded immediately and steps be taken to resolve these problems so that the general aim of remaining friends forever be not diverted or lost. And experience shows that at the conclusion of contracts there is never any mistake about the general aim: all misunderstandings that occur concern particular points and sufficient provision to resolve these can never be made. It is not possible to continue to insist that before a contract is finally concluded everything must be conditioned in detail and the parties should so conduct themselves that in future no rewording is required, for human understanding cannot foresee every contingency: circumstances always change. If it should really be impossible to compose and draw up contracts in such a way that our principal intention and general aim becomes perfectly clear, then surely all contracts would only give new food for debate and war, and this is obviously a ridiculous conclusion. In my opinion the more details one puts in a contract of alliance or friendship when concluding it, the more one deviates from one's general aim to remain friends forever. Thus one had better not enter into too much detail, but rather add a clause enabling, even compelling, all ensuing differences to be settled by friendly discussion. This ought to be self-evident as the contract has been concluded in good faith.

By the way, how, when concluding the Pacification, could the States have possibly made provision for all such contingencies as might arise afterwards? Certainly they did not have the time to consider the situation carefully. For, so closely oppressed as they were, on one side by the Spaniards, on the other by the common people reduced to commotion by the sack of Antwerp,[6] they were compelled to come to a decision without even thinking of all the contingencies we have mentioned above. Given the circumstances this was to be expected. The States were therefore satisfied

---

[6] The Spanish Fury of 4 November 1576.

to have so settled things that the provinces of Holland, Zeeland and their associates would return to the community of our state. As to the future, they intended to adapt their policies to circumstances. At present we can see that to preserve the state we must concede their freedom to adherents of the reformed religion as has been done in Holland and Zeeland; otherwise we shall endanger the whole country. But as it was made a condition when conceding this freedom to adherents of the reformed religion in Holland, that they should give no offence to the other provinces,[7] similarly it must be made a condition that the adherents of the reformed religion in the other provinces should not give offence to the Catholics of their towns nor disturb them in their practice. In making these provisions the States do not violate the Pacification; they wish to prevent disputes arising in the other provinces because of difference of religion. And this is the principal aim of the Pacification.

That the States have reserved to themselves, that is to the Union, the power of settling all differences which might arise afterwards, appears from the clause in the Union, in which it is said that no member of the Union may privately offer any counsel or advice, nor have any secret understanding with people who are not members of their Union, nor reveal to them what is or will be discussed, advised or resolved in their assembly; and that all shall be obliged to conform to whatever their general and unanimous resolution implies.[8] This was put in such a way because they were convinced that after concluding the Union with the object of remaining friends forever and maintaining the liberty of the country, the particular points laid down in the Union would always be subject to distortions, and therefore the best thing was to leave everything to the States.

It is nonsense to maintain that because His Majesty confirmed it the States cannot interpret, moderate or alter the Pacification without the king's consent. After agreeing to it, the king himself immediately violated it and later expressly declared in his letters that he did not wish to hear about it any more.[9] But, apart from this, since the king has so far forgotten his duty towards his subjects that he does not deserve to be mentioned by them, it is quite unnecessary to respect him when order must be established in this country. His Highness, His Excellency,[10] the Council

---

[7] See the Pacification, Document 23.

[8] See the First Union of Brussels, Document 24.

[9] It was approved by the ratification of the Perpetual Edict at the beginning of 1577, but disavowed in the letters from the king transmitted by John Noircarmes, baron of Selles, at the end of this year.

[10] Matthias and the prince of Orange.

and the States must establish order and they possess for doing so the same authority they had before.

39

Discourse of Elbertus Leoninus, councillor of State, to the States General at Antwerp, 11 April 1579[1]

Elbertus Leoninus, born in Gelderland, was a professor of law at Louvain and one of the delegates of the States General at the negotiations for the Pacification of Ghent (Document 23). He was a member of the Council of State under Matthias in 1578 and delivered in April 1579 the following address to the States General. His thinking was so exclusively political that he did not even mention the religious issue.

From His Highness's[2] proposition Your Honours have sufficiently realised that the need of the country has come to such an unhappy pass that in none of your previous meetings so much distress or such great difficulties have been represented to you as at this time. In former times the general assemblies of the country gathered to bid a new lord or prince a joyous welcome or to see the late emperor, Charles V, blessed be his memory, resign the provinces to his son and heir, their prince[3] or for similar purposes. At that time the provinces were at peace with each other and were flourishing. But nowadays the States assemble in very dangerous and alarming times when the provinces are disarrayed, harassed, ruined, engaged in war and oppressed by the Spaniards and other enemies. This present meeting has been called to give advice and take measures to protect our lives, possessions, wives and children from the danger which is threatening us and to avert eternal, unbearable slavery and the complete ruin of the provinces. This is apparently at hand now if you choose to persevere in the old bad ways with every one seeking to pursue his own interests and no one prepared to appease the domestic quarrels or obey and contribute readily, if need be. But if Your Honours (in whom all the provinces put their faith) proceed sincerely and assiduously in this

---

[1] 'Oratie van doctor Elbertus Leoninus, raedsheere van State, aen de Generale Staten, 1579', Bor, *Oorsprongk*, II, pp. 49ff.
[2] Archduke Matthias.
[3] At the meeting at Brussels on 25 October 1555.

assembly and show in fact that you take the preservation of your own country to heart, as is your bounden duty, then in spite of the afore-mentioned difficulties, there is a sure way of putting things straight again and of not only giving assistance to our compatriots and allies who are now closely besieged, but also of preventing further troubles and dangers by means of a good war and safe peace. This is sure to follow if the enemy sees that we remain united, and that our fixed intention is indeed to employ all means, allowed by God, to keep our persons, possessions and privileges in lawful freedom. If, however, we show ourselves to be coward-ly and faint-hearted, if we give way in any respect through fear, then we shall multiply the pride and wilfulness of our enemies and increase our misery and distress. It is appropriate to quote the saying of our fore-fathers: those who desire freedom, must not negotiate for conditions of peace before they have defeated the bulk of the enemy or before they have made their forces equal to those of the enemy. For the character of the peace depends on the outcome of the war.

Almighty God has given us the opportunity of aiding and relieving the inhabitants of Maastricht, who desire this.[4] If we desert them and let them fall piteously into the hands of the enemies, then these will impose their will upon us when making the peace, the negotiations for which started at Cologne.[5] But if united we put all our forces into the field to help them, as we can and should do, then we shall gain honour and our enemies will readily be satisfied with such reasonable conditions as we shall offer them. Therefore I ask Your Honours on behalf of His Highness and his councillors to consider the matter and to come to a conclusion soon, as is fitting, and I assure you that you can never perform a more profitable and honourable act nor will such an excellent opportunity for your rescue offer itself again. For you may meet your obligations and fulfil the oath concerning your allies and loyal compatriots[6] who have per-sistently held out against the common enemy and still do, and at the same time hold an important and fine town, on which in this union the pros-perity and safety of all the provinces depends. You will moreover deliver

---

[4] Since the beginning of March 1579 Maastricht had been invested by Parma's troops.

[5] Negotiations for peace in the Netherlands were conducted through the inter-mediary of the emperor at Cologne in 1579.

[6] Because of the threatening situation Matthias and the Council of State wished to strengthen the general union of the provinces which was still in existence. The provinces of Hainault, Artois etc. which had concluded the separate union of Arras on 6 January 1579, were however absent from this meeting.

the provinces from oppression and have the proper means to comfort the poor subjects, so long tormented, by the good and safe peace which will undoubtedly ensue, if the town of Maastricht is relieved and retained. This should be seen to. And provinces which formerly so readily accorded millions of guilders to enable the duke of Alva, the Great Commander[7] and other oppressors of their freedom to oppress them still more cruelly, should accord even more now and should show the love in which every one holds the common prosperity, liberty and safety of their lives, possessions, wives and children. This can be well accomplished if they be willing and determined to execute this. For all the damage and disorders which happened in the past, were caused not by lack of means or the weakness of the provinces, nor by the power and strength of the enemies, but by carelessness, inaptitude and lack of determination and delay in providing the necessary contributions. Formerly when the provinces were separate,[8] each one had individual means of self-protection and of waging open war against kings and potentates: the chronicles of Brabant, Gelderland, Flanders, Utrecht, Friesland and other provinces give evidence of this and the examples are so well-known and still so fresh in our memory that there is no need to relate them at length. For that reason it would be to our everlasting shame and ignominy if all these rich provinces now united and assembled could not find the means of taking a firm stand and raising a considerable army to help the afore-said town of Maastricht with all their resources and to put order into their affairs generally. Therefore I pray Your Honours to persevere in this union, and not to let slip this opportunity, which will never again occur. And I pray you to take a prompt, beneficial resolution on the items and articles proposed by His Grace,[9] in particular and above all on the decrees of war and on the relief of Maastricht, without starting a discussion about privileges or other matters in detail. For this war concerns all provinces alike and if a prompt decision is taken, you may expect that this miserable war will be happily and laudably brought to an end with a safe peace. If this is not done, you must expect a protracted war with endless harm and distress. But we can now deliver the provinces from such disasters by fighting determinedly and briefly for three or four months.

[7] Alva as well as his successor Requesens made heavy financial demands on the States of the loyal provinces in the years 1572–4 (see Documents 16 and 20).
[8] Before their union under the Burgundian–Austrian rule.
[9] Matthias had laid these matters before the States General, the religious peace being among them.

40

Letters from the States of the Netherlands to the Electors and other commissaries of His Imperial Majesty sent to Cologne to make peace, 10 September 1579[1]

In this letter the States General answered the proposals of mediation made at the Cologne peace conference by the imperial commissioners (the electors of Cologne and Treves, the bishop of Würzburg and the count of Schwartzenberg). These negotiations opened in May 1579 in the presence of the papal nuncio. The duke of Terranova was there for Spain.

When the inhabitants of the provinces learned that the king refused to allow them to abide by the Pacification of Ghent and that a general war, leading in its turn to serious domestic quarrels, was fought to ensure that those who had forsaken the Roman Catholic religion and would not come back to the old religious rites prevailing at the time of Charles V, would be banished or massacred in violation of the Pacification of Ghent, which they were not allowed to keep, things had come to such a pass that to ward off the complete ruin of the provinces it was necessary to take further action and to restore the peace of the inhabitants firstly by letters in which the parties promised to respect each other's religious persuasion[2] and later by religious peace[3] and other agreements. Therefore people who accuse the inhabitants or the States of inconstancy and almost of perjury for exceeding the limits of the Pacification of Ghent by permitting the exercise of another religion should be bitterly hated and blamed. For it was the king, the king's commanders and councillors who were the first to reject the afore-mentioned Pacification[4] under the pretext of the Perpetual Edict and some letters as being dishonest and scandalous. They strove to abolish it by force of arms and to restore the former cruel conditions of the inquisition. In fact the States and the inhabitants were not allowed to keep the Pacification though they wanted and desired it (with

---

[1] *Brieven der Staten van Nederlant aen de keurvorsten ende andere commissarissen der Keyserlicker Maiesteyt nae Cuelen ghesonden om den peys te maecken* (Knuttel, no. 484).

[2] At the second Union of Brussels of 10 December 1577.

[3] See Document 38, note 2.   [4] See Document 38, note 9.

permission and under the protection of the clerics) to avert further misery and difficulties; the king's captains and soldiers made this impossible. Apart from the fact that the inhabitants may have wanted to alter the Pacification concluded by them, it was the king's severity, the distress of the provinces and the desire to prevent the imminent dangers (which one feared because of the war that was started and the ensuing domestic quarrels) that made the States introduce some necessary alterations. This obviously suffices to justify the States' policy. A man prevented by a stronger person from doing what he wants to do cannot be blamed for his actions; nor may he be blamed if he is forced by circumstances to alter his conduct, for instance, if the country's distress requires new measures to prevent domestic troubles or the threat of hostile armies. All laws and statutes should be made conducive to the peace of the commonwealth and ordinances, dispositions and treaties should be observed as long as circumstances do not change and remain as they were before. Only those can be accused of breach of faith and inconstancy who do not do what they promised so long as circumstances remain as they were at the time when the promise was made. However if circumstances change or if those who made the promise are prevented from carrying it out, the situation becomes totally different – especially in the present case when both the changes and the impossibility to carry out one's promises are caused by the very people with whom negotiations were conducted and when there is a real danger of disturbances (as the Spaniards had certainly expected when they revoked the Pacification)...

And because His Royal Majesty once rejected the Pacification of Ghent so resolutely and strove so hard to abolish and annihilate it entirely and spent so much money on this war, we rightly call into question the fine words addressed under pretext of the Pacification to the nobles and burghers. We fear that the only reason why there are so many foreign soldiers about is to try to deceive the people and to stir up greater dissension and to mislead and to surprise all the towns and provinces. For since the king rejected the Pacification when the provinces were in a more favourable condition, who will believe that now after having brought so much woe upon the provinces and having spent so much money on the war, he will wholeheartedly approve of the Pacification and lay it before his subjects in full earnest? The opposite seems clear from the veiled wording of the articles[5] and from the fact that the Pacification has been altered not only with regard to the authority of the prince of Orange and

[5] The proposals of mediation made on 18 July 1579.

the assurance given to Holland and Zeeland but also because the Perpetual Edict is interpreted as an integral part of it and the two new articles concerning religion contain explicit binding regulations, according to which the inhabitants of the other provinces are more strictly obliged and with more stringent stipulations than in the preceding Pacification to profess the Roman Catholic faith in accordance with the pretended obligation of the Perpetual Edict. This is clear from the vague and diffuse words of the afore-mentioned articles and from the excepting clause which follows. According to these the religious stipulations of the Pacification of Ghent are valid only with regard to the inhabitants of Holland, Zeeland and Bommel. And though in the second article dealing with religion, under the pretext of merciful generosity, those who have forsaken the Roman Catholic religion, are said to be tolerated, this toleration is immediately restricted to exempting them from the rigour of the king's religious edicts. People who left these provinces must have their possessions administered by Catholics. When they return they must live as Catholics and make it clear to the local priest and magistrate that they really do so. This is quite contrary to the Pacification of Ghent which allows every one to arrive in, to stay in, to trade in, to depart from, and to return to these provinces without being obliged to profess any particular religion, and to entrust the administration of his goods to whoever he chooses.[6] Thus the Pacification of Ghent is highly praised in order to increase domestic dissension, while in truth its benefit is entirely lost and annihilated. In fact the old conditions have been restored in which any one was liable to the inquisition, excommunication, first indictment, second indictment, invocation of the secular authority and the rest of the usual practices. In the present situation, however, such means cannot be used without creating everlasting mutual hostility between the provinces and towns, without causing disturbances and internecine killings by the inhabitants with great danger that what remains of the Catholic religion as well as of the king's authority will be totally lost.

[6] See Pacification, Document 23.

41

A brief discourse upon the peace negotiations which are now taking place at Cologne between the king of Spain and the States of the Netherlands, 1579[1]

This discourse expounds a clear Calvinistic view concerning the peace negotiations at Cologne of 1579. It emphatically defends the policy of the States General.

Among the people who presume that the States General are responsible for continuing the war are on the one hand subjects and inhabitants of the country who remain loyal to our cause, and on the other hand the enemies: the Spaniards and their adherents. By ignorance or by malice they hold opinions about affairs which do not square with the safety and conservation of the state. We may suppose that those inhabitants of the united provinces who quite wrongly believe that it is the States who protract this war, are not well acquainted with what is happening and, secondly, are moved by a great desire to see the country at peace again and fully flourishing. Although their error is excusable because their intentions are good and laudable, they should however before forming a judgment take the trouble to enquire and to learn the reasons for the long duration of the disturbances and civil wars. If they do this, they will realise that the States General are constituted by people who appear and assemble on behalf of the nobles and the towns of the provinces. This means that the inhabitants themselves, who have delegated them, have also the power and authority to delegate others, if those who have this commission now or in future, do not do their duties in such a way as their state and charge requires. Therefore to calumniate them amounts to criticising oneself.

Moreover there is no reason in the world which could move the States to prolong the dissension and war. For it is a well-known fact that they have not had and have not now any money available to spend to their profit and advantage. And from the very beginning of the assembly, the shortage of money has continually been such that it was always allocated for war necessities before it had even been received. The situation the States have been in during these recent peace negotiations is common knowledge. They have indeed kept aloof from all financial administra-

[1] *Brief discours sur la negotiation de la paix, qui se traicte présentement à Coloigne entre le Roy d'Espaigne et let Estatz du Pays bas* (Knuttel, no. 492).

tion, because the public revenue is bonded to the merchants and all other monies are especially allocated for the support of the foot and horse which are still in active service. It is therefore neither the management of finances nor any other ambition which could move the States to want to keep the provinces in this disastrous state of civil war. For in peace time too, the States will still be the leading institution they are now, whether as States general or provincial, and the provinces and towns will always have the same power to delegate and employ whomsoever they like, without restrictions. The pensionaries and town-councillors will never be short of work, nor will there be fewer opportunities of promotion in times of peace than in the hard and bad times caused by such a detestable civil and intestine war. And it should not be presumed that there are people so wretched and miserable that they would imperil and endanger a whole country for the little good a war might bring them. Any one who pictures to himself the condition of the state, the need for money, the devastation and ruin of the countryside, the poverty of the towns, and the complaints made daily to the States about soldiers who commit thousands of oppressive and insolent acts for lack of pay, and to discharge debts, can easily imagine whether or not it is entertaining to be involved in such complicated and difficult matters without the means to apply suitable remedies, and whether the States have any reason to deprive the whole country and themselves of the benefit and happiness which a good and secure peace could bring. And even our enemies and their adherents who maliciously interpret all the States' actions in bad part in order to idealise their own unjust and tyrannical schemes could not rightly maintain that the States have ever postponed peace negotiations...

It would take us too long to discuss all the points of the instruction given to the deputies of the States[2] to show that the conditions which are put forward are necessary to maintain the privileges, liberty of conscience and free exercise of the reformed religion and to assure and secure that the promises made about these are kept. I will mention here only what the States have earnestly requested about the exercise of religion. They have asked that until a legitimate assembly of the States decides otherwise the exercise of the reformed religion may continue in those places where it is already in practice.[3] This is the most controversial article and has been

---

[2] Amongst the delegates of the States General at Cologne were the duke of Aerschot, the abbot Van der Linden and the Frisian Agge Albada who acted as spokesman.

[3] As in the Pacification of Ghent the ultimate decision on the matter was expected from the States General.

flatly refused by the king's ministers, so that we must examine whether the States are demanding something unlawful and whether the king has reason to reject it flatly. As to the States, it is easy to demonstrate that their demand is just and reasonable because every one can see that the greater part of the inhabitants of the country profess the reformed religion.[4] As the States represent the whole nation and all the inhabitants of the country, it is reasonable that they comply with the just and respectable wishes and feelings of the inhabitants for the general welfare of the provinces. Of old and within the memory of man, the States in the Netherlands have represented the whole nation, to defend their rights and to maintain peace and tranquillity for them and to guard them from all injuries, violence and oppression against every one, even their princes. It is not easy to imagine a state, a kingdom or another sovereign government without a subordinate magistrate and States, which represent the provinces. However according to the privileges or constitutions with which the magistrate or the States are provided, this is more evident in some states than in others, so much so that in some countries the venerable name of the States with very little authority left to them has all but gone. This is by no means the case in the Netherlands. Here the States have always had so much authority and respect that the dukes and princes have not been able to make any alterations in the matter of sovereignty or been able to levy duties or other taxes, to have new money minted, or to make peace or war without the express consent of the States. This and many other rights and prerogatives are clear from their privileges, the laws and constitutions of the country. When the States grant subsidies to their princes even for an essential war against an open and declared enemy, this is described as a request, not as an aid or as taxes levied by the prince, to demonstrate that the States are not obliged to pay that money but grant it at the prince's request. And in order that these States shall always be respected and preserve their authority, they have never given an eternal and absolute consent to raise subsidies, but have always restricted it to a certain sum and time.

As it is clear enough that the States are authorised to take up arms against princes who exceed the limits of their office by overt acts of tyranny,[5] they are free beyond doubt to propose and demand such things as they think conducive to the well-being of the inhabitants of the provinces; and in consequence they should obtain these from their prince. As a great many inhabitants profess the reformed religion, it is clear that the States' de-

[4] This is of course a gross overstatement.
[5] Cf. the argument of the *Vindiciae contra tyrannos* published in the same year.

mand is justified. The States are obliged to protect all subjects of the provinces alike and to support their requests provided they are not unreasonable. Obviously the requests cannot be regarded as unreasonable unless it is proved conclusively that in one country two religions should not be allowed. If this is proven, the true religion should be maintained and the false one rejected. Consequently it would also be necessary to prove that the reformed religion is false. In my opinion, however, it is superfluous to debate about tolerating the two religions because in large countries in Christendom such toleration is actually practised and has been practised for several centuries.[6] Certainly it is more desirable to have one religion, just as it would be nice if all men were of the same opinion, had the same desires, were of the same condition and possessed an equal amount of wealth, and above all, were all virtuous and happy, but when this cannot be brought about, one has to govern the country in the best manner possible and to proclaim such laws in the matter of religion, that all are satisfied. Should the States which see that many people follow the example of their neighbours and profess another religion than the Roman, allow the king to ruin the country, expel and massacre the subjects rather than to tolerate both religions? And having seen that the king's unfair stubbornness and cruelty has been useless and that the reformed religion has achieved a great success, and the number of its adherents has increased rather than decreased, notwithstanding the fact that the king has had innumerable people burned alive, has expelled and exiled an infinite number of men and women of all ranks, declared their lives and possessions forfeit and sent the poor children begging – should the States then allow this for ever or should they rather oppose such barbarous tyranny for the defence and protection of the inhabitants of the country? And if it has been proved that there are no grounds for permitting two religions, one should examine which is the true one. And as the adherents of the reformed religion say that they are prepared to have their articles of faith examined by a free council and offer to prove that these are in conformity with the Scriptures,[7] should we not hear them rather than condemn them unheard? For it is true that the Council of Trent has only served the purpose of the ecclesiastics who cannot be judges in their own cause. Neither France nor Germany, Poland, England or other countries and kingdoms have obeyed this council or obey it now.

[6] In this context it was customary to refer to the practice of some Roman emperors (see Document 2).
[7] In fact the adherents of the Reformed Church suggested a national council in their supplication of 22 June 1578 (see Document 33).

As to the king, he must choose one of two things. Either he must grant his provinces the freedom to exercise the reformed religion or he must refuse this on the grounds of conscientious scruples. If he can grant toleration without feeling such scruples, what use to him is this long war and shedding the blood of so many of his poor subjects? Why else but to use the difference of religion as a pretext to exterminate all worthy people and to ruin the country completely by fire and sword as was suggested by his late secretary Escovedo,[8] and to have a means of bringing all into total enslavement? But if his conscience forbids him to tolerate the reformed religion, what can the country expect from him? What else but a firm and resolute determination to continue the war and to achieve his aims by force or by ruses and intrigues and to raise expectations of peace in order to sow dissension and to deceive both sides? Thus in any case he wants to force his subjects to abandon him and to look for other ways of protecting and defending themselves. And the king's feigned conscientious scruples, his desires and wishes deserve no regard for he has no control over the conscience of the people. Have the States of the country, who have reserved to themselves the power to decide on all matters concerning the sovereignty, allowed the king alone to dispose of the conscience of his subjects? Can such permission be given at all, considering that neither the king nor the States but everyone personally must account to God for his faith and conscience? Everybody must examine the Scripture personally, so it is more appropriate to take the whole of the people into account than the king's desire alone. For when our salvation is in question, we should obey God and not men or kings.[9] And as it is evident that in the Perpetual Edict the king of Spain has permitted the exercise of the reformed religion in Holland and Zeeland, and offers to continue it there,[10] we must say that the king's real intention is to abolish this right in those provinces too by force or by ruses. Otherwise he wrongs his other subjects by refusing to grant them the same benefit.

[8] See Document 27. Escovedo was assassinated in Spain in 1578.

[9] See Document 35, note 5.

[10] The Perpetual Edict indeed confirmed the Pacification as did the proposals put forward at Cologne on 18 July 1579 (see Document 40).

42

Advice and counsel of the prince of Orange on some articles sent to His Excellency by the deputies of the Union, 28 September 1579[1]

After January 1579 when some provinces joined together in the Union of Utrecht the administrative situation became extraordinarily complicated. The prince of Orange stayed with the States General which continued in assembly at Antwerp, but in August he was called to Ghent because of the crisis developing there. In September 1579 some delegates from the Union of Utrecht were sent to Ghent. On 18 September they handed the Prince proposals concerning the peace negotiations at Cologne, the levying of taxes, the negotiations in progress with the duke of Anjou and the government of the country. The prince answered them in the document of 28 September.

As to your third article dealing with the question of the duke of Anjou, His Excellency has this to say. He acknowledges the admirable way in which the provinces and all the subjects have done their duty and sees on the other hand that the king has not displayed the least sign of regard towards his subjects and even less towards the reformed religion. His governors and servants bitterly attack the country, and the articles propounded by those who negotiated with the States in former times and by the duke of Terranova[2] during the recent peace negotiations at Cologne are fallacious. Therefore, His Excellency answers that unless peace is offered by the deputies of the king on terms favourable to the fatherland as well as to religion, and assurances are given that there shall not be the slightest reason for the suspicion that on the pretext of peace the king and his servants should want to tyrannise once more over the country and exterminate religion, the provinces may want to choose a prince as their protector. All things considered His Excellency thinks that in that case no lord or prince could be found whose authority and means are of greater importance and consequence than those of the kingdom of England or the

---

[1] *Advijs ende raedt van den Prince van Oraengien op sekere articulen aen zijne Excellentie ghesonden van weghen der ghedeputeerden van der Unie* (Knuttel, no. 503).

[2] The representative of the Spanish king at Cologne.

duke of Anjou. The princes of the Holy Roman Empire have been asked several times to take these countries under their protection, and His Imperial Majesty himself has also been asked very humbly by His Highness[3] and the States General both in letters and by nobles and other distinguished persons sent thither, but His Imperial Majesty or the princes of the empire could not be persuaded to render any assistance to these countries, though they are members of the empire.[4] On the other hand His Excellency has been informed on good authority that the queen of England intends to agree to become the protectress of these provinces and that she is favourably disposed toward the duke of Alençon and feels affection for him.[5] She has, in fact, written this to the States, adding that in order to perform such a magnificent task it is necessary to have a prince and lord who can perform it in person. His Excellency thinks (and if he is wrong the united provinces and towns should correct him) that no other means is left but to have recourse to the afore-mentioned duke of Anjou. However, the condition must be that the country is given the assistance of soldiers and sufficient means to put up a stubborn defence against the Spaniards and drive them away. Religion and the privileges of the country as well as its freedoms and jurisdiction must be fully guaranteed and it should especially be ensured that each province separately remains in full possession of its old fiefs and other prerogatives and that no alterations be made to them now or later on. But if the provinces think it more advisable not to elect a prince as their protector, His Excellency will comply with their discretion and counsel. In that case too he promises to serve and assist them as much as he can in all matters that they may consider advisable for the benefit and prosperity of these countries. And he urges and admonishes them always to give heed to the best and most expedient means to withstand such a powerful and terrible enemy as is theirs...

Your fourth point concerns the government of these provinces. In this matter His Excellency leaves it to the provinces and their deputies to take the decisions they think appropriate. As to His Highness, the Archduke Matthias, he approves of what has already been advised by the deputies.

---

[3] Archduke Matthias.

[4] Marnix of St Aldegonde addressed the Diet at Worms in the name of a delegation from the Netherlands on 7 May 1578 and referred to the treaty of Augsburg of 1548 concerning the Burgundian circle (see Document 19, note 8).

[5] The title of duke of Anjou was conferred on Francis of Alençon in 1576. In August 1579 he paid a visit to Queen Elizabeth concerning his proposal of marriage.

But as to His Excellency himself, His Excellency will not refrain from calling the attention of the deputies to the fact that he has not been able to rectify the many great and gross faults and abuses which have been committed because he was not obeyed. All of us know that commands and orders are vain unless they are obeyed and complied with by those who should do so.

On this subject many serious complaints have been lodged by all sorts of people for various reasons. Some of them are wise people. They know that the source of the evil is partly the lack of proper obedience, partly the fact that the money necessary for carrying on the war has not been raised in due time or has not been spent on what it was destined for or was held back by evil practices and cunning devices. Nevertheless it is His Excellency whom they deftly hold responsible for all such irregularities, as if His Excellency could have done everything on his own without any means and without the assistance of those who should help him. What made it even more difficult for His Excellency to act in the required manner was the fact that people who defended our case and had taken our side raised many obstacles because they had different opinions and pursued private designs, as became clear afterwards.

Many others, not so clever though not of really evil nature (mankind being naturally inclined to calumny particularly against those who govern them) have rejoiced at these and similar propositions and have been so stupid as to air them at their tables as well as in the streets and other places where they found themselves. They did not perceive that the inventors of such calumnies intended to bring about the utter ruin of the provinces, and that they helped these men by repeating their denunciations. Some of them, incidentally, had undoubtedly been bribed by the enemy.

His Excellency, seeing the ingratitude of people who witnessed the arrest of his son, taken away in custody,[6] and the loss of His Excellency's three brothers,[7] and who know that he has got head over heels into debt and lost all his possessions, had reasons enough to accept the excellent and profitable offers which were made to him had he been willing to listen to them and to come to a private agreement during the peace negotiations. And His Excellency might well have been inclined to such dealings when he noticed that people who behaved previously as if they were totally

---

[6] Philip William (see Document 23, note 12).
[7] Adolph (born 1540) was killed in the battle of Heiligerlee in 1568. For Louis and Henry see Document 19, note 2.

devoted to the religion, very ungratefully declared to be his enemies.[8] But nevertheless His Excellency's only purpose remains to further the honour and glory of God and the welfare of the fatherland. He has treated all these forms of ingratitude and unfairness as matters that must be forgotten as soon as possible. And without any or with very small resources, but aided by the confidence His Excellency has inspired in the soldiers, he has so far with the utmost exertion prevented the enemy from invading the country further, when the latter attacked the provinces from all sides by force of arms as well as with ruses and evil practices. The enemy was, moreover, strengthened both by the imprudence and by the wickedness of some of us, who pretended to be on our side but in fact did more harm to the country than all the violence of the enemy. Indeed it is very surprising that the whole country has not been entirely lost.

As the afore-mentioned united provinces now offer His Excellency the post of lieutenant-general of these provinces[9] His Excellency declares that he is willing to obey some other person whom the afore-mentioned provinces would like to appoint, and that he promises to spare no pains in the service of the provinces and to do his utmost as he has done so far. If however the provinces persist and pray His Excellency (who has devoted himself wholly to the service of God Almighty and the fatherland) to accept the post of lieutenant-general, then His Excellency desires that the provinces will understand the causes of the afore-mentioned abuses, in order that they may take appropriate measures.

[8] The Ghent extremists, who disapproved of his negotiations with the duke of Anjou. In order to take action against them the prince had been in that town since 18 August.

[9] Viz. those of the Union of Utrecht.

43

About the constraint upon conscience practised in Holland. A conversation between D.V.C. and N.V.L., 7 November 1579[1]

Derick Volckertsz Coornhert (1522–90), a Haarlem notary of christian humanist conviction, is the best known advocate of religious toleration in the Netherlands in the second half of the sixteenth century.

[1] Dirck Volckertsz Coornhert, *Wercken*, I (Amsterdam, 1630), pp. 470ff.

His independence over problems of faith and ethics frequently brought him into conflict with the ministers of the Reformed Church. He held this conversation with the Haarlem burgomaster Niclaes van der Laan.

c.: We have now agreed that Moses never commanded that heretics should be killed and that such a command is not to be found in the Old Testament generally, either in clear and explicit terms or couched in the form of a metaphor or a story. We see too that when Paul expressly mentioned a heretic, he clearly indicated how he should be punished, namely by keeping out of his way and avoiding him after admonishing him once or twice.[2] This is undeniably a law on the punishment of heretics given to us by the apostle inspired by the Holy Ghost. Moses never wrote down a law about this. Nevertheless you do not hesitate to ignore the clear evangelical law about heretics given by Paul and to look for one in Moses, or even to invent one which is not there. This is what the Ebionites did.[3] It means ignoring and failing to keep God's law, rejecting the Holy Scripture and following one's own pleasure and human reason. Is this what you want to be called following God's commandments? Obeying God and seeking God's honour? What else is this than despising God, repudiating His Word, offending, defaming and humiliating His Name? Don't you worship God in vain in this way with your human commandments? Do you want this to be called seeking God's honour? This is not Christ's opinion. When talking of such people he said explicitly: Those who kill you will imagine that they are doing God a service.[4]

v.: You are mistaken here.

c.: Correct me, if possible, try as hard as you can to quote one single clear sentence from the whole Bible in which it is said that God has ordered the political authority to kill heretics, to protect His church by their sword of steel, or to nourish, guide and preserve the souls of the subjects. You will not be able to do this. By the prophets God charges the prophets and teachers with this task, saying that he will demand his sheep back from the false prophets, not from the political authority.[5] For it is the prophets and not the magistrates God entrusts with the care of souls, and it is to the apostles and not to the political authority that Christ gave the power to bind and to loose in matters which regard our souls.[6] The

---

[2] Titus III, 10.

[3] Ebionites, an early Jewish Christian sect in Palestine. They rejected the authority of Paul and denied the doctrine of the virginity of Mary.

[4] John XVI, 2.   [5] Ezekiel XXXIV, 10.   [6] Matt. XVI, 19.

political authority has no jurisdiction or power over souls; it is not allowed to kill, wound, ensnare or banish souls. Why then does the political authority have the presumption to lay down rules in matters in which it has no competence? You see, it is impossible for you to prove that you have been ordered by God to rule, order or compel souls and to deal with he retics. I have made it clear that there is no text to be found in which such an order is given to you. Now you see to what conclusion this necessarily leads us.

v.: What?

c.: Quite the opposite of your opinion.

v.: In what respect?

c.: In this respect, that when you take upon yourself to banish or to exterminate the heretics, and to protect the churches of God by means of your power, you do openly what God did not order you to do, and you do it without, nay against His will. You dare honour Him at your own discretion. By thus being disobedient, you openly dishonour Him, despise His commandments and blaspheme His Holy Name. That is far from honouring God.

v.: May a Christian authority silently and with good conscience allow so many thousands of souls to be tempted and damned?

c.: Maybe the authority is wrong in thinking that those souls are damned and tempted; in reality they may be on the right road and guided well. Under King Philip's reign a few years ago the king was convinced that he was killing heretics, but in fact he killed members of the Christian church and made them into martyrs. But even supposing that the authorities were able to form a correct judgment in this matter, are they allowed to prevent such things?

v.: Why not?

c.: Because doing this the authorities forgo the legal means and employ means found to be wrong.

v.: What do you think to be the legal means?

c.: Just what Calvin said when he was still under, not beyond the power of the authorities: 'there is no other means to exterminate all impious sects and heresies but to give place to the pure truth of God. Only this dispels the dark by its clearness, as experience teaches well enough'.[7] That is well said by Calvin. For truth, not the sword has the power to chase away and kill lies, error and heresy. Now the States and the preachers

---

[7] Jean Calvin, *Contre la secte phantastique et furieuse des libertins qui se nomment spirituelz* (Geneva, 1545).

too dare forgo the right means.[8] They do not risk trying to justify their doctrine against me by claiming that it corresponds with the truth revealed in the Holy Scripture. But they hope that the authorities may condemn me as a rebel for reproving the preachers for their teaching, and thus will overcome me with the sword of the executioner or by putting me in prison or banishing me. This is the means we have found to be wrong. It was employed by Charles and Philip but it was like oil on the flame as the great increase in sects and sectarians clearly proves. What have they gained by it? Have not a hundred nay a thousand men replaced one? Do we intend to make the same mistake again and again and (to use the praiseworthy words of the States General[9]) do we still try by force of arms to exterminate what lies hidden in the inmost of the souls and can be reshaped by no one but God? What else can such policies produce but impious or hypocritical people? Impious I call people who forsake God to save their skin, and hypocritical people who pretend to agree with you while firmly sticking to their former opinion. Is that the profit you expect to gain by allowing the political authority to exert compulsion? Compulsory service displeases the free God, who does not admit hypocrites nor impious persons into His kingdom. Is this the way to prevent many thousands of souls from being tempted and damned? You add to their number those who are made impious or hypocritical by your fault. If you wish to become persecutors yourselves too, you should consider whether you will save your own souls. It is written: blessed are those who are persecuted,[10] but nowhere: blessed are those who persecute others in My name. It is written too that all who wish to live the religious life in Christ Jesus,[11] will be persecuted, but nowhere that they will persecute. The Lord sends sheep, not wolves. He says: beware of men,[12] but not: kill men. He says that His flock will be hated, handed over and killed,[13] but nowhere that His flock will hate, hand over or kill any one. Be careful, friend, which side you choose. For one is the Christian side, the other the side, way and manner of tyrants and murderers. Do not be drawn to this by false doctrine, interpretation and glosses of people who follow in the well-trodden footsteps of the Catholic murderers, if you won't be brought so far as to forsake the merciful Father in heaven and to say Father to the

---

[8] By a resolution of 23 August 1579 the States of Holland instructed the town of Haarlem to forbid Coornhert to continue his assaults on the reformed ministers in speech or in writing on penalty of being prosecuted as a peace-breaker.
[9] See Document 30.
[10] Matt. V, 10.   [11] II Tim. III, 12.
[12] Matt. X, 17.   [13] Matt. XXIV, 9.

devil from hell, who is fierce and has been a murderer from the outset. For thus the so-called honour of God sought outside of, nay against His commandments, at your own pleasure and with human commandments, would not only be in vain but damning to yourself, offensive to the Gospel and blasphemous to God. You must consider this in good earnest.

v.: You have spoken a long time and I have listened a long time, now then what is your opinion? That one should allow every one to do as he likes in religious matters and so create a Babylonic confusion?

c.: My long speech was to the point, you were free to interrupt, you have not done so. Therefore I went on talking, thinking you had nothing to say against it. As you ask for my opinion, I will not give you mine, but that of our Lord Christ himself.

v.: How is that?

c.: That the weeds may grow beside the wheat, without being weeded out, lest the wheat is weeded out at the same time: at the Lord's express command both are allowed to grow until harvest time, when the Lord will give His orders to the reapers.[14] Do you wish to hear more? Add to this Paul's advice about which we have spoken to avoid heretics. This is the command of Christ and the apostle Paul. As long as you are true believers, you need not worry about sinning if you do not do what is nowhere ordered but explicitly forbidden in the Holy Scripture. Do not on your own authority accept anything which has not been given to you from Heaven.[15] But render unto God the things which are God's and unto man the things which are man's.[16] God alone is entitled to authority over men's souls and consciences, men are entitled to freedom of conscience. Let the authorities choose a religion they like best, and let them with their civil power and the sword of justice protect the preachers from violence when preaching and exercising it, but let the preachers, outwardly protected in this way, themselves protect their doctrine with the spiritual sword of truth. Then you are doing what you should do and so are the preachers. Then God will not neglect to do what it is His right to do, that is to further His glory and to protect His church.

v.: You have said many fine things, but I do not expect that people will accept this. I can in no way agree to killing people for the sake of religion. But to permit several religions to be exercised is, in my opinion, not right.

c.: If you did not attach greater value to your own judgment than to that of the States General which made the Pacification of Ghent, you would not consider such a permission wrong.

---

[14] A text frequently quoted in the literature on toleration: Matt. XIII, 29, 30.
[15] John III, 27.   [16] Matt. XXII, 21.

v.: They have not permitted this.

c.: Not only I myself, but so far every one has interpreted the Pacification of Ghent in this way: that all the inhabitants of the Netherlands were granted freedom of conscience.

v.: That is correct. They have acquired freedom of conscience. But does this mean that they are permitted to exercise any religion they happen to choose? I cannot interpret it in this way at all.

c.: Yet I do think it is true, unless it is thought that thanks to the Pacification we have acquired freedom only in name but not in reality.[17]

v.: Is not every one now allowed to believe whatever he likes without being punished?

c.: Even before, every one was allowed to do so. Who could prevent this? Neither emperor nor king, pope, cardinal, inquisition or whoever else. If we have got no more freedom now than we had before, what use has the Pacification of Ghent for us on this point? By their cruel edicts the emperor, Charles, King Philip and the Spanish inquisition did not allow any one professing another religion than the Roman Catholic to have different preachers, to administer sacraments in a different way, or to reprove or to contradict their doctrine and their preachers. You won't have this done to your preachers either. Does not then constraint upon conscience remain?

v.: Not in the same way. Who is killed now? Whose possessions are confiscated?

c.: What I am going to say is already well-known. You confess (who can deny it?) that compulsion has remained, but you add that punishment has become less severe. That may be so. They don't kill as much as formerly: the time is not yet ripe for this and the people would not yet permit it. But even if the punishment be a fine only, there is nevertheless compulsion and want of freedom. The compulsion remains, although so far the punishment is less severe. Accordingly we have still to do without the freedom of conscience every one was longing for and promised in the Pacification of Ghent; we have only a mitigation of punishment. Well! Did I say mitigation of punishment? I find that to me punishment is beginning to be measured out, not less but more frequently and more severely and with much less appearance of justice than ever in the times of papistry.

[17] Here Coornhert interprets the Pacification in the same way as the reformed supporters of religious peace.

44

Proceedings of the peace negotiations at Cologne, in the presence of the commissaries of His Imperial Majesty, 1581[1]

This pamphlet contains not only the proceedings based on the official reports of the delegates of the States General but also a commentary written by the Frisian lawyer Agge Albada who played an important part at the Cologne conference. He frequently quotes authoritative texts such as Sebastian Castellio's treatise on the persecution of heretics (1554) and the *Vindiciae contra tyrannos* (1579). In the following passages he comments on the acceptance of Archduke Matthias by the States General in December 1577.

There are many elements which indicate that the king's dominion is bound under contract to the States or the people. However if one takes the contracts of all provinces into consideration, and in particular that of Brabant, it cannot be said that the king received supreme dominion from them. In almost all matters concerning the community he is not allowed to exercise his power without the people's approval. If you wish to criticise me for advancing propositions not specified in these contracts or alliances, the States answer that these contracts and alliances have the same purpose, to wit that the lives, honour and possessions of the common people should be preserved. They think this purpose has become far more important now, since things have come to such a pass that all we stand for is being openly challenged and contested by the Spaniards on behalf of the king. Now the common people have no other human help and remedy than force of arms to protect themselves and their possessions. Moreover, it can be proved that the princes are made for the benefit of their subjects and not the subjects for the benefit of the princes...The States know better than the king which persons are disposed to keep the peace and which to stir up new revolts, and whether or not such persons are respectable and capable of governing and administering justice, and to whom functions and offices should be given. To a wise man therefore it will not seem unjust or strange that the States want to appoint people who are agree-

---

[1] *Acten van den vredehandel gheschiet te Colen, in de teghenwoordicheyt van de commissarissen der Keys. Maiesteyt*...(Van der Wulp, no. 493).

able to them as well as to the king until the state has been restored to its former shape and stability.

So that no one should think it was unjust and illegal for the States to elect and appoint Archduke Matthias, I would like to add the true words spoken by Philip Marnix, lord of St Aldegonde in an address to the delegates of the empire delivered on behalf of the archduke and the States of the Netherlands at the diet at Worms.[2] The States of the Netherlands realised, he said, that since Don John of Austria had only the ruin of the fatherland in mind, they would need another leader and captain, thanks to whose authority and high rank the provinces might be kept united in their feelings and desires in such a dangerous and precarious situation, and the neighbouring countries'[3] proposals and intrigues designed towards occupying these provinces and withdrawing them entirely from loyalty to the king of Spain and house of Austria, might be prevented. It seemed to them in all respects fit and proper, to entrust His Most Serene Highness Prince Matthias, archduke of Austria, with state affairs – which were in an almost desperate condition – partly to prevent so great a ruin of their fatherland and partly to preserve and protect the right and dignity of the very illustrious house of Austria in Lower Germany or, to put it briefly, to maintain the alliance and great friendship which for various reasons they have with Germany. He is twice, nay thrice related to the king of Spain;[4] he possesses a good and honest nature and thanks to his strict and perfect education in all sorts of virtues his manners differ totally from those usual in Spain. In word and deed he has always shown himself to be kindly disposed towards the Netherlands. Thus Matthias may surely be relied on to calm the tempest and readily to persuade the king his uncle to resume his old friendship and kindness to his subjects as well as to persuade the Netherlanders to restore their old loyalty and respect to their king. He will take the necessary steps to make the country prosper again for, while introducing in the Netherlands the methods and decrees concerning religion which prevail in the German Empire, he will retain for the people the statutes and privileges of our own country.

Truly His Serene Highness did not belie the just desire and expectations of the States nor did he refuse to accept their offer but he went thither as rapidly as possible, taking little rest at night.[5] Then he was entrusted with

[2] The speech summarised here was delivered by Marnix on 7 May 1578.
[3] France and England.
[4] Matthias' father Maximilian II was Philip II's cousin; his mother Mary was Philip's sister; his sister Anne was Philip's fourth wife.
[5] In October 1577.

the government with the unanimous consent of all States[6] and to the great joy and mirth of the people in these turbulent times, until by the will of the king and the consent of the States, other arrangements should be made. No one who examines this carefully can consider himself entitled to criticise the States for their conduct. Their laws, privileges and decrees and the examples of their ancestors show that their policy was perfectly legal. In the privileges of Brabant it is explicitly stated that even if the prince himself (not to mention the prince's deputy) should break the laws and rights of the country, not only the States in general, but every one concerned of whatever rank he might be, is allowed to refuse him obedience and respect, for as long as the king fails to comply entirely with the statutes and privileges.[7] But a person appointed by the prince to act as governor, who undertakes something against the statutes and privileges, is considered by such deeds to have immediately forfeited his office and must be regarded by the whole population as being dismissed. No one is allowed to support him; without any further formal legal procedure he must be judged not only unfit to hold any public office but infamous and not qualified to make his will.

A striking instance of this is an action performed by our ancestors in recent history. For by decree of the States they deposed Duke John of Brabant, son of Anthony and grandson of Philip the Bold, duke of Burgundy and brother of the king of France, from all his administrative and governmental offices, when he showed too much favour to some of his close friends, giving them permanent office in the service and administration of the country and doing much that was contrary to the rights of the country and laws he had sworn to observe. His brother Philip was appointed his substitute until John had repaired the avowed offence and, with all those who had offended against the privileges and rights of the country excluded from office, had entirely complied with the statutes and laws of the country to the satisfaction of the States. He gave them a letter signed in his own hand and sealed with his seal, in which he declared on behalf of himself and his successors that the States had acted

---

[6] See Document 28.

[7] The passage in question in the *Joyeuse Entrée* of 3 January 1356 runs as follows: 'And if the case be that we, our heirs or our offspring violate, infringe or order the infringement of these afore-mentioned points, articles and agreements in general or in detail, in whatever manner that may be, then we consent and permit the afore-mentioned worthy persons that they perform no longer any duties towards us, our heirs or our offspring nor are any longer subordinate to us, until we have redressed and requited it to them completely.' Van Bragt, *Blijde Inkomst*, p. 106.

well and lawfully and to the benefit of the commonwealth and that they might do this with perfect justice in accordance with the laws and statutes of the country and that therefore all their successors would be allowed to follow this example as often as necessary.[8] At the time of the very Serene Lady Mary, wife of Maximilian the First, Roman emperor of that name, blessed be his memory, this law or privilege, which pertained only to Brabant, was by public treaty and contract made common and universal in all provinces of the Netherlands:[9] this is stated in public papers and further documented in the annals of the realm which may serve as evidence. In former times the inhabitants of Holland and Zeeland and also of Flanders often did the same thing, as the history books show. As it is customary in all countries, even in Germany, to follow in one's ancestors' commendable footsteps, no one may now justly criticise the States of the Netherlands for using their right to oppose, not the prince himself, but the man sent from far away, from Spain, as the king's stadholder; the man who, following foreign Spanish advice,[10] not only openly and shamefully offended against the privileges and laws of the country, but also against the general peace and firmly founded Pacification of Ghent, applauded and confirmed by all States, even by the king himself.

[8] See Documents 47 and 50.
[9] The Great Privilege of 1477 that was revoked in 1494.
[10] Don John of Austria.

45

Remonstrance made to the deputies of the States General at Antwerp, by the prince of Orange, 9 January 1580[1]

The prince wanted the deputies of the provinces at the States General in Antwerp to impress upon the various provincial States the urgency of taking binding decisions on administrative reform. Shortly after this he left Antwerp for a journey to the Northern Netherlands.

We do not think it necessary, gentlemen, to expatiate on the articles of peace sent to you,[2] for all the provinces together have unanimously and

[1] *Vertooch ghedaen aen myne heeren de ghedeputeerde van de Staten generael by mijn heere den Prince van Orangien* (Knuttel, no. 524).
[2] From Cologne in 1579, see Document 40, note 5.

without any objections judged that these should not be adopted or approved of as they are not in any way conducive to the safety or prosperity of the country. Therefore we shall (as we should) regard them as a matter on which your masters, the provincial States, have taken a definitive decision; at present, we do not want to oppose this resolution nor contest it, but feel obliged to declare that we think it praiseworthy and useful.

Because after mature consideration and deliberation you have resolved not to approve of these articles whereas the articles sent by you have been rejected by the enemy, it is obvious and already manifest, that the enemies want to attack you openly and to persecute you by main force. As peace is out of the question, gentlemen, it will be necessary to take the other course and protect ourselves by force of arms. It is not necessary to waste more words on this, as we believe and have understood that at present you make no objections to this conclusion.

Nevertheless it is surprising that although all of us think it advisable to take up arms to secure the freedom of the country, our possessions, honour, wives and children and are convinced that precise decisions on the special problems facing us are urgently required, we should usually injure and even wreck our cause by taking wrong decisions when dealing with those particular aspects of an action which we think in a general way to be absolutely necessary. Consequently all our labour and efforts are so purposeless and fruitless that the total destruction of the country and of ourselves is inevitable.

Your first and foremost mistake is that as yet neither you nor your masters, the provincial States, have established any assembly or council on behalf of the States,[3] which has the power to take decisions beneficial to the whole of the country. Everyone in his own province or town acts as he thinks is beneficial to himself and his particular affairs without realising that when some town or province is under attack, it may be useful not to help it for the time being so that in the end the whole country, including these towns and provinces, may be saved.

That is why we are forced to fight not in areas chosen by ourselves and indicated by the interest of the country but in areas determined by the enemy who attacks one part of the country this time, and another part the next time, so that we must follow him as if he alone has the power to decide both on the time and the place to give battle. As a result we are always compelled to stay on the defensive without daring to attack because each

[3] At the time the prince was striving to establish a general council composed of representatives of the provinces to serve as a central administrative body.

time it is difficult for us to use more than the army of a single province. This of course is not sufficient to resist the forces which the enemy can easily concentrate while our army is scattered.

The cause of this unhappy situation is the fact indicated above, that you have not established a superior body or council which should be obeyed by the subordinate authorities. Such a council may meet dangers as they occur; these may be frequent and great in some places and absent in others. The result of your particularism is that if some provinces are attacked, they ask us for help (though often in vain); the others, that are no longer threatened, want to get rid of the soldiers either by disbanding their troops altogether or by transferring them to the charge of other provinces which are already heavily burdened. As soon, however, as they perceive the slightest trace of the enemy, they immediately want to be given aid and assistance, as if it were possible for us to extract the soldiers, first dismissed, out of the ground by stamping our foot.

You know well enough, gentlemen, how often we have told you, all of you as well as each province separately, that some horse and foot should be kept in readiness. We should have been able to bring them together at short notice and draw them up in order. If we had managed to persuade some province to accept five or six companies of German horse, the districts of Tournay and West Flanders would without doubt not be in the desperate state they are in now.[4]

Last year when we received reliable information that the enemy had raised many soldiers and made them ready to attack us, we asked several times that orders should be given to keep our soldiers in service for some time at least, waiting for the enemy to strike first. We would then have destroyed his army or divided it. But we did not succeed in persuading you to do this, and thus we lost the town of Maastricht, which could have been relieved had soldiers and some means been available.[5]

But it is impossible to levy any soldiers or raise an army for lack of authority from Your Honours to rally the army once it has dispersed and also because of lack of means, should each town or province immediately after the enemy's departure, wish to get rid of the soldiers. Meanwhile the towns which could be defended by a small garrison, should a field army able to stop the enemy be raised, are looted and completely ruined by excessively large garrisons which it would be fatal to remove, since there is no other army to protect those places. This is a very grave abuse.

[4] Tournay was closely threatened by Parma's troops. It was the only Walloon member on the side of the Union at this time.
[5] The town of Maastricht fell into Parma's hands on 29 June 1579.

The field army, raised to oppose the enemy, would also serve to defend the towns and could live mostly off the enemy's territory instead of eating up, plundering and ruining our own country. The best solution is to establish a supreme council with power over the army.

Various honest persons with little understanding of the essence of state affairs, think it strange that so many misfortunes take place every day, that towns or whole provinces are lost or rise in revolt, that the country is ransomed and pillaged by the enemy, that many leave us and side with another party,[6] that others become less zealous and no longer display their earlier ardour, but are flagging like a sick body that is drying up. This malady, gentlemen, comes from the deepest corners of our own body. Looking beyond our own borders, we see that no monarch, king or prince or foreign nation is well-disposed towards us or tries to obtain our friendship or alliance,[7] and that no one leaves the ranks of our enemy to come over to our side. All this we see daily and, as was said before, with astonishment; most people do not know who is to blame, but often criticise those who are least to blame. But the true cause of all these disorders is our own indecision. We meet often enough and deliberate long enough, but are as negligent in implementing our decisions as we are diligent in deliberating at length. Yet, gentlemen, there are undoubtedly still many pious and honest inhabitants in this country; it is like a fire smouldering under the ashes: if you take them away it burns high again but will soon be dead if you let it consume itself.

[6] Many nobles and clergymen from the southern Netherlands (the duke of Aerschot, abbot Van der Linden *et al.*) went over to the Spanish side after the failure of the Cologne peace negotiations.

[7] The negotiations with the duke of Anjou were still in progress, mainly through the prince of Orange.

46

The return of harmony in the Netherlands by the return of Madame, 1580[1]

This pamphlet published at Mons advocates the reconciliation of the Netherlands with the king according to the example set by the

[1] *Le retour de la concorde aux Pays Bas par le retour de Madame* (Knuttel, no. 543).

Union of Arras of January 1579. In September 1579 Margaret of Parma was re-appointed as regent, but when she arrived back in the Netherlands in the summer of 1580 to take over government, her son Alexander prevented her from exercising any influence.

If you hope to gain advantage from having a man like the prince of Orange as your chief, and from our having a woman as our regent, you are very much mistaken. For if Madame's sex is an obstacle, so is his lack of courage. Tell me, how many times has he been at the head of your regiments when it was time to fight? Do you remember seeing him assemble and command your army with the diligence and zeal appropriate to a commander-in-chief? Did you see him come to the rescue of the town of Maastricht after a siege lasting four months[2] or (a little time before) go to meet the prince of Parma? The prince of Parma hastened rashly to the gates of Antwerp and cut your army to pieces before the eyes of the prince of Orange,[3] who remained paralysed within the walls of Antwerp and gave neither the assistance nor the orders which one must expect in such a situation from a commander-in-chief.

You, soldiers, who love military glory and who have borne arms on his side, did you not feel ashamed of him for cowardice so great that he even lacked the courage to send off five hundred harquebuses to support you when you had retreated as far as the counterscarp of the moat of Antwerp? Do you not remember that at the critical moment his authority over the horse (who are of his nation) failed and they deserted him? Do you not see that it is always so with him? How long will it be before you see that all his strength lies in his ability to deceive those among us who are carried away by his fine words, but that his actions are to little or no avail?

You must therefore confess that if Madame does not bear arms herself nor takes part in fighting, your prince of Orange does not do this either. His share consists in giving good advice. Well let us see which of the two wins the prize for giving the better advice, for putting into practice his own advice best and for looking after his soldiers better and paying them better. Madame advises us to make war only on foreigners and disturbers of the public peace and cordially receives all the king's subjects who are willing to live in accordance with the Pacification of Ghent, confirmed by the recent treaty of Mons.[4] The prince of Orange advises us not to keep

[2] From March until June 1579.

[3] On 23 February 1579 Parma sent his soldiers from his camp at Visé near Liège to positions immediately before the gates of Antwerp.

[4] By the treaty of Mons (September 1579) the stipulations of the peace of Arras of May 1579 between the Walloon provinces and Spain, including withdrawal

the Pacification and secretly orders the Catholics to be either driven away
or to be harassed everywhere. Madame sincerely advises the re-establishment of peace and harmony between the provinces; the prince sows as
much discord and dissension as possible in the whole country, so that one
of the parties may be his stronghold. Madame has the fear and the glory
of God in mind, and she attunes her decrees and counsels to this. The
prince has the ambition to usurp power but he conceals this under the
mask of Calvinism or the confession of Augsburg.[5]

What this princess swears or promises she really wishes with all her
heart and she keeps her word with total sincerity; the prince's aim, however, is to deceive and to hoodwink people with fine words without effect-
ing what he swore and promised. She is sure to get money from the resources of the king of Spain to pay His Majesty's army (though he takes a
long time); he will not have the four million guilders necessary to levy
and put into the field a new army next summer unless with Aldegonde,
Villers and Taffin[6] he fabricates new lies to lull the people of the towns
and countries he occupies, into granting him this large sum in addition
to the ordinary loans for his garrisons. She has the power and the will to
reward the good services of the captains and soldiers of His Majesty's
army with good jobs in the provinces loyal to the king; he has only his own
goods at Dillenburg to give away[7] and should he give away the other
men's goods, he will suffer the misfortune of Seius and his horse.[8]
As those among us who have observed her actions will testify, the heart of
the princess is so full of the fear of God and a Christian desire to re-
establish the old harmony of these countries, that nothing inimical to
these aspirations may enter it. He has his heart full of discord and cruelty;
all he devises is to take a town by surprise, to sack another, to chase away or
molest all the Catholics, in short to introduce everywhere disorder and
dissension among the subjects of the king under the veil of religion, to
ruin one party with the help of the other, until he is checked in his course

of the Spanish troops and replacement of the governor, Parma, were chiefly
confirmed.

[5] In 1566 the prince advised the adherents of the reformed religion in the Netherlands to accept the Augsburg confession in a somewhat modified form. From
1573 he himself was a member of the reformed church which was based on the
Calvinistic confession of 1561.

[6] Marnix of St Aldegonde, and the court-chaplains Loyseleur de Villiers and
Taffin were held to be Orange's chief advisers at the time.

[7] Dillenburg, residence of the counts of Nassau.

[8] The Latin proverb 'ille homo habet equum Seianum' refers to Seius (1st
century B.C.) who possessed a horse that led all its owners to disaster.

by the Catholics united and joined together for the king. And that is how the general peace desired by all virtuous men of this country will return.

47

Emanuel and Ernest. Dialogue of two persons on the state of the Netherlands, 1580[1]

> Gerard Prouninck, alias van Deventer, who emigrated to Utrecht from his native town Bois-le-Duc, which had taken Parma's side, is probably the author of this work. He makes a strong plea for accepting Anjou as sovereign of the country and therefore promotes Orange's policy. Cf. Document 64 for a later version of Prouninck's theory.

EMAN.: If we agree that because of the inequality of the inhabitants a popular government is impossible here, would there be any objection to the States governing the country in an aristocratic manner?

ERN.: I have already given you part of my answer, Sir Emanuel, but will now develop it further. If the Spaniards estimate the time this state can be expected to last by looking at the corruption of the people, they may set their greatest hope on the corruption of the States. I was in Cologne when the States General assembled in the town of Antwerp.[2] All worthy men rejoiced at it, the Germans even said that almost the whole of Christendom looked forward to the outcome of this honourable and very solemn assembly. But the king's adherents held quite a different opinion. They maintained that the assembly would turn out to the king's advantage. Firstly, the States would spend nearly all their time there in disputes and contentions; the niggardliness of some and the cowardice of others would prevent effective decisions on war-finances; the provinces, jealous as usual, would not agree to establishing one single Council of State, but would have several with equal authority in several places. But even to these councils they would not grant powers and commissions as comprehensive as necessary. The cause of all this is their irresolution. And this

---

[1] *Emanuel-Erneste, dialogue de deux personnages sur l'estat du Païs Bas* (Knuttel, no. 545).

[2] In April 1579 (see Document 39). At Cologne the peace negotiations were started in May with the emperor as intermediary.

irresolution is the simple consequence of the fact that they were too weak to unite into one strong body. Moreover, the king's adherents said, it would be impossible for the States to keep anything secret; there were far too many people there and some of the members were elected not because they were experienced in state affairs, but because they were enormously stubborn and particularly good at fighting for the rights, exemptions and advantages of their towns and provinces. For a long time one had been used to sending to the court, where most of the time the issue was whether one should grant subsidies, people bold enough to refuse taxes and to defend the interests of their towns and provinces. It was not to be expected, the king's adherents said, that the Netherlanders would act differently in the present situation because they like to stick to their old ways.

EMAN.: Good heavens, how right they were! Obviously they were well informed.

ERN.: Certainly. The king spares no expense on spies and scouts. Soon we learned at Cologne that the States had sworn not to leak any information about their work. Yet we were told that some provinces almost refused to take part in the discussions if the replacement of the king was not put first on the agenda. We also learned that when the power to be granted to the new Council of State came to be discussed, as well as on other occasions, the representatives of Holland and Zeeland were not prepared to give up any of the rights obtained by them at the Pacification of Ghent, and even began an extremely intemperate dispute with some of the deputies of Flanders. And many such reports on the smallest details reached us daily.

EMAN.: What did the king's partisans say about all this?

ERN.: Of course, they were delighted. They were particularly glad about the behaviour of the deputies of Holland. They fear nothing so much as to see Holland unite its power with that of the other provinces, so nothing is more pleasant for them than to notice that mere trifles give the Hollanders, who started the revolt, cause for getting angry with people to whom they should be a spur and an example. I heard a gentleman of some importance (who seemed to be angry at this confusion, because he loved his country) say this: By what misfortune, what ignorance, what blindness have these people been struck? Their whole future, their state, their honour, their reputation, or their shame and total ruin depend on whether or not they succeed in remaining united. I pity, he said, the poor prince of Orange, who is a slave to their confused minds and destined to lose his life as well as his honour there. He will be severely criticised for all the evil consequences that are bound to follow – for certainly they will not achieve good results. As to the prince of Orange, the others answered, we must confess that the king has greatly erred by so ill-treating him. No monarch in the world would not deem himself exceedingly happy to have at his side so accomplished a man, endowed with such rare virtues. His patience is surprising, his mind is unbelievably brilliant. Though people keep chattering to him from early morning until late at night and though we have often expected that he would break down or at least get exhausted by the constant stream of unpleasant new developments and evil tricks he has to deal with, in fact his mood has always remained cheerful, his mind lively, his judgment well-considered. What would become of the States if the prince were not at the helm? Although the prince is the king's and our enemy this we must say to his honour that never since the creation of the world has any other seignior been able under an aristocratic government to preserve against a monarch as powerful as King Philip a country that so short a time ago decided to refuse obedience to its legitimate prince and is so divided by faction and full of self-seeking. There were others who attempted something similar but no one else achieved such results and no one else remained firm and cool among such baffling vicissitudes. The king and the whole Council of Spain are profoundly astonished. Had they understood that the prince of Orange's policy could secure order in such confusion for so long a time, they would doubtless have offered peace on more favourable terms. This, Sir Emanuel, is, briefly put, the opinion of the king's adherents, and really, they are right. For the nobility in this country possesses idiosyncrasies which are incompatible with an aristo-cratic government. In the first place they are too corrupt, too envious, too partial; they have lost the virtues which were the strength of their fore-fathers. Secondly their power, rank and jurisdictions are too unequal.[3] And finally they are so used to being ruled by a superior authority, that is to say, by their prince, that their manners and qualities are adapted to a monarchical form of government and unfit for an aristocracy.

EMAN.: I agree with you, Sir Ernest, and the more so when I also take into account both the power of the king of Spain and the fact that in such a new state one usually makes few friends and many enemies for obviously such innovations are prejudicial to a number of people who forfeit both the glory and the profits which they drew from managing the king's affairs. Neither the people under a popular government to which they are not accustomed, nor the nobles in an aristocratic state which is

[3] The opposite is maintained in Document 32.

equally unfamiliar, will be able to surmount these difficulties. What we need is a prince. But this prince should be a person of great authority, wise, brave and virtuous. Only such a man will be able to resist attempts against the state and to reform our totally corrupt government. This is not the sort of work which can be done by a group of people for they are likely to disagree among themselves and to despise one another. One single man must take up this task.

ERN.: Your discourse, Sir Emanuel, makes me admire the wisdom and foresight of our forefathers. There is a law in the province of Brabant which their Duke John ordered to be proclaimed in the year 1421 saying that 'in case he, his heirs or successors should fail to observe the rights, franchises and privileges of their subjects, the subjects were to be absolved from their oath and obedience and the States enabled to choose a regent or protector of the country, whom the inhabitants would be bound to obey as their own prince, until and in so far as the errors and infractions should have been duly redressed'.[4] This law reflects the wisdom of the prince as well as of the States. Although the nature of the people and the nobles was at that time less debased and corrupt than it is now, it was realised that a country used to being ruled by a prince, could in those difficult circumstances not survive without a protector endowed with the same power, greatness and authority...

ERN.: You are right, Sir Emanuel, but many people wonder whether the legitimate prince can be deprived of his old patrimony. The argument that the prince is a tyrant, they say, can only be directed against conquerors. In His divine providence God sends us good or bad princes to chastise us or to restore us to grace. The bad ones remind us of our sins and God employs them to make us repent. He calls them His servants, and He wants us to obey them even if they compel us and our children to be their slaves, to plough their ground, to reap their harvest, to give them a tithe of our arable land and vineyards and even if they take the pick of our vineyards and olive-groves and wheat and take and use our servants, male and female, and our cattle and asses for their own ends.[5] The Lord Himself has predicted that the world will end amidst many such tyrannies.[6] Shall we resist His ordinance? How will the Scriptures be fulfilled?

EMAN.: You are perfectly right. When a monarch starts so to torment his subjects, they must nevertheless obey him because he is their sovereign

---

[4] John IV of Brabant was temporarily deposed as duke in 1420 and replaced by his brother Philip of St Pol as regent. Thus a wider interpretation was given to the stipulations of the *Joyeuse Entrée* of 1356.

[5] I Sam. VIII, 11–18.   [6] Matt. XXIV, 21.

prince. They must wait patiently for the promised time to come when Almighty God who directs the hearts of kings and the fate of kingdoms, removes the scourges by which we are chastised and replaces them with rulers who will do justice to the oppressed. But there is a great difference between a sovereign monarch or prince and a prince to whom the people themselves give jurisdiction. For the people make the princes and not the princes the people. If the people willingly give all power to their princes without retaining any themselves, there is no reason for them to complain, even if they have afterwards to endure a government as severe as that which at God's command Samuel predicted for the people of Israel: kings totally sovereign and the people totally subject as was current in the neighbouring countries, whose example Israel, in asking for a king, wished to follow.[7] But if the people have retained the right to give jurisdiction to the princes, the princes cannot overrule this jurisdiction and usurp sovereign rights and power such as those predicted for Israel's children. The people have no obligations beyond the limits of the power they have given to their rulers. And these, Sir Ernest, are the limits within which the people of the Netherlands, who declare they have been a free people since time immemorial, wish to remain. The duke of Brabant (to take the leading province as an example) does not by any means have the right to compel the inhabitants of this province to plough his ground, and reap his harvest or to do any similar servile work.[8] He swears to keep all their rights, franchises, liberties and privileges...

EMAN.: [If the duke of Anjou were to die] the States of the country should, I think, forthwith make it an elective principality, because for their recovery and maintenance they need successors no less powerful and competent than the predecessors have been. For one prince's life-span, however long it may be, is hardly sufficient to restore a state abounding with factions and abuses. Two or three excellent princes succeeding each other (the surest way to achieve this is by election) would be sufficient to consolidate the state and to free it from its imperfections, and even to raise it to the summit of greatness. The new prince will have no cause for complaint. There are very many kingdoms and seigniories, there is even the Empire, where leaders are appointed by election. And even if their children apply themselves to virtuous works, they should not be preferred to others. This will not only incite them to exert themselves still more but will remind them anew of the benefits and honours conferred upon them. This much is certain: nothing is so efficacious and beneficial to a free

---

[7] I Sam. VIII, 20.   [8] On the grounds of the *Joyeuse Entrée*.

seigniory, or one endowed with many privileges, as elective princes. For if the most recent ruler committed faults or were deceitful, this can be redressed by a new election and should no other remedy be found, the States may gradually and easily transform the principality into a true aristocracy. If election cannot be introduced, I would at any rate like to see the Salic law established by a solemn and irrevocable decree of all the States of the country, on such terms that in default of a male heir, capable of ruling the state, the States would be entitled to appoint the prince whom they thought would be most beneficial to the country. Thus the principality would not come into the power of a person who governs as the Spaniards governed.

48

Apology or Defence of His Serene Highness William by the grace of God prince of Orange etc. against the ban or edict published by the king of Spain, 1581[1]

On 13 December 1580 the Apology was presented by the prince to the States General assembled at Delft; it was published in February 1581. The court-chaplain Loyseleur de Villiers was probably the author. The royal ban against the prince of Orange, dated 15 March 1580, was published on 15 June.

Does the king not realise that if he is duke of Brabant,[2] then I am one of the principal members of Brabant because of my baronies?[3] Does he not realise his obligations towards me, my brothers and companions and the good towns of this country? And on what terms does he govern this state? Does he not recall his oath? Or if he does, does he attach so little import-ance to what he promised God and the country or to the conditions con-nected with his ducal rank? I need not remind you, gentlemen, of what he promised us before we swore to serve him. Most of you know it only too

---

[1] *Apologie ou defense du tresillustre prince Guillaume, par la grace de Dieu prince d'Orange. . . contre le ban et edict publié par le roi d'Espaigne. . .ed.* A. Lacroix (Brussels, 1858), pp. 100ff., 150ff.

[2] Philip II was inaugurated as duke of Brabant in 1549.

[3] The baronies of Breda, Diest, Grimbergen and Herstal.

well. But there are many others who will read this defence, and so I would like to imprint once more upon your memories a summary of his oath.

You know, gentlemen, the obligations which bind him, and that he is not free to do what he likes as he can in the Indies. He may not by force compel any of his subjects to do anything unless the customs of the local courts of justice, which have jurisdiction over him, permit it. Nor can he change the general state of the country in any way by ordinance or decree. He must be satisfied with his customary and regular income. He cannot levy and demand any taxes contrary to the privileges of the country or without its express permission. He may not bring soldiers into the country without its consent. He may not debase the currency without the permission of the States. He cannot have a subject arrested until the local magistrate has examined the case, nor can he send a prisoner out of the country.

When you hear even so brief a summary, gentlemen, do you not realise, that if the barons and nobles of the country entrusted with its defence by virtue of their prerogatives, did not rise in opposition, when these clauses are not only broken but tyrannically and haughtily trodden under foot – not one single clause, but all of them, not once but a million times, and not only by the duke himself but by barbaric foreigners – ; if I say, the nobles did not honour their oath and obligations and force the duke to make reparation for his misdeeds, would they not then themselves be convicted of perjury, disloyalty and rebellion against the States of the country ? As for myself, I have a special and more personal reason for acting as I do, for contrary to the privileges and without any form of justice I have been robbed of all my goods.[4] Moreover what happened to my son the count of Buren[5] is such a clear proof of the enemy's lack of faith and disregard of privileges, that no one can doubt my right to take up arms.

If in my first campaign I did not obtain a foothold in the country[6] (with this I am upbraided), is this so new ? Has this not happened to the greatest captains in the world ? Did it not happen to him, on the many occasions when he entered Holland and Zeeland with large and powerful armies and was shamefully driven out of the country by a handful of soldiers with the help of the States of these provinces ? Did it not happen too to that great captain, the duke of Alva and his successor,[7] so that the king does not now have in these provinces a square foot of land at his

[4] By a sentence of the Council of Troubles in 1568.
[5] Philip William, see Document 23, note 12.
[6] In 1568.
[7] Requesens had succeeded Alva at the end of the year 1573.

disposal nor, I hope, with your assistance, will he have in the rest of these countries in the near future?...

The threats which accompany this ban are intended to shock you into leaving me. They make it seem that this war is being waged against me and not against you, just as the wolf would like to make the sheep believe that he intends to fight only against the dogs, and having killed them, would be on good terms with the herd, for it is the dogs who always start the fights. But, gentlemen, after I had left for Germany,[8] were there in my absence no more burnings at the stake? Was there no more blood-shed? Were there no longer any people drowned? Was your freedom maintained by that gentle man, the duke of Alva? Was it not at that very time that your ambassadors, the lords of Bergen and Montigny, died so piteously in Spain?[9] Was it not at that time that the heads of your most prominent captains and governors were displayed and presented to you on spears?[10]

The other thing they intend above all, is the extermination of the true religion. I will not discuss here, gentlemen, which is the true religion, the one in which God is truly served and invoked according to His Word. I leave this to people better trained in this area than I am, especially as every one can gather what my beliefs are from the profession I make. But I tell you frankly that the condition of your country is such that if the practice of the reformed religion is no longer allowed the country cannot survive for even three days. You see how miraculously the numbers of its adherents have increased and that hatred of the pope has taken deep root in the hearts of all the inhabitants of the country because his evil practices against this whole state have been so clearly exposed. Who can pride himself on loving this country and still recommend that so many people should be driven out of it, people who will leave the country desolate, poor and waste and will populate and enrich foreign countries? But if they refuse to go away, who can force them to do so? Let us look at our neighbours and at what happened in our own country; unless we are raving mad we will never follow such evil advice, advice which will completely upset this country.

Moreover, gentlemen, it is true that among the adherents of the Roman Catholic Church there are many honest and patriotic men and some of

[8] In April 1567.
[9] The marquis of Bergen died a natural death at Segovia in May 1567. Montigny was secretly executed at Simancas in October 1570.
[10] Lamoral, count of Egmont and Philip Montmorency, count of Hoorne were beheaded at Brussels on 5 June 1568.

them have done their duties honourably; among those who are devoted to the [reformed] religion, however, there is definitely not a single person who has any understanding or association with the enemy for all of them are unanimously hostile to him. Though there are some among them who, like wanton and mischievous children, have by their imprudence given trouble at home,[11] they certainly had no dealings with the common enemy.

As you know the enemies' intention, gentlemen, you must start taking appropriate measures. How? By giving effect to what you keep saying and to what is symbolised by the sheaf of arrows which you gave orders to be engraved on your seal. No limb of this fine body should look after its own interests indifferent to what concerns the whole body; no part of the body should usurp the food prepared for the whole body but each should allow the stomach (which stands for the council you will establish) to digest it and then send it on through the veins to all other parts of this state; and medicine should be sent swiftly to wherever a malady may manifest itself; and the sick should patiently bear their pains for a time so as to enjoy their recovery the more deeply later. We are governing so fine a state and possess such fine means, that it would be to our everlasting shame if we allowed ourselves through miserable avarice and the desire to get rich at the expense of our fellow-countrymen – one party pulling with all their strength on one side, the other on the opposite – to be crushed at a stroke by our mortal enemies. Remember, gentlemen, how much this state's riches declined after Duke Charles died, merely because of trivial debates between the provinces over pretended privileges and some advantages, whilst the people's true interests were neglected.[12] And do not suppose, gentlemen, things being as they are, that I can resist the enemy for long with the very few means that you know I have at my disposal. But on the other hand, having some experience as I have, in the field of government and war, knowing well, as I do, the country and the power of the enemy, be sure that should all the armies of Spain and Italy (which already threaten us) attack us, they would accomplish next year as little or even much less than the duke of Alva did in Holland and Zeeland. If it is within your power (as in truth it is) to make preparations and if you fail to do so, what shall we say of such dereliction, committed by you, gentlemen, now assembled here? All these honest men rely and depend on you. They take you for their fathers and protectors, and are ready to embrace a good ordinance as a gift from heaven (if only you will

[11] The Ghent Calvinists (see Document 42, note 8).
[12] In the turbulent years after Charles the Bold's death (1477), when the States succeeded in obtaining the Great Privilege from his daughter Mary.

issue it). Have pity on yourselves. And if you cannot be moved by your own needs, have pity at least on the many poor people utterly ruined, on the many poor widows and orphans; think of the many murders and bloodshed committed in the bowels of your country, of the many churches destroyed, of the many pastors wandering with their poor flocks. Remember the cruel and barbaric execution carried out by Count Mansfeld at Nivelles.[13] All such disasters you can avoid. And you can easily transfer all the misery of this war to the territory of the enemy, simply by holding aloof from faction and harmoniously and with courage making use of all you have, without sparing, I do not say that which lies at the bottom of your purses, but which abounds therein.

And as for myself in particular, you see, gentlemen, that it is this head they are after, it is this head they have destined for death, putting upon it so high a price and so large a sum of money,[14] and saying that as long as I remain among you this war will not come to an end. I wish it were God's will, gentlemen, that either my eternal exile or even my death could indeed deliver you from all the evil and misery the Spaniards have in store for you. I have so often heard them deliberating in the council and giving their opinion in private, and I know them inside and out.[15] How sweet would such a ban be to me and how delightful a death for such purpose! For why did I leave all my goods at the mercy of the enemy? Was it to get rich? Why did I lose my own brothers,[16] who were dearer to me than life? Was it to find others? Why have I left my son so long under arrest, my son whom did I correctly call myself a father, I should long for? Does it lie within your power to give me another or to give him back to me? Why have I risked my life so often? What price or reward could I expect for my long trouble and toil in your service, in which I have grown old[17] and lost all my goods, other than to win and buy your freedom even, if necessary, with my blood? If gentlemen you therefore believe that my absence or even death may be of use to you, I am willing to obey. Bid me go to the end of the world, and I shall willingly do so. Here is my head over which no prince or potentate but you alone have power; do with it what you please to bring prosperity to you and to maintain your

---

[13] Nivelles in Walloon Brabant had been conquered for Parma in September 1580 by Peter Ernest Mansfeld, stadholder of Luxemburg.

[14] 25,000 crowns.

[15] An allusion to the part played by Cardinal Granvelle, who became the king's councillor at Madrid in 1579 and inspired the ban against the prince of Orange.

[16] Adolph, Louis and Henry (see Document 42, note 7).

[17] Orange was born in 1533.

commonwealth. But should you think the small experience and little diligence I have attained through such long and unremitting toil, should you think that what is left of my goods and my life will still be of use to you (for I devote it entirely to you and to the country), make up your minds to do what I have proposed to you. And should you think I have some love of the fatherland, some capacity to give good advice, then believe that this is the only way to protect and save yourselves. This done, let us go forward together with a good heart and will, and let us together undertake to protect these upright people who are only in need of good counsel and are eager to follow it. If, in so doing you should continue to show me favour, I hope, through your help and God's grace (of which I have so often in the past been conscious in desperate circumstances) that what you decide for your welfare, and the survival of yourselves, your wives and children and all holy and sacred things,

Je le maintiendrai.[18]

[18] 'I will uphold it': the device of the House of Orange.

49

Edict of the States General of the United Netherlands by which they declare that the king of Spain has forfeited the sovereignty and government of the afore-said Netherlands, with a lengthy explanation of the reasons thereof, and in which they forbid the use of his name and seal in these same countries, 26 July 1581[1]

The States General considered this resolution at their meeting on 22 July 1581 at The Hague. The text of the edict was finally approved four days later.

The States General of the United Netherlands greet all those who will see or hear this read.

It is common knowledge that the prince of a country is appointed by God to be the head of his subjects to protect and shield them from all iniquity, trouble and violence as a shepherd is called to protect his sheep, and that the subjects are not created by God for the benefit of the prince, to submit to all that he decrees, whether godly or ungodly, just or unjust,

[1] C. Cau ed., *Groot Placaet-Boek*, I (The Hague, 1658), pp. 26ff.

and to serve him as slaves. On the contrary, the prince is created for the subjects (without whom he cannot be a prince) to govern them according to right and reason and defend and love them as a father does his children and a shepherd does his sheep when he risks his body and life for their safety. It is clear therefore that if he acts differently and instead of protecting his subjects endeavours to oppress and molest them and to deprive them of their ancient liberty, privileges and customs and to command and use them like slaves, he must be regarded not as a prince but as a tyrant. And according to right and reason his subjects, at any rate, must no longer recognise him as a prince (notably when this is decided by the States of the country), but should renounce him; in his stead another must be elected to be an overlord called to protect them.[2] This becomes even more true when these subjects have been unable either to soften their prince's heart through explanations humbly made or to turn him away from his tyrannical enterprises, and have no other means left to protect their ancient liberty (for the defence of which they must according to the law of nature be prepared to risk life and property) as well as that of their wives, children and descendants. This has often happened for similar reasons in many other countries at various times and there are well known instances of it. And this should happen particularly in these countries, which have always been governed (as they should be) in accordance with the oath taken by the prince at his inauguration and in conformity with the privileges, customs and old traditions of these countries which he swears to maintain. Moreover, nearly all these countries have accepted their prince conditionally, by contracts and agreements and if the prince breaks them, he legally forfeits his sovereignty.[3]

After the death of the emperor Charles V who is remembered with respect and who left all these Netherlands to him the king of Spain forgot the services which these countries and subjects had rendered his father and himself and which made it possible for him to achieve such glorious victories over his enemies[4] that his fame and power came to be talked of and respected throughout the world; similarly he forgot the admonitions made by His Imperial Majesty in the past and lent his ear to and put his trust in members of the Council of Spain which was at his side. These persons, most of whom knew of the wealth and the power of these coun-

---

[2] For a similar demonstration based on natural law of the right to depose a tyrannical prince see Document 50.

[3] Privileges like the *Joyeuse Entrée* only permitted obedience to the prince to be refused temporarily.

[4] During the wars with France, e.g. that of 1556-9.

tries, envied them and their liberty, because they could not be made governors of them or acquire high office in them as they could in the kingdoms of Naples and Sicily, in Milan and the Indies and other places within the king's realm. This Council of Spain or some of its most prominent members repeatedly remonstrated with the king, asserting that it would be better for his reputation and majesty if he conquered these territories again so that he might rule them freely and absolutely (that is, tyrannise over them at his will) instead of governing them according to the conditions and under such restrictions as he had been bound on oath to agree when he took over the sovereignty of these countries.[5]

Ever since, on their advice the king has been trying to deprive these countries of their ancient freedom and to bring them into slavery under Spanish rule. First he intended to appoint new bishops to the most important and powerful towns under the pretext of protecting religion.[6] He endowed these magnificently by appending to their sees the richest abbeys and attaching to each of them nine canons as councillors, three with special responsibility for the inquisition. Through the incorporation of the abbeys the bishops, who might equally well be foreigners as natives, would have acquired the foremost places and votes in the assemblies of the States of these countries, and would have been the king's creatures, totally submissive and devoted to him. Through the appointment of the canons the king would have introduced the Spanish inquisition in these countries where (as is generally known) it has always been held to be as abominable and odious as the worst slavery. When once His Imperial Majesty proposed to establish it in these countries, his subjects submitted a remonstrance which made him withdraw the project. Thus he displayed the sincere affection he felt for them.[7]

Various written remonstrances were submitted to the king by towns and provinces and verbal complaints were made by two prominent nobles of the country, the lord of Montigny and the count of Egmont.[8] With the consent of the duchess of Parma, then regent of these countries, and on the advice of the Council of State and the States General, these nobles were in turn sent to Spain. Although the king of Spain gave them verbal assurances that he would comply with their request, shortly afterwards he sent

[5] At his investiture in 1549.
[6] See Document 6, note 9.
[7] In 1522 Charles V appointed Francis van der Hulst inquisitor general for the Netherlands, but he had soon to be relieved of his office because of general opposition.
[8] Montigny was sent as delegate in June 1562, Egmont in January 1565.

written orders[9] that the bishops should be received immediately, on penalty of incurring his wrath, and put in possession of their bishoprics and incorporated abbeys, and that the inquisition be enforced where it had existed before and the decrees of the Council of Trent be executed (this was in various ways contrary to the privileges of the said countries). When all this became generally known, it naturally gave rise to much alarm among the people and the great affection which as faithful subjects they had always felt for the king of Spain and his forebears greatly diminished. They were particularly shocked by these events because they noticed that the king was not only trying to tyrannise over their persons and possessions but also over their consciences. For these they thought to have to answer to none but God alone.

Thus, in 1566, out of pity for the people the most prominent members of this country's nobility submitted a remonstrance to his Majesty.[10] In this they asked him to mitigate his policy relating to the strict inquisition and punishment in matters of religion, in order to appease the people and to prevent all sedition, and moreover to show thereby the love and affection which as a merciful prince he felt for his subjects. At the request of the regent, of the Council of State and of the States General[11] of all these countries, the marquess of Bergen and the lord of Montigny were sent to Spain as ambassadors to explain all these matters further and to speak with greater authority to the king of Spain. They were to make it clear how necessary it was for the prosperity and tranquillity of the country to abandon such innovations and to mitigate the rigorous penalties for infringing the religious edicts. But instead of listening to these envoys and providing against the ill consequences about which he was warned (these had already started to manifest themselves among the people in most provinces since the necessary remedies had been delayed so long) the king surrendered to the pressures of the Spanish Council and declared that the people who had submitted this remonstrance were rebels and guilty of the crime of *laesae majestatis* and as such liable to punishment by death and confiscation.[12] Moreover (because he firmly believed that the duke of Alva's violent measures had totally subjected the provinces to his power and tyranny) he acted against all fundamental rights, always strictly maintained by even the most cruel and tyrannical princes, and committed

[9] Of 13 May 1565 from Valladolid.
[10] Of 5 April 1566 (see Document 4).
[11] The States General did not assemble at all during these years.
[12] All this was carried out when the Council of Troubles was established by the duke of Alva in 1567.

the said noble envoys to prison, had them put to death and had their possessions confiscated.[13]

And although the disturbances caused in the year 1566 by the actions of the regent and her adherents had been virtually quelled and many of those who defended the liberty of the country had been driven out and the others subjugated, so that the king no longer had the remotest reason for suppressing these countries with force of arms, he nevertheless – showing, contrary to his duty as their prince, protector and good shepherd, his lack of affection towards his loyal subjects – gave in to the advice of the Spanish Council. It is clear from the letters – which were intercepted – of Alana,[14] the Spanish ambassador in France, to the duchess of Parma, written in those days, that the council had for a long time been seeking and hoping for an opportunity to abolish all the privileges of the country and to have it tyrannically governed by Spaniards like the Indies and newly conquered countries. Thus the king sent the duke of Alva and a large army to these provinces to suppress their liberties. The duke was notorious for his severity and cruelty, he was one of the principal enemies of these countries and was accompanied by advisers of the same nature and mentality.[15]

The duke of Alva entered these countries without meeting any resistance and was received by their poor inhabitants with great respect and honour. They expected only mercy and clemency, for in his letters the king had often hypocritically promised them this. He had even written that he intended to come personally to these countries[16] to arrange everything to everybody's satisfaction. At the time of the duke of Alva's departure[17] the king had a fleet of ships equipped in Spain to carry him and another in Zeeland to meet him – which put the country to great expense – in order to deceive and ensnare his subjects. In spite of this the duke of Alva who was a foreigner and not related to the king, declared immediately upon his arrival[18] that the king had appointed him commander-in-chief, and shortly afterwards even governor-general of the country. This was contrary to the privileges and ancient traditions. And making his intentions quite clear he immediately put troops into the principal towns and for-

---

[13] See Document 48, note 9.

[14] The intercepted letters from Francis d'Alana to the duchess of Parma have already been mentioned in the Warning of the prince of Orange of 1568 (Document 11).

[15] Especially Vargas and Del Rio, members of the Council of Troubles.

[16] See Document 6.   [17] In the spring of 1567.

[18] Alva arrived in Brussels on 22 August 1567 and was appointed governor in October.

tresses and built castles and fortifications in the most important and powerful towns to keep them subdued. On behalf of the king and in kindly terms he bade the highest nobles come to him under the pretext of needing their advice and of wishing to employ them in the service of the country. But those who complied with his invitation were imprisoned and contrary to the privileges removed from Brabant where they had been seized. He had them tried before him, although he was not competent to be their judge, and then, without completing their trial, sentenced them to death and had them publicly and ignominiously executed.[19] Others, more aware of the hypocrisy of the Spaniards, left the country but were for this condemned by Alva to forfeit their life and possessions.[20] Thus the poor inhabitants, having lost their fortresses and the princes who could defend their freedom, would be helpless in the face of Spanish violence.

Moreover he put to death or drove away innumerable other nobles and excellent citizens so as to be able to confiscate their goods; he lodged common Spanish soldiers in the houses of the other inhabitants and these molested them, their wives and children and damaged their property; and he levied many and manifold taxes. He forced the people to contribute to the building of new castles and fortifications in the towns – erected for their own oppression; he forced them to pay the hundredth, twentieth and tenth penny[21] for the support of the soldiers whom he brought with him and those whom he recruited here and who were to be used against their fellow-countrymen and against those who risked their lives to defend the liberty of the country. Thus the people would become so poor that they would not be able to prevent him from fully carrying out his plan to execute the orders he had received in Spain – to treat the country as though it were newly conquered. For this purpose he also began to alter the existing system of justice in the most important places and to remodel it after the Spanish fashion (an innovation which ran counter to the privileges of the country[22]) and to appoint new councillors. When finally he considered he had no longer anything to fear, he set out to introduce forcibly a tax of ten per cent on all commodities and manufactures[23] despite the numerous protests and remonstrances submitted by each

---

[19] The counts of Egmont and Hoorne were already in prison in September 1567. They were then removed to Ghent, to be executed at Brussels on 5 June 1568.
[20] Orange, Marnix of St Aldegonde, Brederode, Hoogstraten, *et al.*
[21] These taxes were proposed to the States General assembled for this purpose in March 1569.
[22] New criminal ordinances were issued in July 1570 at Alva's instance.
[23] In August 1571, when the two years' term of commutation expired.

province individually and by all of them together, for it was feared that the country whose welfare depends entirely on trade and industry, would be totally ruined by this new tax.

The duke of Alva would even have carried this plan into effect by force had not the prince of Orange, several nobles and other distinguished inhabitants who after being exiled by the duke of Alva, had followed His princely Grace and were now mostly in his service, together with other good citizens who had remained in the Netherlands and who cared greatly for the liberty of the fatherland, shortly afterwards caused the greater part of Holland and Zeeland to abandon the duke and to put themselves under the protection of the prince. First the duke of Alva and then the Great Commander[24] (who was sent by the king to replace him, not to introduce any improvements but to continue the tyranny, although less overtly) forced the other provinces – kept in subjection to Spain by their garrisons and newly built fortifications – to help them with all means in their power to subdue these two provinces. However, the Spaniards had as little regard for the provinces which were forced to help them as they had for their enemies. They allowed the Spanish soldiers who, they pretended, had risen in mutiny to force their way to Antwerp in the presence of the Great Commander and to live as they wished there for six weeks at the burghers' expense. In order to rid themselves of these violent Spaniards the citizens were forced to pay the arrears of pay, amounting to 400,000 guilders, which they claimed to be their due.[25] Thereafter the Spanish soldiers, committing yet more abominable infamies and violence, had the impudence to take up arms openly against the country.[26] First they intended to capture Brussels and to turn the traditional residence of the prince of the country into a robber's den. When they failed in this design they surprised first the town of Alost, then the town of Maastricht. Finally they seized Antwerp, where they ransacked, pillaged and massacred, and which they set on fire and treated as badly as the most cruel and tyrannical enemies of the country could have done, causing unmeasurable damage not only to the poor inhabitants but also to most of the world's nations which had stored their merchandise and money there. The Council of State, which after the death of the Great Commander[27] was

[24] Requesens, governor from November 1573.
[25] This happened in April 1574 after the battle of Mook.
[26] The mutiny of the Spanish troops began after the surrender of Zierikzee at the end of June 1576. Alost was taken by surprise in July, Maastricht in October, while the Spanish fury broke forth at Antwerp on 4 November 1576.
[27] Requesens died on 4 March 1576.

charged by the king of Spain with the government of the country, publicly and in the presence of Hieronymo de Rhoda[28] declared these Spaniards to be enemies of the country because of the damage they had caused and the force and violence they had used.[29] Yet this Rhoda accepted the leadership of the Spaniards and their adherents on his own authority (or, as may be presumed, by virtue of secret instructions from Spain). Without regard for the Council of State, he used the name, authority and seal of the king and acted publicly as the king's governor and lieutenant. This caused the States to make a treaty with the prince and the States of Holland and Zeeland.[30] This treaty was approved by the Council of State as the legitimate governors of the country, who thereby agreed jointly and unanimously to fight the Spaniards, enemies of the whole country and to drive them away. However, as loyal subjects they did not fail to approach the king as soon as possible in all proper ways.[31] In humble remonstrances they asked him to order the Spaniards to depart because of the troubles and disturbances which had already occurred in these countries and which would doubtless continue and, as a solace to the people who had suffered and a warning to others, to punish those who were responsible for the ransacking and ruin of his principal towns and who had thus done his poor subjects unmeasurable harm.

But the king, though pretending that all these things had happened against his will and that he intended to punish the leaders responsible for them and wished to provide for order and peace with the great clemency that is proper to a prince, not only failed to judge and punish them but made it quite clear that everything had been done with his consent and on the prior advice of the Council of Spain. For shortly afterwards intercepted letters written by the king himself to Rhoda and the other captains[32] who caused these disasters, showed that he not only approved their actions but praised them for what they had done and promised to reward them, Rhoda particularly, for their exceptional services. Indeed on his return to Spain he rewarded Rhoda and all the others who had helped him establish tyranny in these provinces. At the same time the king tried to blind his subjects still more by sending a near relative of his, his bastard brother Don John of Austria, to these provinces as governor general.[33] Though

---

[28] Rhoda was a Spanish member of the Council of Troubles and of the Council of State. He fled from Brussels to Antwerp in August 1576.

[29] For this resolution of the Council of State see Document 23.

[30] The Pacification of Ghent of 8 November 1576.

[31] By letter, as early as October 1576.   [32] In October 1576.

[33] He arrived at Luxemburg at the beginning of November 1576.

pretending that he approved and agreed with the treaty of Ghent, that he was in favour of the States, that he would have the Spaniards leave the country, and have those people who were responsible for past troubles and violence punished and that he would restore order to the provinces and reestablish their ancient liberty, Don John in fact tried to divide the States and to subdue one province after the other. Thanks to the will of God (enemy of all tyranny) this was shortly afterwards revealed through letters which were seized and intercepted.[34] These showed that the king had ordered Don John to conform to the instructions and advice Rhoda would give him. But to conceal that plan Don John was forbidden to meet Rhoda and ordered to behave suavely towards the principal nobles so as to gain their confidence until, with their help and assistance, he was able to subdue Holland and Zeeland. After this he might treat the others as he pleased.

Although in the presence of all the States Don John had solemnly promised to uphold the Pacification of Ghent and a certain agreement concluded between himself and the States of all the provinces,[35] he violated both and used the colonels who were in his service and devoted to him to win over to his side the German soldiers who at that time occupied all the principal fortifications and towns. Thus he aimed to secure these fortresses and cities.[36] Indeed he had already won over most of the soldiers and thought that the towns held by the troops were at his disposal. By these means he intended to force even those who were unwilling to make war on the prince and the inhabitants of Holland and Zeeland and to start a civil war more severe and cruel than ever. But what a deceiver does contrary to his real intentions cannot remain hidden for long; so this plan was discovered before he had completely carried it into effect and it therefore failed. Nevertheless he started a new war which is still going on instead of bringing the peace which on his arrival he was boasting he would bring.

All this has given us more than enough legitimate reasons for abandoning the king of Spain and for asking another powerful and merciful prince to protect and defend these provinces. This is particularly clear because for more than twenty years during all these troubles and disorders these provinces have been abandoned by their king and been treated not as subjects but as enemies, whom their own lord sought to

[34] In December 1576.
[35] The Perpetual Edict of 12 February 1577, sworn to by Don John upon his arrival in Brussels in May 1577.
[36] Antwerp, *et al.*

subdue by force of arms. Moreover, after the death of Don John the king made the baron of Selles[37] declare quite clearly – although he claimed to be offering some proper means of achieving an agreement – that he was unwilling to endorse the Pacification of Ghent which Don John had sworn to on his behalf, and his conditions grew harsher every day.

Nevertheless we have not ceased to attempt through humble letters and through the mediation of the most important princes of Christendom to reconcile ourselves and to make peace with the king. Indeed, until quite recently we kept envoys in Cologne,[38] hoping that through the mediation of His Imperial Majesty and the Electors who took part in the negotiations we might obtain a firm peace guaranteeing some freedom granted in mercy, principally freedom of religion for this mainly concerns God and men's consciences.[39] But from experience we learned that we could obtain nothing from the king by such remonstrances and meetings, for the only purpose of these negotiations was to sow discord among the provinces and to divide them. Thereafter the king hoped that he would be able to subdue them more easily one after another and to realise with the utmost severity what he had from the outset intended against them. This was afterwards clearly shown by an edict of proscription[40] which the king published in order to render the inhabitants of the provinces universally hated, to impede their trade and to bring them into utter despair. For he declared that we and all the officials and inhabitants of the united provinces and their adherents were rebels and as such had forfeited our lives and estates; furthermore he set a large sum of money on the head of the prince of Orange.

Therefore, despairing of all means of reconciliation and left without any other remedies and help, we have been forced (in conformity with the law of nature and for the protection of our own rights and those of our fellow-countrymen, of the privileges, traditional customs and liberties of the fatherland, the life and honour of our wives, children and descendants so that they should not fall into Spanish slavery) to abandon the king of Spain and to pursue such means as we think likely to secure our rights, privileges and liberties.

Therefore we make it known that for all these reasons, forced by utter

[37] Noircarmes, baron of Selles, was sent by the king as delegate to the States General at the end of 1577, when Don John was still alive (Document 38, note 9).

[38] The peace-conference at Cologne dragged on from May till November 1579.

[39] This is the only explicit reference to religious freedom in this edict.

[40] The ban of 15 March 1580 against Orange and those who remained loyal to him.

225

necessity, we have declared and declare herewith by a common accord, decision and agreement that the king of Spain has *ipso jure* forfeited his lordship, jurisdiction and inheritance of these provinces, that we do not intend to recognise him in any matters concerning him personally, his sovereignty, jurisdiction and domains in these countries, nor to use or to permit others to use his name as that of our sovereign. Consequently we declare all officers, judges, lords with lower jurisdiction, vassals and all other inhabitants of these provinces, whatever their condition or quality, to be henceforward released from all obligations and oaths they may have sworn to the king of Spain as lord of these countries.

As, for these reasons, most of the united provinces have put themselves by common accord and with the consent of their members under the lordship and government of his most serene prince, the duke of Anjou, upon certain conditions and articles concluded with His Highness,[41] and because His Serene Highness, Archduke Matthias, has resigned the office of governor-general of the country,[42] and we have accepted this, we also order and command all judges, officers and others whom this may in any way concern and regard, to use the name, title, great and small seals, counterseals and cachet-seals of the king of Spain no longer. As long as His Highness the duke of Anjou remains abroad, engaged on urgent affairs for the benefit of these provinces, they shall (as far as the provinces which have concluded an agreement with the duke of Anjou are concerned)[43] provisionally assume and use the title and name of the lords and the Council of the Land,[44] and until these lords and councillors have been formally and actually appointed and have taken up office they shall use our name. That is to say that in Holland and Zeeland the name of the very noble prince, the prince of Orange[45] and that of the States of the same countries shall be used until the actual installation of the afore-said Council of the Land. Thereafter they shall act in conformity with the consent given by them to both the instruction of the aforesaid council and to the treaty with His Highness. Instead of the king's seals, our great seal, counterseal and cachet-seal shall henceforward be used in matters of general government which the Council of the Land, according to its

[41] According to the treaty concluded at Plessis-lez-Tours on 19 September 1580 Anjou was to receive sovereignty over the Netherlands.

[42] In June 1581.

[43] The provinces of Utrecht, Gelderland and Overijssel had not accepted Anjou.

[44] The new council to be established to advise Anjou.

[45] The supreme authority over these provinces was entrusted to Orange in July 1581.

instruction, is authorised to conduct. But in matters of public order, the administration of justice and other matters concerning each country individually, the provincial and other councils shall use the name, title and seal of the respective country where the case arises, and no other, on penalty of having all letters, documents and dispatches issued or sealed in any other way annulled. And to ensure that this be effected we have ordered and commanded, and order and command herewith, that all the seals of the king of Spain which are now in these provinces must upon the publication of this be immediately handed over to the States of each province, or to such persons as the States appoint and authorise; possessors of seals who fail to do this will risk discretionary punishment. Moreover we order and command that henceforward the name, title and arms of the king of Spain shall not be struck on any coin of these countries; but such a form shall be placed there as shall later be commanded when new coins of gold and silver, with their halfs and quarters, are struck. We likewise order and command that the president and the other members of the Secret Council[46] as well as all the other chancellors, presidents and members of the provincial councils, that, further, all the presidents or chief treasurers and the other members of all the chambers of accounts in the said provinces and all other officers and judges shall (since we hold them discharged from the oath they have according to their commissions sworn to the king of Spain) be bound and obliged to take a new oath in the presence of the States of their respective province or their special deputy swearing to be faithful to us against the king of Spain and his followers, in conformity with the formula drawn up by the States General. And, instead of new commissions annulling the former ones, we shall give the councillors, judges and officers who are in the service of those provinces which have signed the treaty with His Highness the duke of Anjou, instructions to continue them in their offices, but only provisionally, that is to say until His Highness arrives. And we shall give the councillors, judges and officers who are in the service of provinces which have not signed the treaty with His Highness new commissions in our name and under our seal. This does not apply, however, to those who may be found to have forfeited their office by violating the privileges of the country, by improper actions and the like. We order, finally, the president and members of the Secret Council, the chancellor of the duchy of Brabant, the chancellor of the princedom of Gelderland and of the county of Zutphen, the president and members of the Council of Flanders, the president and

46 A council established by Charles V in 1531 charged with the supervision of the judicature.

members of the Council of Holland, the treasurers or high officers of Zeeland East and West of the Scheldt, the president and members of the Council of Friesland, the bailiff of Mechlin, the president and members of the Council of Utrecht and all the other judges and officers whom this concerns and their substitutes and each of them in particular, to make known and proclaim this edict in all places under their jurisdiction and wherever public announcements are usually made, so that nobody may plead ignorance. And we call upon them to maintain and uphold this edict strictly and not to allow infringements, and to punish severely all offenders without delay or deceit, for we consider this to be necessary for the welfare of the country. And to all and each of you whom this concerns we grant full power, authority and special instructions to carry this and everything related to it into effect. To make this known we have had our seal appended to this edict. At our meeting at The Hague, 26 July 1581.

50

A true warning to all worthy men of Antwerp, 1581[1]

This pamphlet was undoubtedly written in 1581, although author, place and year of publication are not indicated. The author tries to refute the arguments used by people opposed to the declaration of the States General on Philip's dismissal. Agreeing that the privileges such as the *Joyeuse Entrée* do not allow the subjects to depose a prince he develops a theory obviously derived from the *Vindiciae contra tyrannos* and other writings.

God has created men free and wants them to be governed justly and righteously and not wilfully and tyrannically. This is why He did not give any single man in this world permission to do what he likes nor declared any one exempt from punishment. He has set His will alone as a rule for justice. Justice and God's will serve for man's guidance. For this reason the people and States of the country bind the king or lord whom they install and swear him in to conditions which they think useful and fitting for the country. Thus it is made clear that the king does not own the provinces. Otherwise we should all be unfree and slaves, and all our

[1] *Een trouwe waerschouwinghe aen de goede mannen van Antwerpen* (Knuttel, no. 575).

possessions, even ourselves, our wives and children would belong to the king in the same way as a horse or an ox belongs to an owner. But the lord of the country is only a vicar of God, a shepherd of the people, a father of the country who administers righteousness and justice to all. For that reason is he chosen and installed and to this end is all his power and authority given to him. It is true that he may be called the hereditary lord of the provinces; but it should be understood that the right of succession was given and granted to him by the provinces themselves, that is to say by God by means of the States or of men authorised by the provinces to install and accept the lord; therefore all his rights and power are dependent on the States of the country.

In some countries the kings are always chosen anew without right of succession, as in the Empire and in Poland; in other countries only the sons succeed and not the daughters, as in France; elsewhere, the child chosen by the States succeeds, whereas there are also examples where only the eldest child has the right of succession. In short, all countries have such usages and rights as they themselves have wished to establish and accept. From this it is clear that the right of succession that some of the kings and princes have, and all the power and authority they may attribute to themselves has been granted and given to them by the countries, that is, by the States of the countries which represent the whole body of the community.

In law, therefore, royal rights and power are defined in the following manner: the people of the country charge and entrust the king or lord with his power, on such conditions as are usual according to the constitution of that country; but in all countries, whatever their nature, the king is always charged to administer right and justice and to be submissive to God's law and the rights of the country. If he becomes instead of a father a murderer, instead of a shepherd a butcher, instead of a prince a tyrant the provinces are no longer bound to obey him. They resume the power and authority which they had given to him, because he is not fulfilling his obligations towards them and is breaking the conditions upon which they installed and accepted him as their lord and prince. The right of succession does not hold in these circumstances. The provinces resume their original rights and return to the position their ancestors were in; they are no longer bound to him, they may choose a new protector and lord and put such conditions to him as they think best for the safety of the country and the prosperity of the commonalty. It is true that this is not stated explicitly in the conditions put to the prince at his installation; one does not usually mention this as one always hopes for the best and does not expect a king to forget his oath and become a tyrant. And, in fact, it is not even necessary to mention it. It is a self-evident conclusion drawn from nature and human intelligence and it is graven in everyone's heart. For men have been created free by God and cannot be made slaves by people who have no power over them save that which they themselves have granted and given their rulers.

Our forefathers were wise and prudent men; in addition to natural law which the lords were of course bound to keep they made them accept many conditions and agreements which specified their rulers' obligations. These conditions and agreements are the privileges of the country. If the lord violates them he forfeits his subjects' obedience until he has made good and redressed the abuses. A good example of this is the case of Duke John. Duke John confessed in a document,[2] that the people whom he had charged with the government of the country had in many ways offended against the privileges. These men were publicly criticised by the towns for trying to estrange the duke from the duchess his consort.[3] And, the document says, this was why the States chose and appointed a regent, as, according to their privileges, they may do. This also appears explicitly from the following words of the *Joyeuse Entrée*: 'If it be the case that we, our heirs or descendants transgress or violate this,' etc. The wording clearly shows that the whole procedure is only applicable when one or more of the articles which in the text precede this clause are infringed.

But this restriction does not imply that our forefathers deprived themselves or their descendants of the power and the right, based on God's will and on justice, to punish their lords by making war on them or even by deposing them for ever, when they realised that their rulers had become oppressors and tyrants instead of lords. If they search deep into their consciences and carefully consider the text of the privileges, even the good souls who have been emphasising the restrictions of the *Joyeuse Entrée* must be able to grasp this. If they really wished to interpret the privileges under discussion as literally as they claim, they would have to punish and condemn themselves for having waged war against the king their lord,[4] for the text of the privileges does not say that the inhabitants may wage war against him if he infringes the privileges. This is not the purport of the text. The only thing it says is that until the prince has redressed the grievances

---

[2] See Document 47.

[3] John IV of Brabant was married to his cousin Jemina of Bavaria, who left him in 1420.

[4] The States General had declared the royal governor Don John to be an enemy of the country in December 1577.

and repaired the abuses to the satisfaction of the States his subjects are absolved from their duty to obey him and to submit to his command. In other words, the text does not refer to a tyrannical misgovernment so crude and general in its nature that the inhabitants feel entitled to take up arms. It simply refers to cases where the privileges are infringed on particular points and when it is easy to remedy and redress the situation. In such circumstances there is no reason to expect that the prince and the inhabitants are estranged for ever. However, the words we have referred to – 'until the abuse will have been redressed and repaired' – also indicate how the subjects should conduct themselves when the prince commits contraventions and offences of a general nature, offences which cannot possibly be redressed or repaired and which cause total and lasting estrangement between lord and subjects. When there is no hope of redress or repair, each of us is entitled, according to the right given by God and by nature, to protect and defend himself against all unlawful violence.

51

A fraternal warning to all Christian brethren, who have been ordained by God to elect the authorities and magistrates in the towns of the united provinces, in which the Holy Gospel is preached and the reformed religion is exercised, 6 August 1581[1]

The fraternal warning was published by dedicated adherents of the reformed religion shortly after the abjuration of Philip II. The author discourses in a seemingly democratic spirit upon the way local government committees are to be chosen.

Each man called to take part in the urban elections must remember God's words. Then he will not restrict his choice to nobles or notables, to people exercising a particular craft or trade, to burghers of the town or men born in the country. He will make his choice out of the whole population, out of

---

[1] *Broederlijcke waerschouwinghe aen allen Christen broeders, die van Godt veroordent sijn tot de verkiesinghe der overicheyt ende magistraten in de steden der gheunieerde provincien, daer het heylich Evangelium vercondicht ende die ghereformeerde religie gheexerceert wort* (Knuttel, no. 577).

all God-fearing men, who observe God's law and shun Mammon's commandments, who trust in Christ alone in true faith, ardent love and firm hope and despise the Antichrist, who are adherents of the reformed religion and hostile to the popish heresy, who cherish virtue, abhor vice, are gentle and not resentful nor envious, but peaceful and meek, not bumptious nor ambitious, but friendly and merciful, not hard nor cruel, but steady, not wavering nor double-hearted, but truth-loving and lie-hating, not miserly nor avaricious, but who are faithful, not false swearers nor grasping, not frequenters of laden tables, but who seek the prosperity of the town and its inhabitants more than their own profit, in short people who are not tainted by any evil passion.

Undoubtedly some will object to this statement and say that we started this war to maintain the privileges and that I would be wrong if I wished to neglect or abolish these. I agree that we do indeed wage our just war for the sake of the privileges. However I make a clear distinction between privileges and abuses. I call it a privilege to be toll-free, exempt from taxes, benevolences, excises and similar matters. I call a privilege the right which exists in some countries according to which all fiefs are inherited by the oldest child, or that of other countries where they all go to the youngest. It is a privilege that makes it illegal to torture a burgher without the court's permission, for this does not apply to foreigners; it is a privilege when – as is the case in some towns – the house of the burgher is so free that no officer is allowed inside that house to seize anyone unless that person has not paid his debts; it is privileges that guarantee payment of certain kinds of debts before others; and there are many more exemptions of this nature. I also call privilege the rule that the duke of Brabant may not raise new taxes without the consent of the States of the province and that the States may choose another lord should the duke not treat them in accordance with the regulations laid down in the *Joyeuse Entrée*; and it would be possible to enumerate many other instances of this kind of privilege but that would take us too long.[2] On the other hand I call abuses those usages which have been allowed to creep in over a long period of years owing to the cunning of ambitious, greedy people, avid of high rank and driven on by insatiable thirst for power.

In my view – and I claim that my opinion on this matter is correct – one of these abuses is the old-established practice of restricting eligibility for the magistracy to a number of private persons, or to the old families of the city, or to some guilds, and to exclude foreigners. Rules like these cause

[2] See Documents 47 and 50.

disputes, sedition, discord and quarrels between the citizens and between towns and provinces; they are far from forwarding and sustaining unity among the burghers. It is not only permissible to abolish such trivial regulations, it is just and necessary to do so.

But so as not to leave the impression that I am speaking without reason and foundation I ask those people who are so deeply attached to these so-called privileges that they think it verging on sacrilege to criticise or attack them, whether it is profitable for the country and the common cause to maintain privileges which restrict eligibility to some private persons and thus to accept that all the others are discontented, without any firm opinion or openly hostile. Would it not be better to abolish these abuses (at any rate during the turbulent times we are living through), to declare all inhabitants without exception eligible and then to elect God-fearing men of the calibre I have already described? Any man in his senses will, I think, readily admit that need knows no law and that, if it is required by the circumstances, one should make a virtue of necessity. It is therefore better for the country and our common cause to make the choice of candidates for elections free than to restrict it. If one does restrict the choice the situation may arise when one is compelled to elect and admit to the magistracy persons who are bitterly opposed to the policies of the town and States; in many guilds only three or four persons are eligible for office, all of them hostile to our cause. If they change their attitude in view of the elections they do so only to acquire and keep their seats in the States.

It is often said that there are as many loyal papists as members of the reformed church but, with respect, I say that is not true. No one is so foolish as to take his own life in order to help some one else, particularly if the other person is his enemy. Is it conceivable that an adherent of the Holy See would help sharpen the sword with which to kill the pope, the life of his soul? It may be that the papists trim their sails to the wind, but that is mere hypocrisy and dissimulation for how (humanly speaking) can anyone favour those who seek to injure that which alone can ease his sorrowful conscience? I cannot be hot and cold at the same time; and so a man cannot be both a good patriot and a papist.

It is also often said, that the people in question have already been magistrates for a long time; they have been through the mill and know all the secrets. Yet it does not follow that for that reason they should be elected. Where would we be if (as may happen and has happened) God were to let all of them die all at once? In that case a virtue should be made of necessity (as I have said afore) and newcomers be appointed; and really no persons will be employed who cannot tell good from bad or just from unjust, and are unable after some study to understand the old books, registers, charters and forms.

To conclude briefly, it is unreasonable in turbulent times to stand so much on privileges, old traditions and persons. Even if all the arguments I have advanced are false (which they are not) one should realise that in the times of the pope the magistracy was composed of people known to be the most fanatical zealots for the religion of the Antichrist. Therefore, now that another reigns, to wit Christ, let us ensure that only ardent adherents of the reformed religion, faithful to their church unto death, are appointed to the magistracy. Then all magistrates and authorities will work together in perfect harmony; God's glory will be spread; the Gospel will be preached and the country will be safe from riots, seditions and hostile attacks. These are the most important things to be striven for in all states and under all forms of government, for they are the sinews which bind the citizens together in unity.

52

Remonstrance of His Excellency at Antwerp to the States, 1 December 1581[1]

The prince of Orange delivered this discourse to the deputies of the States General at Antwerp where he was again residing. Since Archduke Matthias' departure in the summer of 1581 the States General had governed the country themselves, while awaiting the arrival of the new sovereign Francis of Anjou. As lieutenant-general of the Union the prince of Orange had retained some vague authority shared with the General Council, which had meanwhile been established.

I will not conceal from you, gentlemen, that next year we shall get into even greater trouble for much the same reasons. For two months have passed already, it is now winter, two full months since the States should have assembled in this town and yet to all appearances we shall not see

---

[1] *Remonstrance faict par Son Excellence en Anvers ce premier iour de decembre à messieurs les Estatz* (Knuttel, no. 579).

them here soon and they will not establish order in our affairs. They act as if we had no enemy at all! Nevertheless we can hear even in this distant place the cannon which are battering Tournay[2] and, as it were, visualise the assaults made upon that city. And yet (blind as we are) we take no notice of the surprises which the enemy is preparing for us for the coming year. This negligence, gentlemen, is a tremendous evil. It is caused not so much by lack of understanding or of industry, but by the fact that everyone has his private rather than the public interest at heart. With regard to the people, I am conscious that the cause of this evil is that they do not understand that this war is their war. As if we were not fighting for their freedom and for their freedom of conscience! And this is why they react to requests to provide the financial means without which neither I nor any one else would be able to wage this war, in the same way as they did to requests made by the late emperor.[3] They should realise, however, that if the means to carry on the war are absent, it is not me who is without them but they themselves and that if they say: 'we do not wish to contribute more', this means: 'we wish to give up the country and the religion'. I do not say this because I am eager to obtain public money. As you know, I have never taken possession of any of it even though some detractors who really knew better said I did. I say this to make you understand once and for all, gentlemen, that the war being fought in this country is your war, and that during your discussions you should remember that you are discussing only your own business. And, as we have a common cause, we must be united. So far we have never achieved unity. Each province has its own council, almost every town and every province has its own army and its own money, with the result that resources which would in total be considerable, are fragmented. It is true that a council has been established[4] but it has no power and if it has no authority, how could it supervise military discipline, finances, justice and everything else? And as to authority, people who have not a farthing to spend, like myself and the council, will never possess authority. This, gentlemen, is a short analysis of the mistakes we have made, and in which we continue. To exculpate myself, I tell you these will ruin us, unless God by His grace provides a solution. And yet I pray you to listen to me and to pass on my advice to the whole people, so that they will not blame me for what has gone

---

[2] Tournai was conquered by Parma's troops on 30 November 1581, the day before this meeting.

[3] Charles V before 1555.

[4] The general executive council that was to govern the country in co-operation with the duke of Anjou.

wrong. However, if you yourselves are willing to exert yourselves to improve the situation, you will learn by experience that I will spare no effort to help you (as I feel obliged to). The matter is very urgent and you must act quickly for the government, which you and the States have established, will not last longer than the end of January. Then there will be no governor at all in the country, unless you make other provisions.

53

Advice of the prince of Orange as to which course to take in the critical situation in which the Netherlands find themselves, 7 February 1583[1]

This advice was drawn up by the prince at the request of the magistracy of the town of Antwerp and presented in February 1583 to the States General there assembled. The prince discusses three possibilities after the failure of the duke of Anjou's attack on Antwerp on 17 January: (a) reconciliation with the king of Spain, (b) reconciliation with Anjou, (c) carrying on the war on their own.

Religion can perhaps, if God helps us, be better maintained by negotiating with His Highness, the duke of Anjou, than otherwise, for it is very much to be feared that, if we do not negotiate, several churches in the small towns (which we cannot abandon without offending God) and perhaps also in large towns will be in danger because of our inability to help them. And if the towns which are in the duke's power,[2] are turned over to the enemies, the exercise of the true religion will undoubtedly be totally forbidden there. This would be, of course, a very great loss for the churches of God.

If some people say that negotiations with a prince who is not wholly of the true religion are inadmissible, I confess that I am not a great enough theologian to be able to solve this problem. Yet I see that no churches in Christendom have raised objections to such dealings. The churches of France, aided by French and German princes,[3] have negotiated several

---

[1] Gachard, *Correspondance de Guillaume le Taciturne*, v, pp. 109ff.
[2] Although Anjou's *coup d'Etat* failed in Antwerp his agents were successful in Dendermonde, Dunkirk, Dixmuyde and other places.
[3] John Casimir of the Palatinate in particular repeatedly interfered in the affairs of France.

times with their king; the Swiss have an alliance with each other in spite of being of different religions and they concluded a treaty with the king of France a month ago; the Protestants of Geneva have come to an agreement with the king of France, who was a great help to them last summer, the kingdom of England has not broken its alliance with the Netherlands concluded at a time when only the Roman Catholic religion was practised there, nor with the king of Denmark; Scotland keeps its alliance with France, now 800 years old; these provinces keep theirs with the Empire and the Empire with us; the Teutonic towns are allied among themselves, although having different religions; the German princes have together chosen the emperor as their chief, although he is not of the same religion as the majority of the electors and other princes of the Empire; the churches of Poland have chosen a king who is not of their religion either;[4] the Vaudois allied with the king of Bohemia; the inhabitants of the valleys of Angroine[5] with the duke of Savoy. Thus I must ask to be excused if I dare not condemn so many, nay all the churches of Christendom. However, I will always be of the opinion that whatever accord is concluded, it must guarantee, as far as is in our power, the safeguarding of religion.

I think these arguments should be considered carefully for our relations with the duke of Anjou raise serious difficulties because of the difference of opinion among the towns. If we decide to seek an agreement with the duke, there is a danger that some towns may secede and if we decide not to negotiate, there is a danger that other towns, feeling that they are left alone and helpless, will seek support wherever they can. This deserves careful consideration...

[If we refuse to be reconciled with either the king of Spain or the duke of Anjou we must adopt the third course and] defend ourselves without any outside help. If we decide to do this, we should realise that we are first of all badly in want of native commanders and soldiers because many of them have been killed in the war and the country is small. The enemies have not only large numbers of native soldiers but also the greater part of the soldiers born in the Netherlands, who formerly served the king of Spain. An additional cause of our difficulties is that the people of this country tend naturally more towards trade than towards the military life. So we are faced with the fact that we need a sufficient number of foreign soldiers. However, we have treated them rather badly in the past and it

---

[4] Stephen Bathory was chosen king of Poland in 1575. Before that he had put religious toleration into practice as prince of Transylvania.

[5] In the Cottian Alps.

will not be easy to find foreigners prepared to serve here unless we guarantee that they will get their pay. Nor will it be easy to find out where we can raise soldiers. But we can discuss this later when we have decided to take this course of action. This much, however, is certain, those of the religion are always more trustworthy than others.

As to money, we know how difficult it has been in the past simply to pay the garrisons: it is surprising that so far we have kept our fortresses without disturbances. Money is indeed the sinews of war and if it is lacking, everything we decide is in vain.

So, if you want to take this decision, you must appoint – if you wish only for a limited period – one leader or more, who must be sure of being really obeyed, not only in words but in deed, and establish a council of worthy people. After this, every one must confine his activities to his own task and business without seeking to interfere in affairs of state and of war, and rely upon the persons we have elected. These men will conscientiously and honourably do what must be done and they will have to be obeyed without contradiction; their orders must be promptly executed and only after obeying them shall we have the opportunity to make the comments we think appropriate. But these measures will serve no purpose, if the means to obtain enough money are not readily to hand; and we must be able to show the councillors we hope to appoint that such means are indeed available, if we wish to induce them to take on this task and to fulfil it voluntarily and dutifully...

Though I do not want to criticise people who say that one has to trust God (for that is right and true) I am quite sure that when one wants to attempt something without money, and what is worse, when the money is withheld through avarice, this is not trusting but tempting God. Trusting God is to use the means it has pleased Him to offer us and to pray Him for His blessing.

Gentlemen, I have now discussed at some length the various courses open to us; if you ask me my own opinion, I reply that whatever decision we come to, we must first of all and very quickly supply money. Whatever our decision, an agreement about this must not be postponed one hour. So far appropriate measures have clearly not been taken. With regard to the three possible courses of action which I have discussed, I declare that it is the third that I prefer and have always preferred, and which made me take so much trouble, four years and more back, to keep all the provinces together on the basis of a solid agreement.[6] And, notwithstanding the

---

[6] In the years 1578-9 when the general union was still in existence.

power of the king of Spain, we would with the help of God, have driven Don John and others out of the country if the provinces had not become disunited much against my advice and for reasons which are well-known. But when I noticed that the members of the States and even those who had undermined the union, were saying that they did not have the means to defend themselves, I changed my mind and decided that we ought to look for aid elsewhere. I was not the only one for others too, who originally did not want to send for a foreign prince, now opted for that plan.

But as I have already said, I do not think that a man endowed with wisdom will be prepared to act as our leader unless the conditions I have enumerated are complied with. Otherwise we shall only be making empty speeches without effect, and causing the destruction of many fine churches; we shall destroy them while intending to save them. We must keep in mind the fact that we are obliged to care for other churches just as much as those of Antwerp. And even if we set aside the question of whether the churches of Antwerp would be safe if the others were lost (which God forbid) we must remember that God loves the small churches as much as the large ones.

If this proposal is not agreeable to you, although I do not believe this can be so, or should there be too many difficulties in carrying it out, I state openly that I will never approve of negotiating with the Spanish king. But if we have to come to an agreement with the duke of Anjou, we must ensure that none of the towns is put in danger and that we get soldiers, and especially commanders of whom both the States and His Highness's council approve. However, as I have said, if the third course of action is feasible, I would infinitely prefer it but upon certain conditions, for otherwise we run the risk of ruin, together with many worthy people.

54

Answer from a good patriot and citizen of the town of Ghent to the notorious pamphlet entitled: Advice of a citizen of the town of Ghent, who has become embittered by the calamities in his town, 1583[1]

This is Marnix of St Aldegonde's answer to a pamphlet published in the same year by Frederick Perrenot, lord of Champagny (Granvelle's brother), detained at Ghent since 1578. The latter had attacked the policies of the prince of Orange in particular.

The prince of Orange has always defended us against your schemes and those of your brother and of people like you, and when we were oppressed by tyranny, he proved that he truly pitied our misery. When he was called in by some of our country to help us,[2] he not only risked his life and used all the means he could lay hands on, but he pledged nearly the whole estate of his brothers, the counts of Nassau. Though God did not at that time allow him to achieve his aims and to deliver us as he hoped, yet he has always remained loyal and full of affection towards us. When there was a new opportunity for helping us, he was again asked to take advantage of it by the States of the country,[3] and he once more brought a large army to our aid. Thanks to that army and to the sympathy he had built up in the country, he was able to take the first step towards our deliverance.

Everyone seeing how much he has suffered since for the sake of our liberty and the bitter pain caused by the death of the counts Louis, Adolph and Henry his brothers, and that of Duke Christopher, killed in battle for our sake,[4] may judge the value of your remarks about the hatred which the house of Nassau feels for these provinces and the grudge you say they harbour against us. Those who stake their lives and possessions on delivering us from our misery and calamities, do not provide any evidence of being hostile to us. Rather do those, who feign to lament our misery and calamities, but in reality intend to return us to the yoke of the king of Spain.

You accuse him of wanting to establish his own dominion; when did he

[1] *Responce d'un bon patriot et bourgeois de la ville de Gand au libelle fameux intitulé Avis d'un bourgeois de la ville de Gand, qui se ressent amerement des calamitez de sa ville* (Knuttel, no. 633).
[2] In 1568.   [3] In 1572.   [4] See Document 19.

ever show such ambition? What evidence have you to convict him? Had
he tried to become seignior of these provinces, had this been his principal
aim, he would not have been so slow to seize opportunities and would not
have refused the offers made to him. We know the powers we have often
offered him and that on many occasions he could have done what you
accuse him of. But honest people also know that he always refused our
requests, perhaps too often. A man who prefers another prince to himself
cannot rightly be judged to aspire to the sovereignty. A man who puts the
crown on the head of another cannot be as ambitious as you represent
him. Discerning people will never believe that he thought fit to call in
other princes in order to establish his own authority, or that he has
always kept in reserve some way of disposing of them; they know that
supreme authority is never shared. Crowns, like marriages, cannot be
shared; a man who aspires to the sovereignty and has the means to obtain
it, will never be so foolish as to share it with others. Thus it is not easy to
depose a prince elected and established in a country by the general consent of the people, especially if he is of royal rank, as is His Highness, son
and brother of the kings of France. And if the ugly affair of Antwerp had
not taken place so soon, before his authority was firmly established,[5] we
would have seen abundant proof of the fact that such princes are not to be
played with.

You claim to suspect the prince of Orange of aspiring to the sovereignty
of Holland. What in fact happened was that he had so proved his fidelity
and love for the people of Holland – of whom he had been governor for
very many years – that they asked him to agree to become their protector
under the title of sovereign.[6] He for his part did not think it wise to let the
duke of Anjou receive complete power over the whole country all at
once, for he feared that this young foreign prince, who did not know the
disposition of the inhabitants and was not well-versed in their laws,
customs and privileges, could easily be misled by his followers' bad
advice or by the sinister practices of the pensionaries of the king of Spain.
Thus with His Highness's consent he decided not to reject the request of
the people of Holland, as he had rejected that of several other provinces,[7]
whose safety depended in his opinion on the support of a prince of greater
power. What objections can one raise to this? What trace of ambition can
one discover here? None, of course. Indeed, is there more convincing

[5] The French fury of 17 January 1583.
[6] In July 1581 the province of Holland had entrusted high authority to the prince
of Orange for the duration of the war.
[7] Gelderland, Overijssel and Utrecht.

proof not only of his great caution and love for these countries and his aspiration to preserve all of them in their liberties, but also of singular moderation and modesty, free from any greed and ambition? The course of events has shown everyone how wise was his decision.

There is nothing that you do not use as a basis for your slander and you model and remodel your lies as an actor does a nose of wax. One and the same subject serves you for different calumnies, entirely at variance with each other. First you say that he perfidiously handed the country over to His Highness; then, that he set the provinces against His Highness and himself tried to make His Highness hated by those of the religion, because he has never cherished any goodwill towards the duke. But all your efforts to disguise your lies are fruitless. There is one single fact that convincingly proves you a liar and cuts through the knot of all your tangled fabrications. When the prince was at death's door and in so serious a state of health that there did not seem any hope of him surviving, he told us that he did not know a more suitable prince than His Highness to help us, nor a prince who could with greater confidence be expected to govern the people peacefully. And he therefore ordered us to honour and love His Highness and to consider him the father of this country. This was his farewell to the States General and his last will and testament.[8] This was the opinion he had conceived of His Highness and evidence of the sincere esteem in which he held him. Who will now believe what you say about his excessive hypocrisy? It is clearly totally unfounded. Surely at the moment of passing from this world there is no room for hypocrisy. This single fact proves you a liar; it will give dignity to the rest of the prince of Orange's life.

If His Highness has since been ill-advised or has himself meant harm, the prince, of whose fidelity and love of the country we have had so much evidence, cannot be blamed for it. The prince considered His Highness a very honest man, capable of delivering us. If the contrary has proved the case, the prince of Orange must not be blamed. People who judge the actions of others on the grounds of their results and not of their motives, do not deserve ever to be happy or to succeed in their undertakings. Sensible people always do otherwise; they offer advice based on solid arguments and are not cast down by the outcome, which God alone decides.

And if, even after disasters as great as those at Antwerp, Bruges,

---

[8] On 18 March 1582 the prince was seriously wounded by Jean Jaureguy's attempt on his life. He then communicated his ultimate wishes to Marnix.

Dixmuyde and elsewhere, the prince does not angrily and hastily pro-
nounce sentence on His Highness (as some people think he should), does
not deprive him of all authority nor declare him to be deposed of his
rights and prerogatives, it is not because he does not love the public good
and does not seek the best means to deliver the country. It is because
great practical experience and clear judgment have taught him that a rule
always held by statesmen is true, that one should reflect a long time before
doing something which cannot be undone and that one should be slow to
give a definitive answer, for time accomplishes gently what cannot well be
brought about by violence.

55

*A discourse outlining the best and surest form and frame of government to be
established in the Netherlands in these times, 1583*[1]

This discourse was undoubtedly written shortly after Anjou's unsuccessful *coup d'Etat* on 17 January 1583.

Though there can be no form of government in the world which is without
disadvantages, and which may not be abused, yet it is clear that no more
efficient or lasting form of government may be devised or established in
these evil times than aristocracy combined with democracy, that is
government by the best nobles and the wisest commoners. Under such a
system the most suitable and capable inhabitants and citizens are chosen
to govern their fellow-citizens on certain conditions and for a fixed
period of time. The citizens obey their chosen masters readily and loyally,
but retain the power and the freedom to dismiss the members of the
government whom they find incapable of governing or not behaving as
they should in government, and to fill the vacancy properly. After shaking
off the yoke of the tyrants, the Swiss, to their honour, established such a
government and so far have honestly kept it. It is clear that our fatherland
which endured under the Spaniards a tyranny incomparably more
savage than the Swiss ever suffered and which recently experienced the

---

[1] *Discours verclaerende wat forme ende maniere van regieringhe dat die Nederlanden voor die alderbeste ende zekerste tot desen tyden aenstellen mochten*
(Knuttel, no. 651).

murderous and treacherous disloyalty of the French,[2] has much more reason, ability and opportunity to establish such a government or a similar one, than the Swiss have ever had.[3] Indeed, the duke of Alva, Requesens, Don John of Austria and the prince of Parma are now conscious that our Netherlands have the ability and opportunity to establish a fine government of this sort and that we have many forces and strongholds...

It is not only the chronicles that testify that our fellow-countrymen themselves have strong hands and feet. Recently this was made abundantly clear in Holland and Zeeland and there would have been more such examples if our nation had been allowed to bear arms and train in the use of them and had it not been considered better to enlist foreigners. For as a result our countrymen were unable to discover their own strength and allowed themselves to be treated only as milch-cows. In fact the inhabitants of Antwerp recently proved (the eternal credit be to God alone) that when necessary they could behave like men. Others could do this too, if they were well-drilled and well-commanded and not hindered and obstructed. Therefore the author of the dialogue in which Ernest and Emanuel hold a discussion,[4] should feel ashamed of despising all the inhabitants of our country as if they were all drunkards, tipplers and misers and as if no brave man was to be found. His fellow-countrymen the French will convince him of the contrary. This author would better have used his tongue and pen (which for so long he has hired out, nay sold for money) for a better purpose, but he will surely get his punishment.

Now it is time for us to stop looking and hearing with foreign eyes and ears; it is time to stop protecting ourselves by means of foreign hands; we should open our own ears and eyes and use our own hands and people for our deliverance and protection, provided we have God's paternal help. For what are we short of? Do we not like other countries also have strong men to bear cuirass and lance and to use the arquebus? Does our country not excel above all others in experienced sailors, mariners and seamen? We have listened far too long to counsellors who took advice from Marciovelli and wished everything done by foreign soldiers so that ignorant of our strength we might be fleeced to the bone.[5] Men who aspired to become tyrants have always used such methods of warfare but all who strive for the deliverance and liberty of the country and the people provide the inhabitants of the country with arms. Men fight best for the

[2] The fury at Antwerp on 17 January 1583.
[3] For an earlier reference to the Swiss example see Document 35.
[4] Document 47. Prouninck was born in Brabant.
[5] In fact in *The Prince* Machiavelli maintained the opposite of what is said here.

protection of their own wives and children, houses, land and property, and for their own lives, much better than soldiers called for money from foreign countries...

The government just described should not seem new or improper to us, Netherlanders. It was only a generation ago that we came under a monarch or chief and to this very day the marks of our ancient freedoms are still manifest in our right to convoke and summon the States and the members of the provinces. No better form of government can be devised because by it the magistrates are obliged to govern prudently and wisely and with all humility for otherwise they are dismissed and disgraced. Thus the subjects are induced to love, honour and obey their government, for it is the government they have chosen themselves and which they have sworn to obey. This form of government is no rebellious disorderly *ataxia* or confusion, as the flatterers of tyrants are wont to call it, but a just *isonomia*, as the Greeks call it, that is an equality of justice, because in such a government law and justice are to be enjoyed equally by everyone without favouritism and irrespective of rank. In all free imperial towns in Germany a very similar form and frame of government is to be found. We might well follow the German example and as far as the privileges and old freedoms of every province and town permit, unite and ally into one body to resist together the common enemy sharing costs if he attacks or harms any one of us. Thus we might relieve and free our allies in the way that was devised and decided at Utrecht...[6]

If the form of government described above is established, it is to be hoped that the provinces, which broke away from us[7] to satisfy the ambition of some individuals, will again unite with us to resist the common enemy and to protect and champion the freedom of the common fatherland. They have reason to do so. They find themselves reduced to the greatest poverty, a poverty that will get even worse because they gave in to the passions and aspirations of some of them and allowed the Spaniards to establish themselves firmly. They now know what is to be expected from the Spaniards, should they get the upper hand again and become masters of the country. It is true that there are as yet no proper ways to introduce the exercise of the true religion into the alienated provinces; but should they be willing to allow freedom of conscience and permit those who have other and better feelings, to depart elsewhere, whenever it suits them, with goods and chattels, we may with a good conscience conclude a civil

---

[6] See the treaty of the Union of 23 January 1579, Document 37.
[7] The Walloon provinces which had united in the treaty of Arras.

alliance with them for the protection of the common fatherland and in the hope that God will open their eyes and give them the knowledge of His Word as by His Grace He has done in other provinces. For this is still happening daily in Germany and Switzerland and the afore-said provinces agreed to such an arrangement in the Pacification framed at Ghent,[8] and will therefore have no objection to what is being proposed here.

[8] This is a very narrow interpretation of the Pacification of Ghent.

56

An explanation of the advice published in the name of the prince of Orange with a corollary, 1583[1]

This polemic against the prince of Orange's Advice of 7 February 1583 (Document 53) obviously comes from those circles at Ghent which had always been ill-disposed towards him and were inclining towards reconciliation with Parma and the king of Spain.

Let us deal briefly with the three courses of action which according to the prince of Orange are the only possible means of extricating ourselves from these troubles. The first one, reconciliation with the king, is, he says, objectionable because we would be accused of inconstancy. But would it not be better to redress the disloyalty into which he has forced us by shifting onto him the disgrace which he has brought on us in the eyes of the whole world in general and in particular? Is reconciliation with the king as pernicious as he says? It can, at any rate, not be worse than what he has brought upon us. We have better means of obtaining a good peace with the king than had the French who, in spite of all that had happened in France, did not fail to reconcile themselves with their king.[2]

As to the great secret which thanks to his long experience in the affairs of princes the prince of Orange reveals to us, to wit that those among the Malcontents who propose reconciliation to us, do this with the full knowledge of the prince of Parma, was any of us so simple as to be unaware of this? And was any one so simple as to wish it were otherwise?

[1] *Esclercissement de l'advis publié au nom du prince d'Orange avec un corolaire* (Knuttel, no. 663).

[2] A new peace was made in the religious wars in 1580, during the reign of Henri III.

The prince of Orange is really afraid that the war will end. You noticed how, when there was a lull in it, he used a number of devices to breathe new life into it, for peace would put an end to his great authority, his monarchical power, pomp, suite, retinue, good table and expensive guards etc., all of which he keeps at our expense; he alone costs the country more than all the combined salaries of all the governors whom the late Emperor Charles and his son the king maintained here. As for the tyranny and the actions blamed by him on the Walloons, what greater tyranny do you know of than that he exercises and makes the magistrates appointed by him exercise? What is the use of the privileges when these are at variance with his will? Privileges restored in such a manner give little cause for gratification and satisfaction. Who but he was responsible for the secession of the Walloons? And who but he wanted to be above all others, to dominate and to rule tyrannically? Has any other foreigner apart from him ever before introduced here a town administration consisting of eighteen persons?[3] He will say that all this was done according to the people's wishes – yes at his suggestion and at his intercession. Did he not seditiously usurp the government of Brabant against the free vote of the States, an office held before him by none but the governors-general of the provinces?[4] Did he not want to remove the count of Lalaing from his government? It was only because of this that the count then called in the duke of Anjou,[5] without awaiting the consent of the States which the prince of Orange held in his power. Did he not intend by other means to deprive the baron of Capres of his government of Arras?[6]...Did he not want to suspend the baron of Ville, Count Rennenberg, governor of Friesland who therefore broke away from him?[7] All these men are natives of the country. But John of Nassau, his brother, is not; he does not

[3] A so-called Committee of XVIII composed from the guilds was established at Brussels in August 1577 and at Ghent in October of that year.

[4] The prince of Orange was proclaimed regent of the province by the States of Brabant in October 1577.

[5] Philip Lalaing, stadholder of Hainault, made contact with the duke of Anjou in 1577. This resulted in the duke going to that province the following year. Cf. Document 32.

[6] Oudart Bournonville, baron of Capres, who was governor of Arras, contributed to the reconciliation of his province of Artois with Parma as early as 1578.

[7] George Lalaing, Count Rennenberg, baron of Ville, was stadholder of the north-eastern provinces (Groningen, Friesland and Drenthe). In June 1579 he adhered to the Union of Utrecht, but in March 1580 he went over to Parma and the loyalists who already dominated his native province Hainault and other Walloon parts of the Netherlands.

have any estates in the Netherlands and yet the prince made him governor of Gelderland,[8] contrary to the articles of inauguration of Archduke Matthias.[9] He himself usurped not only the government of Holland, Zeeland and Utrecht,[10] the admiralty,[11] the government of Brabant (as I have already said) and next Friesland,[12] but also wished to have that of Flanders. Thus you see his insatiable cupidity and ambition. It will not end until he has got everything, and quite unjustly for he has no right to all these offices. Do I need to recall those of the other religion, whom he had arrested illegally, simply because they did not approve of his practices? You can decide for yourselves whether they were wrong. Did he not treacherously try to arrest even John of Hembyze to whom he owed so much, and who finally had to go into exile to escape his rage? And master Peter Dathenus too?[13] Not to mention the murders perpetrated on his behalf on Hessel, Visch and others.[14] He publicly acknowledged that he was responsible for them by promoting the murderers to the highest posts in the country, to our everlasting shame, for we allowed it to happen. Who banished the men whose return[15] as is clear from the 'Advice' which we are discussing he fears? What kind of law has been used here?

[8] In 1578 John of Nassau, a Calvinist, had become stadholder of Gelderland, a province with a preponderantly Catholic population.

[9] See Document 28.

[10] Orange was again recognised as stadholder of Utrecht in October 1577.

[11] In fact he held the post of admiral-general, which went with the stadholdership of Holland, from 1572 and this was confirmed by the Pacification of Ghent (see Document 23, note 8).

[12] After Rennenberg's defection in 1580.

[13] In August 1579, when the prince of Orange intervened in Ghent (cf. Document 42, note 8) Hembyze, first alderman of the town, and Dathenus (Document 34) were forced to emigrate to the Palatinate.

[14] On 4 October 1578 councillor James Hessel, a former member of the Blood Council, and bailiff Visch were put to death at Ghent after a year's imprisonment by order of the town-commander Ryhove, who was closely attached to the prince of Orange.

[15] Hembyze was called back to Ghent in August 1583; Dathenus returned at the same time.

57

A warning to all honest inhabitants of the Netherlands, who are united and allied to protect the freedom of their religion, and all persons, privileges and old usages against the tyranny of the Spaniards and their adherents, 1583[1]

This pamphlet was published in May 1583. The reconciliation with the duke of Anjou which it recommends corresponds with the Advice given by the prince of Orange on 7 February. It apparently comes from the prince of Orange's circle.

There is no reason in the world why supporters of the true religion and the freedoms of the country and its privileges should accept that an agreement with the Spaniards or Malcontents[2] (which means the same thing, because they are tarred with the same brush) is desirable. Whatever favourable conditions the Spaniards might put forward regarding freedom of religion and the army, these would not be observed for long. Patriots thinking to achieve a good and lasting peace by such an agreement, as is promised them, would in reality not only be led into eternal slavery and unrest but also into an open and difficult war against our allies, as the inhabitants of Hainault and Artois have experienced.[3] For Holland and Zeeland, not the smallest but the mightiest and strongest provinces, have often warned the other provinces that they are firmly resolved never to be united with the Spaniards and their adherents.

There are people who may be made to believe that the united provinces could be transformed into a republic on the lines of the Swiss or Venetian. If possible and feasible, this would indeed be an excellent solution. Yet one should bear in mind that the nature of these provinces is wholly different from that of Switzerland and Venice. Switzerland is mountainous and barren, not rich and difficult to reach with armed forces. Venice is situated on an island. It has often been attacked by its neighbours and in the past lost all its inland-towns to the Emperor Maxi-

---

[1] *Waerschouwinghe aen alle goede inghesetenen van den Nederlanden, die tot beschermenisse van de vrijheydt van hunne religie, persoonen, previlegien, ende oude hercomen, teghens die tyrannie van de Spaingnaerden ende heuren aenhanck t'samen verbonden ende vereenicht sijn* (Knuttel, no. 655).

[2] The Walloons who since 1579 had sided with the Spaniards.

[3] These provinces had concluded the Union of Arras in January 1579.

milian.[4] If the neighbours of the Venetians were really strong and if the Venetians were not allied to the Turks (to whom in fact they pay tribute), they would be bound to lose their country gradually, as they lost the kingdom of Cyprus some years ago.[5] It must be emphasised that the Netherlands lie wholly open especially on the French side, that they are rich and powerful and have many powerful kings and princes as neighbours. There are very many powerful provinces and towns in the Netherlands, and these are accustomed to seeking their own advantage and robbing one another of their navigation and trade (on which the prosperity of the country chiefly depends) in order to aggrandise themselves. And while some are prepared to pay war-taxes, others are not. Moreover their contributions come in very tardily and they are so slow in coming to a decision that sometimes towns and provinces are lost whilst they deliberate, as experience has indeed shown. Even towns situated in the same province are often involved in disputes and quarrels and have difficulty in coming to terms with each other. Consequently it is totally impossible to rule the provinces in harmony without an overlord and prince, or to issue good ordinances for everything, for example coinage,[6] trade and other political matters which should be made uniform in a state. Moreover, when more than one person is entrusted with the government, they often quarrel among themselves, each of them trying to be the most respected and often instead of one tyrant there are many. This phenomenon has often manifested itself under republican forms of government and this is why most of them were overthrown.

It would take us far too long to list all the reasons why the monarchy with a prince or lord has been considered of old and according to all wise people experienced in politics to be the best, safest and most lasting form of government for a country or state. This is especially so when the monarchy is so conditioned and restricted that the prince may not use tyrannical methods or improper and unlawful violence against his subjects. In these provinces and especially in Brabant these requirements have been met thanks to the *Joyeuse Entrée* and recently the treaty of Bordeaux concluded with His Highness[7] and relating to all the united

---

[4] This happened when all Venice's enemies united in the league of Cambrai in 1508.

[5] The Turks took Cyprus from the Venetians in 1570.

[6] This was settled in article XII of the Union of Utrecht.

[7] By the treaty of Bordeaux of 23 January 1581 the duke of Anjou accepted these conditions in return for which the States General entrusted the sovereignty to him.

provinces. Moreover, as the country is flat and open and the enemy has taken possession of many places and towns in its heart, many towns have to be garrisoned for their protection and to withstand the enemy a large army has to be fed. For this exorbitant sums of money and many soldiers are necessary. Without the help of a powerful prince, all this could hardly be accomplished. For these and other reasons, which it would take us far too long to sum up here and which are surely well-known to every one, we were induced, when all the provinces were still united and the country was incomparably more prosperous and powerful than now, to ask the Emperor and the princes of the Empire for help in order to escape the danger of being again brought under the yoke of the Spaniards. We offered to put ourselves under their rule and, to make them more favourably disposed, we asked that the Emperor's brother, the Archduke Matthias, come here and handed the entire government of the country over to him. We would have been glad to maintain him as our ruler if His Majesty the Emperor and the princes of the Empire had been willing to help and assist us against the violence of the Spaniards. But they refused the requests transmitted to them by various official envoys sent by the States General of the country and by the Archduke Matthias himself.[8] After long and mature deliberations the States and their members could not find a better or more fitting solution than to come to an agreement with the duke of Anjou, the only brother of the king of France, on the terms and conditions included in the treaty of Bordeaux, and to entrust the country to him, on condition that he use the power of the king his lord and brother[9] for its defence.

[8] See Document 44. [9] Henri III.

A humble discourse and simple exposition of the only means of protecting from now on these poor oppressed Netherlands from further destruction and how to end soon this deplorable war, 1583[1]

The author describes the situation in the summer of 1583. The discourse was probably written a little earlier than Document 59, although it appears later in the Knuttel catalogue.

Is it not ridiculous that the States of the united provinces (and especially those of Brabant, where most of the enemy forces are concentrated) are so slow in coming to decisions, although in war it is necessary to react with the utmost speed? Is it not more than six months since the deputies of the States General began to deliberate day after day at Antwerp? But so far they have not decided whether or not they will accept His Highness again,[2] a decision on which so much depends. Why were the king of Spain's interests here so damaged? It was because the king did not appoint a new governor quickly after the death of the Great Commander[3] but allowed the Netherlands to be ruled by the States, who because of their jealousy for each other quickly started to quarrel among themselves in total disorder.

Is it not obvious that all our money or at least the greater part of it, is used to pay the unreasonable fees of the deputies and a vast number of useless commissaries? We must realise that people who can earn money so easily, do not want a short war; they seek rather to run up their expense accounts with travelling expenses or rather fees, travelling to and fro to their constituents as long as money is to hand, to fill their purses. The covetous and wilful men who are ruling us know quite well whether I tell the truth. Should we be surprised that the prince of Orange[4] and other

---

[1] *Een ootmoedich vertooch ende eenvoudighe verclaringhe van den eenighe middel, waer deur men voordaen dese arme bedructe Nederlanden sal behoeden van voorder verwoestinghe, ende deser elendigher krijch haest een eynde maken* (Knuttel, no. 658).

[2] In March 1583 the States General concluded a provisional arrangement with Anjou but in June he left the country.

[3] Requesens died in March 1576. Don John did not arrive in the Netherlands until November of that year.

[4] In fact after Anjou's coup of 17 January 1583 the prince of Orange controlled central government together with the States General.

honest noblemen are aggrieved to see this miserable and slack government and that they do not attend the meetings of the States General as willingly and as often as they used to? It is sad for them to see that a pensionary⁵ or some other mediocrity will dare to speak and argue about military affairs with considerable boldness and very little information and will wilfully oppose every sensible suggestion. Is it anything other than their wish to run up their expense accounts which makes them so bold and audacious? The reason they say with such pleasure that they have not been fully empowered by their masters to take decisions without reporting back to their constituents is simply that they do not want to have such power. Yet they are wrong and what they say is unjust and damages the reputation and honour of their constituents. For in fact deputies are entitled to take definitive decisions, if they wish, and to exceed their instructions. By unnecessarily prolonging the session of the States, to the detriment of the provinces, they seek only their private profit.

Would to God that all honest, wise magistrates and the commonalty of all the towns understood better the intentions of such persons, and reflected deeply upon them; they would then soon realise what these persons have in view and how craftily they try to satisfy the public's wishes when only trifles are involved while leaving undecided important matters on which the prosperity of the country depends. I would that every one knew them as well as they know themselves, so that honest people would no longer be deceived by them. Nevertheless it is quite easy to see what sort of men they are. Look at the state they keep, and compare the wealth they possess now with what it was five or six years ago, before they were in good faith appointed by the burghers to their present office and rank.

Has anyone ever seen or heard of pensionaries, merchants and commoners taking part in discussions on military affairs and sitting on the council of war side by side with the nobility and soldiery, whose job this has always been and who have usually been entrusted with such matters? Has any one ever seen or heard of affairs of state, on which the country depends, being entrusted to such persons? It seems to me, if I am not mistaken, that trade gives the merchants quite enough to do and that the magistrates would have more than enough to do if they only served the commonalty as they should.

If some one should reply that the nobility have not been faithful to the commonalty and that that is why the people have been forced to take control too, my answer is: It is true that the greater part of the nobility and

⁵ A town-official with legal training.

other court dignitaries did not support us and committed grave and ugly errors. They should have treated us and the public cause more faithfully than they did. Yet that is no reason for sensible commoners, for the councillors of all the towns, and especially for the broad council of Antwerp,[6] to permit the rank and authority of those who have proved to be faithful and have remained with us, to be so boldly and disrespectfully encroached upon and the affairs of war and state to be dealt with by inexperienced persons whose knowledge is based only on hearsay. Should we then be so surprised when affairs of state and the war go so badly? Can we really believe that jealousy has not developed because of this suspicion between the nobility and the commonalty? We must not forget that the nobles too are persons who care for their honour and reputation. I am talking of the nobility and old court dignitaries, who are faithful to us and whom the commonalty cannot justly accuse of disloyalty. We should remember that they have always been annoyed, and still are, at the way they are treated and are therefore delighted to see our affairs go wrong although they do not thereby profit themselves.

Let us for God's sake take control before it is too late and repair the damage. From now on let every one keep within the range of his intellect and his trade. Let the nobility and the experienced officers, who have proved to be faithful (being of the religion) administer and conduct the affairs of state and war, together with the leading and most experienced burghers of the towns – those who are more endowed with intellect than with property. Let the magistrates, pensionaries and other town officials guard the customs, rights and privileges of their towns. Let them ensure that order is maintained, that the good are protected and the wicked chastised without favour or respect of persons. This will require all their time and energy. By doing this they will be honoured by the commonalty and their towns will flourish. Let the merchant keep to trade and watch his purse. And if from now on everyone sticks to his own trade, with the help of the Lord everything will undoubtedly thrive.

Is it surprising that the enemy is so sure of himself that he needs hardly pay any attention to us and holds his ground firmly? It is not, for he knows that our affairs of state and war and decrees about the soldiers' pay are entrusted to merchants and inexperienced persons and that the men who have traditionally and for many years dealt with that sort of business are now made subordinate to them. I repeat, and in the end I will be

---

[6] Until then Antwerp had been the residence of the States General. It then turned against the prince of Orange and in July 1583 forced him to leave for Middelburg.

proved right, that if the war, the administration of justice,[7] the collecting and spending of money are not very soon managed more satisfactorily by men of greater authority than merchants or commoners, it will not be possible for the provinces, especially Brabant and Flanders, to drive the enemy out of the regions and the towns he now holds.[8] We know that in the course of time the enemy will take all the remaining towns and fortresses in the Southern Netherlands, and that all the other united provinces will then be in mortal danger. Ultimately (which God forbid) we will all have to bend to the Spanish yoke. All this because of our own bad government and innovations. I say before God that I do not say this to condemn the merchants, pensionaries or commoners (for I myself am one of them) but only that things may change for the better and turn out well.

[7] The Dutch text has 'justicie' which may be a misprint for 'policie': political affairs.
[8] A number of smaller towns in Brabant and Flanders were conquered by Parma's troops during this year.

59

About the present condition of government in the Netherlands, 1583[1]

This pamphlet depicts the situation in the Netherlands in the latter half of 1583, when central authority was virtually powerless. The pamphlet was written after the fall of Zutphen at the end of September, which is mentioned.

Considering our inconstancy it is not surprising that we have changed our government many times. In less than four years we have seen the Archduke Matthias,[2] the Council of State, the Nearer Union,[3] the Council of the Land,[4] the duke of Anjou. And now a new council is about to be set up. Truly we cannot understand why, unless some mischief-makers are seeking their own profit and deceive the authorities by pretending that change from one government to another is an improvement. Yet they know perfectly well that everywhere these and similar changes have been

[1] *Van den staet der tegenwoerdiger Nederlandtsche regierung* (Knuttel, no. 652).
[2] See Document 28.
[3] See the treaty of the Union of Utrecht, Document 37.
[4] See the edict of the States General of 26 July 1581, Document 49.

disastrous for the provinces. This is why they are looked on as a punishment from God. And when we consider our past experiences and what has happened recently, we find that all our misfortunes were accompanied by a change of government, and all changes of government by misfortunes. Recently we lost the town of Zutphen,[5] while the States General were moving from place to place[6] and the discussions spun out from month to month only to bring about a change of government and a new council. Is it not a great pity that we thus promote the enemy's cause and bring on ourselves so much damage that it looks as if we had firmly sworn to surrender these provinces to him? Is it not because of this that we are the laughing-stock of all the nations in the world and are mockingly asked where we think we could find a prince, council or government which might please us for as long as three months?

We earnestly warn all good inhabitants of the country that, if we were to set up a new council every month provided with the most satisfactory and beneficial instruction we can think of, and held in the same esteem as the previous councils, matters would nevertheless finally become a thousand times worse than before. For if we intend to hold the authorities and the council beside them in the esteem due to them and to obey them, what is the point of this lamentable practice of constantly setting up new councils? On the other hand, if we do not wish to hold the authorities in esteem, no council in the world can be of any use to us.

We do not in any way suggest that the common people have damaged the authority of the council. On the contrary, we must regretfully and sadly state that the council's authority was undermined by precisely those men who ought to have strengthened it. And this is the main point to which we must diligently pay attention in this government. For if we can remedy this (and it depends only on our willingness) then we will soon see our welfare and our prosperity daily increase. If not, we shall have to get used to being bowed down beneath the yoke of the Spanish tyranny from now on. For even if Providence itself would wish to save us, it would be in vain. Therefore we pray all burghers, as the only ones who can move the States of their provinces by timely and practical petitions, and the States themselves as the only ones whom God has given power and authority, each to remedy this situation in their own province and seriously take to heart what we have to say on this subject.

[5] Zutphen was taken by the Spaniards on 22 September 1583.
[6] The States General had been convoked first at Middelburg in the summer of 1583, and had then moved to Dordrecht. So, like the prince of Orange, they had left Antwerp for good.

Firstly we think it is a well-known fact that the high or (as it is now called) sovereign authority is in the hands of the States of each of our provinces. For no one among them can command the others, nor is any one province directly subject to an overlord. Each province has its own States and its own ordinary public revenue. But this war has brought them together in a common union, which obliges them to help each other by word and deed, with their lives and property. This union has formed a community which manifests itself when the envoys of the States of each province meet at an appointed place. This is called the States General, not because they represent the States of each province in particular, but because they represent the community of the general union, that is to say, only what is common to them. For that reason their authority does not go beyond what was agreed upon in the union. And just as it would be unreasonable if any one province usurped control over the affairs of the general union, so it would be equally unreasonable if the States General interfered in the ordinary rule of the States of each province. Nay what is more, when the States General have provided the money necessary for waging war and have elected an able leader and a good council, they should withdraw and leave matters to the competent authorities. But the States General must act again when it is necessary to take further decisions about how to deal with an escalation in the war, or the need to raise more money, about whether or not to keep the commander-in-chief or the council, about appointing a new lord, concluding peace, alienating land, changing religion and the coinage or finally calling to account those to whom they have entrusted government. If they interfere any further, they assume the duties of their delegates, and this is in two respects wrong. In the first place, sovereign power should only be concerned with sovereign matters, and secondly state-affairs should only be dealt with by people appointed to do so and not by those who appointed them. This is of vital importance; the most powerful and famous empires have been brought down because this maxim was not heeded. The reason is that no government can exist without authority and no authority without fulfilling the duties of the office to which it has been appointed. If the person appointed to an office is by order of the men who appointed him prevented from accomplishing his duties, authority breaks down and the whole government is thrown into confusion. But the most fearful and fatal defect is not so much that the States General have usurped control over affairs which they had entrusted to their appointed councillors, for this could to some extent be endured. It is rather that each of the individual provinces has successively usurped control over affairs, which should be decided upon by the States General and their councillors appointed for this purpose. This is why things go so badly and why we are in such great danger that it is a wondrous miracle of God that our cunning enemies did not crush us long ago.

It is plain that all the money voted for the protection of the united provinces by virtue of the common union is no longer the property of any one province, though it was levied there, but of the States General. It should be used in the States General's name by the councillors in charge, firstly for the monthly pay of the garrisons, secondly for financing the equipment needed for the men-of-war, thirdly for maintaining the field army and finally for incidental expenses. Have not most of the provinces, we ask, followed the bad example of some of their number and used this federal income as if it were their own instead of belonging to the whole union? We ask the council itself (without whose orders this money should not be spent) if it knows how much money each province has brought in and how much each province owes? And if it has ever received that money at the correct time or has received it other than piecemeal? It will have to confess that this is not so, and that miserable confusion has characterised the two years it has been ruling the provinces, and that it has had to issue supplications instead of orders.[7]

Nevertheless in our opinion it is not the provinces that should be blamed the most for this abuse; they have simply not considered the matter deeply enough. It is to be feared that the devil, the enemy of all unity, has enough evil instruments in each province to cunningly pervert good advice by putting forward what seems better; this can be done most easily in political and religious matters. For assuming (which our gracious God forbid) that in some provinces there are people who are secretly favourably disposed towards the enemy, or who out of self-interest are trying to change our Netherlandish government so that the highest authority would be shifted to places where they themselves possess the greatest respect, credit and power, these people might argue that it would be impossible for them to carry out their plans if the commonwealth of the general union were powerful and unimpaired and thus they must use devious means to undermine this commonwealth and the council set up to maintain it. This they could do very easily and without being noticed if the council were to fall out of favour with the people – a situation which they would soon succeed in creating if they could deprive the council of all

[7] In the territory of the Union of Utrecht an executive council was still in operation. The system of federal taxation developed in article v of the treaty was never put into execution.

finances. To achieve this they must impress upon the provinces that it is to them that the money and the convoys[8] belong, that they must follow the example of their neighbours and inquire whether these do as much as they do themselves, and why one province should be obliged to bring its money in more readily than another. These are the sort of futile questions the common people like to hear and the sort of criticism which they enjoy. And whatever disaster may befall the country in the meantime (for it is impossible to govern without money), all the blame can then be laid on the council and it can be slandered, as if it did not know how to fulfil its duties. Thus these people hope that the council will finally be dismissed or, compelled by the resistance to it and by its lack of money, will hand in its resignation.

[8] Convoy money was paid for by trading-ships and used for the fleet.

60

A missive from the States General to the towns of Ghent and Bruges, 15 March 1584[1]

The States General, then at Delft, react in this letter to the news from the Flemish towns of Ghent and Bruges. Both these towns – hard pressed by the advancing Spanish troops – had contacted Parma, in particular through Hembyze and the prince of Chimay, the duke of Aerschot's son.

Is it probable that what the king was unwilling and unable to do in solemn peace negotiations[2] through the intercession of His Imperial Majesty and the kings of France and of England, when the provinces still formed a more powerful unity than at present and had not yet taken another lord, he will now do for the towns of Ghent and Bruges especially in their present situation? It may be that some agreement has been put on paper but it will be as little respected as the conditions agreed upon in the year 1566,[3] or even less so, for the king has now occupied many more

[1] *Sendtbrief van de Generaele Staten aen die van Gendt ende Brugghe* (Knuttel, no. 683).
[2] In the years 1578–9.
[3] The agreement concluded on 23 August 1566 by Margaret of Parma and the confederate nobles about public Protestant services.

places and because of the war has so many more means at his disposal to strengthen himself and to oppress the provinces. The exiles and refugees, who in spite of what is being suggested will take good care that they are not excluded from the treaty which you intend to make with the king, will obtain nearly all power and will bring everything back to its former state. They will ensure that their own security is guaranteed and that those who sent them into exile are oppressed. This happens in all civil wars when exiles and refugees return. It is bound to happen on this occasion too, for there are in your towns very many people who have always wanted to make peace with the king and who are not at all pleased with the present state of affairs, that you were obliged to garrison your towns. Your Honours yourselves were even forced to surrender the town of Menin because you needed the soldiers to strengthen yourselves with a larger garrison. . . [4]

Your Honours need not fear [to continue the war] if you still possess the courage of your brave ancestors, who often waged long wars, even for small matters, and took very great risks. This is especially true of the town of Ghent, which was prepared to fight even when all other towns were its enemies. This, however, is not the case now; they are your friends and render every possible aid and assistance. But it seems that instead of wishing to persevere staunchly in a good and righteous cause, you want to decree to God Almighty a time and a way in which the country can be liberated and to surrender to the enemy. Do you think that because the hearts of kings and princes are in the hands of the Lord who directs them according to His wishes the king of Spain has changed his mind completely? First you must have proof that the king's heart has indeed changed for the better. The reverse seems to be the case. In all the provinces and towns, which have fallen into his hands, he has had the true religion exterminated and what is worse, he gives the newly appointed bishops authority contrary to the privileges of the country: he has the children rebaptised, the married people remarried, and in general no one under his power would dare to declare that he is friendly disposed towards the true religion. Idolatry has more adherents than ever before and a vast number of the inhabitants of the provinces and towns which came to an agreement with the Spaniards have been driven away or killed, strangled or burned. . .

And therefore we beg Your Honours to cut off the negotiations entirely or to suspend them temporarily both on your own behalf and on that of

[4] Menin yielded to Parma's troops in July 1583.

your neighbours and allies. They could only bring about a general and immediate change and ruin, as Your Honours will realise if you consider the orders and instructions of those who seem to act on behalf of the enemy, and the other reasons given above.

61

A remonstrance to the States General about the restoration and the maintenance of the State of the Netherlands (by a nobleman of Flanders), 1584[1]

This remonstrance dates from about the middle of August 1584, more than a month after the assassination of William of Orange. The situation of the towns of Flanders and Brabant which still held to the Union was then becoming more and more threatening.

It is already a month, or rather almost six weeks ago since our wise prince departed this life.[2] He was the true father and protector of our fatherland and by his unique wisdom and deliberation he was able to steer our vessel like a good and sure helmsman in the midst of the terrible thunderstorm and tempest in which we are in danger of being shipwrecked. With God's help he was able to protect us from being lost. Now the body is without a head, the ship adrift without a helmsman. We will inevitably perish unless in your wisdom you take the necessary measures as soon as possible.

You know, gentlemen, that nowadays every one has his eyes fixed on you. You must put the helm in its right place again, and appoint a good new helmsman. You must ensure that the ship is navigated into a good port in spite of this tempest and that Ghent is relieved, and that Antwerp and Dendermonde are set free from the fetters of the enemies and that wherever necessary everything is put in order.[3] The way to do this is to

---

[1] *Vertooch aen mijn heeren de Staten Generael op de wederoprichtinghe ende behoudenisse van den staet van de Nederlanden (door eenen edelman uut Vlaenderen)* (Knuttel, no. 700).

[2] On 10 July 1584 the prince of Orange was murdered at Delft, a month after the duke of Anjou had died in France.

[3] Bruges surrendered to Parma in May 1584, Dendermonde capitulated on 17 August 1584 and Ghent in September of the same year.

establish immediately a good Council of State,[4] made up of honourable God-fearing men, who understand political and state-affairs as well as warfare, and whose election is not brought about by any sort of favouritism or nepotism. It will be vital too to establish a good council of war of reputable, properly qualified persons, noblemen, colonels, captains as well as other commanders, who are skilled in warfare, as the well-known proverb goes: *Ut tractent fabrilia fabri*.[5] This council must be entrusted with full power and sovereign authority, so that it will no longer be necessary to report back each time to the provinces for this is one of the chief reasons of our present decline. The council of war must restore strict military discipline, for the soldiers have become intolerably disorderly because of the protracted wars, and reform is urgently required.

If we start in this way, things may go well. But what is most necessary, too, is to collect adequate finance immediately so that we can enlist without further delay a large troop of soldiers, foot as well as horse. If you levy about eighteen or twenty thousand men, enough to defeat the enemy or beat him out of the field, it has been calculated it will cost you at most 300,000 guilders a month, including the pay of the commander-in-chief, the fieldmarshal, the artillery commander, the quartermaster-general, and other army officers. Is this sum not very small, I pray you, when you consider that these provinces have a very large number of very rich people, and fine towns too? These towns are still in our possession and if we look for them seriously we shall undoubtedly find there more than 500 rich and prosperous citizens. These will, of course, be prepared to bear the costs of this war for six months; this will not force them to reduce their state of living and daily expenses. If they are made to see, both through written and verbal discourses, what frightful and totally destructive consequences the enemy's victory would have for them and their descendants, their readiness to help and their generosity will increase yet more. All we can expect from the enemy is the cruellest bloodshed, the looting of our possessions and perpetual banishment; and people so foolish as to prefer to await the course of events at home, will every moment of the day suffer pains a thousand times harder to bear than the misery of being banished forever from the country. But what honest man, however rich he may be in ready money as well as in other possessions, would like to banish himself forever from his dear fatherland, from his houses and estates, from daily contact and conversation with all his friends and relations, if by

[4] A new Council of State headed by Prince Maurice was established by the States General on 18 August 1584.
[5] Every man to his trade.

adopting a sensible policy and spending a small sum of money on it he may live in safety? And, what is even more important, who is so evil and has so little fear of God that he would abandon his religion rather than suffer the vexation of making a small contribution, when so many thousands of martyrs in the early days of the Church, and even recently in this world of ours, have maintained it unto death at the price of bloodshed, the loss of their possessions and the complete ruin of their families? I am firmly convinced that it will be possible to find as many as fifty thousand men on our side, whose religious zeal is such that they would not think of abandoning their faith for such a trifle as a small contribution of money. And therefore I would think it advisable to look thoroughly for such men, not only among the adherents of our religion, but also among Roman Catholics. For many Roman Catholics are undoubtedly honest men and God-fearing patriots who would be as distressed as many of us to see their fatherland heading for ruin...[6]

The imposts, excises, tolls and other public revenues[7] will bring in a surprisingly large sum of money during these six months. They must be collected in an orderly way without deceit or fraudulence, and the money must really be used for the purpose for which it was collected: the welfare of the commonwealth. We must prevent private persons from enriching themselves with it at the expense of the poor common people. When the money has been levied and collected, it must be put away and kept in the public treasury and used to pay the garrisons. Part of it must be used for defraying the expenses incurred by the army and by the artillery if we should happen to take the offensive in this war. A fairly large sum will still be left to start enlisting a large troop of men next spring, without having to burden the people too much. If we thus succeed in keeping the field for two seasons, we shall bring our enemies to reason whether they like it or not.

After this it will be very necessary to restore the administration of justice. During these wars the law was totally disregarded not only by the soldiers but also by the magistrates, who were apparently blindfolded for they stopped punishing criminals, even though these were caught treating with the enemy, robbing and stealing money from the public purse and perpetrating many other kinds of pillage and plunder. This caused countless disturbances both in the towns and in the country, and in all places where a considerable number of people were clearly enriching themselves

[6] For an opposite opinion of the Roman Catholics see Document 51.
[7] See Document 59, note 7.

to the unspeakable damage of the poor people. But whereas the malefactors are to be punished, the worthy must be honoured and rewarded. Most of these have received little but ingratitude, all kinds of slander and a bad reputation with the common people in return for their good and faithful services during the domestic wars.

This is the foundation we must establish. Moreover, it is most important, too, to maintain good relations with the neighbouring princes of our religion, to wit the queen of England, the kings of Scotland, of Denmark and of Navarre,[8] the electors and protestants of the Empire, from whom we may expect nothing but friendliness, and from some even assistance. And it would be a very good and necessary thing to have a capable and respectable ambassador who understands state-affairs and intercourse with princes, accredited to the most important of them, especially to the queen of England. And though it is true that the king of France might have scruples about coming to an agreement with us, and in consequence might not want to aid our cause, nevertheless we should not fail to seek his favour and friendship again,[9] and pray him very humbly that, if he will not help us, at least he will not harm us and that it may please him to live with us as a good neighbour.

[8] Henri Bourbon.
[9] At the end of 1584 the States General offered the sovereignty of the Netherlands to king Henri III who, however, declined it.

62

Discourse of a nobleman, a patriot partial to public peace, upon peace and war in these Low Countries, 1584[1]

This discourse dates from about the same time as Document 61. P. A. Tiele[2] may well be right in ascribing it to Marnix of St Aldegonde who at the time was burgomaster of Antwerp which was beleaguered by Parma's troops.

We know that the only reason why this war was started was to ensure that

[1] *Discours d'un gentil-homme amateur de la patrie et du repos publicq, sur le fait de la paix et de la guerre en ces pays-bas* (Knuttel, no. 705).
[2] P. A. Tiele, *Bibliotheek van Nederlandsche pamfletten*, I, p. 36.

the liberties of the country would be respected so that no one might in violation of law and justice be oppressed on the pretext of religion. Undoubtedly to invoke the pretext of religion is the right way to go about abolishing all a country's liberties, rights and privileges. The example of the kingdom of Naples, the Indies and Spain itself bears this out. And we know that in the Netherlands the introduction of the inquisition disturbed first liberty and then the entire state of the fatherland. For as long as he has one single enemy who would destroy him none of us or of our posterity can be confident of not becoming a victim of the false accusations which the inquisitors use. This is as clear as daylight, and does not need proof, for every one sees it and experience daily shows it.

I know that they promise freedom of conscience provided there is no public worship and no offence is given, but this is only to trap and ensnare us. For it is well known that conscience which resides in people's minds, is always free and cannot be examined by other men and still less be put under their control or command. And in fact, no one has ever been executed or harassed merely on grounds of conscience, but always for having committed some public act or demonstration, either in words, which are said to be an offence, or in acts which are described as exercise of religion. There is no difference between so-called freedom of conscience without public worship, and the old rigour of the edicts and the inquisition of Spain. Moreover, it is ridiculous for the Catholics to grant freedom of conscience when they so firmly prohibit public worship. For it is well-known that they differ from the Huguenots not so much with regard to ceremonies or public worship as in doctrine, and in matters pertaining to faith and conscience. There is no Catholic theologian who dares to or can in truth maintain that the ceremonies practised by those of the religion concerning baptism and the Lord's Supper, or that the invocation of God's name through the intercession of Jesus Christ only, without altars, without images, without invocation of the saints and without innumerable other things ordained either by the Church or by the popes in Rome, are not in accordance with the ceremonies which have existed from the beginning of the primitive Church established by Jesus Christ and observed by His apostles in all simplicity. They would not of course dare to condemn the apostles, for they maintain that their ordinances were given to the Roman Church at the time of the apostles through the inspiration of the Holy Ghost. But if this is so, it ought to be no more difficult for them to permit the public exercise of a religion which they confess to be in accordance with the ordinances of the apostles, than to give freedom of doctrine and inner faith which they maintain to be entirely erroneous and pernicious. How is it then possible to grant freedom of conscience without exercise of religion? For what are the consequences for people who wish to enjoy the benefit of this freedom? If they have no ceremonies at all and do not invoke God to testify to the piety and reverence they bear Him, they are in fact left without any religion and without fear of God. But if they do have ceremonies and want to show openly that they honour God, their religious services must be conformable to their conscience as this is allowed to be free.

If neither religion, nor divine worship nor the opportunity to invoke God and to respect Him, are permitted to them they will necessarily become extremely profane, atheistic and wicked.[3] Instead of advancing or planting the Roman Catholic religion, the authorities will succeed only in abolishing it and in its place they will release a torrent of impiety.

If the authorities grant or prescribe to the Protestants a form of religious service which the conscience of these men makes them regard as impious (as undoubtedly is intended under the conditions of this fine peace[4]) this is not freedom, but compulsion and restraint of man's conscience. In that case conscience will not even be free to omit what it judges to be against God and His word.

For if any one should fail to hear mass on holy days, or receive Holy Communion at Easter or go to confession, or does not bow down to the sacrament of the altar or the chrism, or does not have his children baptised in the manner of the Roman Church, or is not married by a priest, the authorities will take this as an offence. In fact this so-called freedom of conscience forces people to act against conscience to avoid causing scandal. Wise men can decide whether this is liberty. And I have not even mentioned that one will not of course be allowed to state what one thinks; any one who says any word detrimental to the dignity of the ecclesiastical state or the Roman religion will be accused of acting scandalously or of desecrating human and divine majesty. But this is only the start. The authorities will go further and search books and cabinets and coffers, they will eavesdrop on private conversation, a father will not be allowed to teach his children how to call on God, nor will we be allowed to use our mother-tongue in our prayers. Soon, as I have said before, it will be thought necessary to restore the edicts and the inquisition in their full severity everywhere, to re-erect the scaffolds, gallows and wheels, to

---

[3] For a similar argument see Document 2.

[4] Similar peace-terms were imposed by Parma on towns captured at the same time in Flanders, with the object of maintaining the Roman Catholic religion exclusively.

relight the fires, to prepare new graves, and to do all that the cruelty of the ecclesiastical order ever devised to maintain its domination.

I do not exaggerate or use rhetorical language. Indeed I think it is impossible to find words for the evil and calamities which the so-called freedom of conscience represents to every one endowed with some understanding, and who pictures to himself a powerful king, victorious, and extremely angry, wanting to maintain the Roman Catholic religion to the utmost of his power and to destroy the other completely, not only inclined himself to do so, but spurred on by the pope, who has absolute power to force him to it and to absolve him of all oaths and contractual obligations, however solemn they may be...

63

A short instruction by one who has at heart the prosperity of these Netherlands, in which it is clearly shown that it is lawful to resist a king or lord of the country, 1586[1]

This pamphlet gives a brief summary of the ideas of Junius Brutus' *Vindiciae contra tyrannos* of 1579. The author Francis Coornhert (born 1519) is Derick Volckertsz' brother. He was at the time town-clerk of Amsterdam to whose burgomasters he dedicated the pamphlet on 28 March 1586. It was published with the permission of the earl of Leicester, who had assumed the government of the Netherlands.

[Having studied the limitations of the king's power in matters concerning religion] we must now consider the question whether there are also secular rights and reasons which make it permissible to oppose and resist a king, prince or lord of the country if, contrary to the oath he has sworn to the provinces and subjects, he wants to rob them of all their possessions and deprive them of their rights and privileges and reduce them to everlasting servitude, slavery and bondage. The vital point here is that before taking possession of his power a king, prince or lord swears to allow the provinces and their inhabitants to preserve their privileges and rights. And after a king, prince or lord has taken possession of his power, he does not govern

---

[1] *Cort onderwijs eens liefhebbers des welstandts deser Nederlanden waerinne claerlijck bewesen wort, dat het wel gheoorloft is tegen te staen een coning ofte here van de landen* (Knuttel, no. 767).

these provinces or subjects absolutely or alone; he has co-rulers and co-regents, who have also taken the oath, and govern with him. These are, for instance, the States of the provinces, the provincial courts and councils, the magistrates, judges etc.[2]

In addition to them a king, prince or lord has his own special councillors, stewards, chancellors, bailiffs etc., but their commission and office come to an end at the death of their king, prince or lord. However, the commissions of the States of the provinces, provincial courts and councils, magistrates etc., are not terminated on the death of the king, prince or lord; they remain unchanged during the life of the king, prince or lord of the country as well as after his death. After the death of the lord of the country the States, provincial courts, councils and magistrates govern the country, administer justice and take complete control (for they took the oath to the provinces as well as to the king, prince or lord of the provinces) until a new king, prince or lord is invested, and to him they then renew their oath.

Moreover the king, prince or lord of the country has no power to pledge or still less to sell the provinces, nor may he tax his subjects without the express consent of the States as co-rulers of the country. Nor may he violate, importune or molest any one, nor take his life or possessions on his own authority and at his own will. He has to submit to and put himself under the sacred law and under the judgment of the States, provincial courts and councils of the country, and he may not wrong the humblest of his subjects. Should he think he has some grievance against any of his subjects, he must take them to law. He may not be his own judge. He must accept the authority of the sacred law and of justice if any one, either one of his subjects or a foreigner, believes himself to have cause for complaint and takes legal proceedings against him. These privileges and rights have been observed for as long as the Netherlands have been the Netherlands.

The States, provincial courts and councils and the magistrates have been expressly appointed and sworn as co-rulers of the provinces to watch vigilantly over the administrative activities of the king as lord of the country. If they discover that the king or lord of the provinces is exceeding his power and that consequently the provinces are damaged, the subjects oppressed or the privileges and rights of the provinces violated, they must prevent this with all diligence and stand up against it. It is not sufficient for them to do good and to govern righteously them-

[2] On the part played by the subordinate magistrates see also Document 41.

selves, they must also prevent evil plans, abuses, bad government or tyranny and defend the interests of their fatherland. And if they do not do this but are hand in glove with the prince or lord of the country or connive at abuses, then they should themselves be considered forsworn law-breakers, tyrants and traitors to their fatherland.

Should it be discovered that a king, prince or lord of the country has exceeded the powers given him when he swore his oath, and has not observed the privileges and rights which he swore to the provinces and his subjects to keep, and has reigned wilfully and tyrannically, all written and natural laws undoubtedly allow the subjects to resist so tyrannical and insane a king, prince or lord, to defend themselves, to protect the fatherland and their lives, wives, children, grandchildren, descendants and possessions against such violence and tyranny, and against the everlasting slavery to which such a tyrant would wish to reduce us, taking from us our rights and freedoms without which life is hardly worth living.

64

Prouninck's Apology, 10 March 1587[1]

Gerard Prouninck (Van Deventer), presumably the author of the dialogue *Emanuel and Ernest* of 1580 (Document 47), was an orthodox Calvinist who hoped eventually to return to Brabant which he had left in 1579. He supported the policies of the earl of Leicester and in October 1586 accepted a post as burgomaster of Utrecht. When the States of Holland came to oppose Leicester and his party they refused to admit Prouninck to the States General. In his apology he sought to refute charges brought against him.

Long before my time and without my knowledge the council of this city decided to offer the sovereignty to the queen of England on condition that the true reformed religion alone should be recognised, our freedoms, rights, privileges and traditional customs maintained while fully respecting Her Majesty's highness.[2] I agree with the council that humanly

[1] Bor, *Oorsprongk*, II, pp. 915ff.

[2] In June 1586 the city council of Utrecht adopted a petition of the burgher captains of the town requesting 'that the whole government and absolute power

speaking these provinces cannot survive in their struggle with a domestic foe in possession of sovereign power without a sovereign head of their own. We all know that our nature is corrupt, that we have for a long time been accustomed to the rule of one supreme command and that distrust, quarrels and discord have been caused among us because numerous provinces hold equal power. But even if we do not emphasise these factors it is obvious that, although we should strengthen ourselves in every way in view of our war against so superior an enemy, rule by many weakens us too much for us to equal him in the very thing that is most important, that is, the best form of government. We have never, moreover, shown ourselves capable of carrying on an offensive war. But as the population is growing weary of the war which inflicts daily losses upon them, it is humanly speaking impossible for us to withstand such a powerful enemy in a defensive war. We will not even refer to the fact that because it is uncertain who possesses supreme authority in the Netherlands, numerous plans to bring them once again under the king of Spain are being considered.

For these and other reasons we obviously need a sovereign head. After vain attempts to find one in Germany and France when we had been abandoned by all kings and princes, God in his mercy has at last made the queen of England take our affairs in hand. Thus there was good reason to offer the government of these countries to Her Majesty in candid gratitude. This is due to her more than to any other potentate because she is assisting us in our emergency and, because our Christian religion is the same, we may and must, after God's decrees, entrust our state to her with the greatest confidence. The only difficulty is to induce Her Majesty to accept this for she has never tried to expand her territory. She is on the other hand wise enough to study carefully the state of our affairs. As we know by experience, it is not he who is in need and forced to ask for help but he who can help and is being asked, who may impose conditions and laws. But nevertheless we would like to acquire Her Majesty's help on conditions specified by us. Is it then unreasonable that we should approach her with fair conditions which will not estrange her from our cause, that is, conditions by which she may accept us as her subjects and protect us without injuring her authority and her reputation? After

over this province be in all humility and loyalty committed to Her Majesty of England, to Her Majesty's pleasure, in such a way that she may decide upon all matters after her own discretion and wise counsel without any conditions and limitation, provided the true Christian religion and the privileges be maintained so that neither these nor Her Majesty's authority are hurt'.

mature deliberation the former magistrate of Utrecht seems to have thought that it would not be good policy for us to prize a queen of England less highly than the princes of the House of Burgundy or Austria who were originally only dukes and vassals whereas the princes of England have always been kings and sovereign lords. Is it reasonable to prescribe conditions and laws to Her Majesty which were never prescribed to previous lords whether of the House of Burgundy or of Austria, not even at a time when these seventeen provinces were in full bloom and peace, whereas now only a corner of the country is left, and we are impoverished, corrupt, in the midst of internal and external war, quarrels and discord? Of course not, for if we put such conditions, we would certainly offend her authority and thus show that we did not desire Her Majesty's protection.

Obviously where many govern, the highest authority is with many but where one head rules, supreme authority cannot be shared. Those who claim the contrary wish to remain masters themselves and cause much distrust between the princes and their subjects and this leads finally either to tyranny or to domestic wars. As far as we are concerned, if we had succeeded in maintaining ourselves under a government of many, we would not have needed to ask for a sovereign head; but because we were not able to govern ourselves in such a way, how then can we help our princes and princesses if we are to be co-rulers? Naval experience teaches us that in a storm a ship at sea must be navigated by a single helmsman of high rank.

We would wish to be too wise and clever were we to presume, without regard to God's ordinances, to provide against all the faults of princes and kings. This would be a rare, nay an impossible thing, on this earth. But by seeking absolute perfection in royal government even though in our actions we proved ourselves very much less than perfect, we encounter so many difficulties that neither those princes nor we ourselves are able to govern us. Thus we must deal reasonably with reasonable princes and for the rest leave it to God Almighty to punish or bless our posterity according to whether we heed His laws and ways or disobey Him...

With regard to the accusation that I have shown insufficient respect for the privileges I should indeed be distressed if I knew one person on this earth who loved the rights, freedoms and privileges of my fatherland more dearly than I do. To defend them I have possibly left more property in the hands of my enemies than has any one of my accusers. I do not want to praise myself but if these people did value the conservation of our privileges more highly than I do, or if some of them did not find more profit in troubled waters than I have sought, I think they would not attempt to hide their shame under unjust accusations. And what could induce me to act contrary to the privileges since I have always, so far as was in my power, myself refrained from yielding to avarice and ambition? Yet there is no question over which we can more easily err during this domestic war than over the matter of privileges. Many privileges which are profitable in time of peace would be detrimental in time of war, particularly those releasing one from the duty of receiving garrisons or from paying capitation taxes, or those ensuring freedom of trade, or hindering the reform of the magistracies and more of such nature. With my own eyes I have seen a town given up to the enemy which could very well have been saved if it had not been for insistence on privileges.[3] The highest law is the tranquillity and prosperity of the people. Privileges must be suspended if otherwise these would be injured. Privileges are there for the sake of the people, the people do not exist for the sake of the privileges. May the privileges therefore not serve us as a pretext for recalcitrance, selfishness or for delaying good resolutions...

[3] Prouninck's native town Bois-le-Duc in 1579.

65

Thomas Wilkes' Remonstrance to the States General and the States of Holland, March 1587[1]

After Leicester's return to England in November 1586 the States of Holland and the States General started to act counter to the power of the Council of State to which the governor general had delegated his authority. One of the English members of the Council, Thomas Wilkes, protested at these procedures in a memorandum in French, summing up various instances and ending with a discussion of the constitutional side of the matter.

...[you ought] at least to give a satisfactory answer with good legal arguments to justify your acts and procedures without alleging either the sovereignty which you have [on various occasions] claimed to possess or unfounded and frivolous reasons that are irrelevant to the matter and are based neither on the treaties and accords nor on your previous actions nor

[1] Bor, *Oorsprongk*, II, p. 921.

on the instruction given to the Council of State. We expect from you arguments based on equity, law, reason and natural common sense. For in the absence of a legitimate prince the sovereignty belongs to the commonalty and not to you, gentlemen, who are only servants, ministers, and deputies of the commonalty and have commissions which are limited and restricted not only in time but also in subject matter. These are conditions as widely different from sovereignty as is the power of the subject from that of the prince or of the servant from that of the master, or, to express it more clearly, as heaven is from earth, for sovereignty is limited neither in power nor in time.[2] Still less do you, gentlemen, represent sovereignty. In giving His Excellency[3] general and absolute command, the commonalty allowed him to exercise justice, administer civil, naval and military affairs, and to take action in all things pertaining to high authority or sovereignty. The governor general however is only a *dispositarius* or guardian of sovereignty until it pleases the prince or the people to revoke it. In this state there is no one else who is allowed to do this for it is the people who through you as their officials and servants have committed this power, authority and government to His Excellency. And as according to the general rule in law *quo jure quid statuitur eodem jure tolli debet* (which means that any thing to be repealed, must be repealed by the law which made it), it follows that if you have been fully authorised by the provinces and towns, or rather by your masters, to commit the government to His Excellency, you need a similar authorisation to take it wholly or in part away from him. And if you have not been charged to reduce his authority or that of the Council of State, indeed, to usurp His Excellency's power as absolute and general governor, you either do not understand what you have been doing and fail to see how extensive this power was or else you are guilty of the crime of disobedience.

[2] Quotation from J. Bodin, *Les six livres de la République* (ed. 1583), book I, chapter III, p. 124.
[3] The earl of Leicester.

66

A short exposition of the rights exercised by the knights, nobles and towns of Holland and West Friesland from time immemorial for the maintenance of the freedoms, rights, privileges and laudable customs of the country, 16 October 1587[1]

This was written by Francis Vranck, pensionary of the town of Gouda, to expound the view of the States of Holland on the problem of sovereignty in the Netherlands.

After previous discussions among the nobles and in the town-councils about the current state of these provinces and after receiving reports of their opinions, the knights, nobles and towns of Holland and West Friesland,[2] well and gravely representing the estates of this country, have considered it necessary, in accordance with their oath and duty, to make clear in the present document the constitutional position of Holland and West Friesland, firmly convinced that every one reading this will judge it in the impartial and conciliatory spirit which is required in the sad state of these provinces.

It is well-known that for 800 years the countries of Holland, West Friesland and Zeeland have been governed by counts and countesses to whom the rule and sovereignty over these countries was legally entrusted and granted by the knights, nobles and towns, representing the estates of the country.[3] They displayed such great discretion and moderation in their government, that they never decided to declare war or make peace, levy taxes or contributions on the countries, or take any other measures concerning the state of the country (although as a rule they received good counsel from the nobles and natives of the country) without hearing the opinion and obtaining the consent of the nobles and towns of

---

[1] *Corte verthoninge van het recht by den ridderschap, eedelen ende steden van Hollandt ende Westvrieslant van allen ouden tijden in den voorschreven lande ghebruyckt tot behoudenisse van de vryheden, gherechticheden, privilegien ende loffelicke ghebruycken van den selven lande* (Knuttel, no. 790).

[2] That is to say: the States.

[3] This is of course an historical myth. In fact the States originated in the fourteenth century when nobles and towns were first summoned with some regularity. However, Vranck's thesis met with unanimous approval and became a dogma in Dutch political thought.

the country who were on all such occasions convoked and assembled for that purpose. But apart from asking for advice themselves, they were always prepared to listen to the nobles and towns of the country, to grant them complete faith and to pass wise resolutions on all suggestions concerning the state and welfare of the country which the States put forward.

This form of government was perfectly legal; it was in no respect less solidly founded in law than other systems. It produced results which did singular credit to the counts and were beneficial to the countries and their inhabitants. And, above all, it caused the counts of Holland, Zeeland and Friesland to be held in exceptional honour and respect by all the princes and rulers of Christendom even though they only ruled a small country, as is shown by the marriage treaties which they concluded with almost all the most powerful Christian dynasties and by the election of William II of Holland as German Emperor in 1247. Still more important was the fact that thanks to this form of government the counts were nearly always victorious over their enemies and able to defend their frontiers against even the most powerful foes – this added much to the respect in which they were held by their neighbours. We may in truth say that in 800 years the state of Holland and Zeeland was never conquered by the sword or brought into subjugation as a result of foreign or civil wars. We doubt whether this can now be said of any other country except Venice. The only reason which can be provided is that there was always unity, love and understanding between the princes and the States of the country because the princes who had no power in their own right were totally dependent on the nobles and the towns of the state and had no ordinary means except revenue from their own domains to meet the costs of the court and the salaries of the ordinary officers.

We also observe that if to the detriment of the country the princes followed bad advice the States had the authority to make them accept again the norms of right and reason, not only by means of remonstrances and supplications but also by severely punishing those who injured the prince's authority or used it improperly. There are many examples of this.

It is also clear that the States of these countries had the task of appointing legal guardians or *gardenobles* on behalf of princes under age; this happened, too, when Count William V became insane.[4]

And finally there can be no doubt that when the countries were not

[4] In 1358.

enjoying lawful government by their princes because these were absent, under age, insane, involved in conflict with the country, or for any other reason unable to rule, it was always the States which legitimately assumed the administration of the countries' sovereignty. For this reason they often elected a ruler called 'guardian' or 'regent'. This happened even when the House of Burgundy was ruling the country, for example after the death of Duke Charles and his daughter Mary, when the regent, Maximilian, brought the whole state into terrible danger by forcefully opposing the authority of the States.[5] And when the Emperor Charles V himself was under age the States also appointed guardians and good rulers on his behalf. Although this freedom was in many respects much reduced under the House of Burgundy, Charles V himself always held the States of the country in great respect because he realised that his position could only thus be made secure. He repeatedly admonished and strongly advised his son, the king of Spain, to act as considerately and discreetly as he had, declaring that Philip would greatly endanger his state as soon as he started to treat the States with disrespect. The king has been able to discover to his own and the country's detriment how right his father was. For, whatever one may say, the only reason for this war was that with the help of Spanish and other foreign soldiers the king wanted to compel these lands, represented by the States, to do things of which they did not approve.

Although we are sure that all this is beyond dispute we have considered it necessary to relate it here because many people are uncertain or mistaken in their opinion about it. Some judge the assembly of the States only according to the merits of the people who take part in the meetings or of the matters discussed there. Apparently they are under the impression that the said people, who are sent by the nobles and the towns to the meetings of the States, act as if they were themselves the States and are therefore personally in possession of the sovereignty and highest power in the country and decide upon all matters concerning the state of the country according to their own discretion. The consequence of this is that the members of the States are personally blamed and hated for all the actions of the assembly. However, people who look more closely at the facts mentioned above as well as at other important things accomplished by the princes of this country with the help of the States, and who consider especially what has happened in Holland, Westfriesland and Zeeland dur-

[5] Charles the Bold died in 1477, Mary in 1482. Her son Philip was only three years old. The States General recognised her husband, Maximilian of Austria, as regent. However, he soon came into serious conflict with the provinces.

ing the last fifteen years, will soon realise that the authority of the States is not identical with the authority or power of about thirty or forty persons who appear at their meetings. Even the agents of the king of Spain who have always sought to undermine our affairs and to bring the authority of the States into discredit by such arguments, have now learned through experience how gravely they were misled.

To ascertain the origin of the authority of the States, we must realise that all the princes, who ruled these countries legitimately, received their power from the inhabitants and needed their consent and approval before starting to rule; and after that they continued to govern in such a way that all members of the assemblies remained inviolate, with powers unabridged and uncurtailed. Since princes are easily circumvented by roguish and ambitious people, this would not have been possible had the inhabitants not always possessed the means to oppose evil practices in an orderly and responsible manner. Not only were they able to keep the prince mindful of his duty to maintain their freedom and prosperity in the name of all members, but they could also oppose him with the means at their disposal, should he be misled into perpetrating an act of tyranny. To this end the inhabitants of these provinces were divided into two orders or estates, to wit, the nobles and the towns.

The nobles form one 'member' of the States by virtue of the dignity of their birth (which is without exaggeration as respectable and old as might be found in any country) and because of the seigniories they have in these provinces and which usually include high, middle and low jurisdiction. On every occasion they deliberate with each other on the state of the country and they appear in the assembly to give their opinion on all matters under discussion; the deputies of the towns do the same.

The government of most of the towns consists of a board of councillors, chosen from the most prominent citizens. These number in some towns forty, in others thirty-six, in others thirty-two, twenty-eight, twenty-four or twenty persons. These boards must be as old as the towns, as no one remembers their origin.[6] Once chosen the councillors serve as long as they live and possess burgher rights. When someone dies or leaves the town, the board chooses a new member from among the citizens to make up their number. These boards alone have the power to resolve upon all matters affecting the state respectively of the province and the town, and the citizens accept their decisions as binding for they have never infringed or opposed these decisions.

[6] In reality the closed town-councils described here came into existence in the towns of Holland only under Burgundian rule in the fifteenth century.

Yearly the boards elect the ordinary magistrates, to wit, four, three or two burgomasters and seven or more aldermen, to serve for one year. In some towns the boards can elect the candidates directly,[7] in others they draw up lists of recommended candidates, and from these the stadholder chooses the required number. The burgomasters are responsible for all ordinary political affairs including both the administration of the town's property and revenue and its prosperity and safety. The boards of aldermen control the administration of justice in criminal as well as civil cases, and possess and exercise all high, middle and low jurisdiction.

These boards of magistrates, all organised in approximately the same manner, rule the towns of Holland, West Friesland and Zeeland absolutely, that is to say, without any interference from the princes of the countries. The prince does not take any part in the government of the towns except in appointing an officer[8] to act as chairman of the law court. This is briefly the true state of the government of the towns of Holland and Zeeland.

From this it is clear that these boards of town magistrates and councillors, together with the corporation of nobles, undoubtedly represent the whole state and the whole body of the inhabitants, and no form of government could be imagined in which decisions could be taken with a better knowledge of the situation of the country or carried out with greater unanimity, authority or effect. It is therefore not surprising that the state of these provinces has not been subject to change and has remained as constant as a state can be. The corporations of the nobles and the towns can only be brought together into one assembly through deputation. Thus when it becomes necessary to assemble the States to discuss important questions, the meeting is convened in a letter which mentions the principal points for deliberation. These points are then discussed among the nobles and in the town-councils and when a conclusion has been reached, trustworthy delegates are sent to the meeting of the States with such instructions and resolutions as they consider to be in the interest of the country.

As many nobles as think fitting appear[9] and the towns send a burgomaster with as many councillors as they consider necessary. During the war, when problems arise in rapid succession, the delegates have always received a general charge to take the decision which they consider most conducive to the good and safety of the country, and, in particular, to

---

[7] This happened at Amsterdam. [8] The bailiff.
[9] According to a decree of 1581 at least three had to be present.

maintain the rights, freedoms and privileges of the country and to oppose every violation of these. And these delegates acting in this way in union with each other represent the estates of this country. They are not the States in person or in their own right. They are the States only by virtue of the commission of their constituents. There is no reason to suppose that any one would obtain such a commission by pushing himself forward out of ambition, for apart from the fact that this people is by nature averse to such ambition and hostile to all ambitious men, it is obvious that such behaviour is impossible in so free an election. Moreover, it is highly unlikely that any one should desire, in the distress which it has pleased God Almighty to bring upon the provinces, to concern himself with affairs of state. It is an activity which brings no profit, but only trouble, enmity and the hatred of the enemies of our cause who often falsely slandered even the most qualified and loyal servants of the country. Therefore the acceptance of these commissions has to be classed *inter munera necessaria*,[10] and all those who have taken any part at all in the government of these countries can bear witness as to the difficulties which have arisen and the constraints used to persuade people who have already served or who are invited to serve to accept the commission with which they are charged.

These delegates must truthfully report on all matters to their constituents after their return.

This is the basis of the government of the countries of Holland, West Friesland and Zeeland. On this foundation these countries have been grounded for the last five, six or seven hundred years, as far as the oldest records go. It is this, that with the help of Almighty God, has in this dangerous war made them hold out against such a powerful enemy with courage and unity, so that during the war no member of these provinces has ever been torn from us except by main force, and the inhabitants have never been seditious nor the soldiers mutinous in the provinces of Holland and Zeeland. We think this is due only, as well as to the help of Almighty God, to the straightforward, frank, grave and open way in which everything has been done. For that purpose small towns, even those which did not before send representatives to the assembly of the States,[11] were granted, if they so desired, free session and a vote in the assembly of the States. Thus every one might have knowledge of the conduct of the common affairs of state and could therefore shoulder willingly the burdens (which would otherwise seem unbearable) and maintain unbroken unity.

[10] Among the obligatory commissions.
[11] Only six large towns – Dordrecht, Haarlem, Delft, Leyden, Amsterdam and Gouda – were convoked; after the Revolt twelve smaller towns joined them.

For the same reason the nobles and towns are free to send to the meeting of the States as many delegates as they think fit, but not, of course, persons who according to the provincial privileges are ineligible.

If there should be proof that there are among the nobles or among the delegates of the towns people who acted contrary to the regulations or to their mandate and commission (though we do not know of such cases), they would be obliged to account for their action to their constituents whenever required. And if they omitted to do so, they would be liable to punishment. People who in good faith strive to reveal such things we regard as true patriots.

However those who defame the States of the country, treating the States with contempt and pouring scorn on their actions, are greatly mistaken if they think that they have to deal with nobles or delegates of the towns as private persons, unless they can prove that the men whom they criticise acted without mandate or exceeded their commissions. Many of course make this mistake because they are ignorant and simple, and one should not blame them too much. But people who slander the States in such a way although knowing full well that they are wrong in not distinguishing between the assembly of the States and the persons of the delegates, are obviously enemies of these provinces, and intend to undermine the foundations of the house so that it shall fall.

This pertains to the prince as well as to the commonalty. For what power has a prince if he is not on good terms with his subjects? What kind of relations will he have with them, what support will he obtain from them if he lets himself be persuaded to take sides against the States which represent the commonalty[12] or, properly speaking, against his very own people? Also, how can the country survive, if the commonalty lets itself be persuaded to take sides against the States, that is, against the nobles, magistrates and town-councillors, who are their protectors and lawful rulers and who for their attempts to support the commonalty often personally incur the ingratitude of the princes and governors? For this reason it is obvious to all wise people that the commonwealth can have no greater, more harmful or more mortal enemies than those who in a general way oppose the States of the country. By this we do not mean people who are able to prove that some particular member of the States exceeded the commission given by his constituents or otherwise gave offence. Thus it should be understood that if people declare that the sovereignty of the

---

[12] See a similar interpretation of the States as representatives of the commonalty in Document 50.

provinces resides with the States, they are not speaking about private persons or delegates, but about the constituents, that is, the nobles and towns of the country whom the members of the States represent by virtue of their commission. Many princes and rulers have understood this as did Her Majesty of England when negotiating with the States General, and His Excellency when he received his commission as governor-general from them.[13] It is a truth that no one in the world can contravene.

We do not think there is any reason for any one to believe that this can be understood in any other way than that in which we here interpret it; else the conclusion would be that the nobles, magistrates and town-councils have no longer the same power to exercise sovereignty as they had formerly (as we have proved above) and which they possessed when treating with Her Majesty and constituting the government of His Excellency. In that case not only the validity of the treaties with Her Majesty and the commission and government of His Excellency but everything that the States have done for their defence these past fifteen years[14] would be called into question. This can only be the work of enemies of the countries.

We therefore think it has been conclusively proved that the authority of the States must be conserved as the keystone on which the commonwealth rests. This cannot be damaged without ruining the state. It is, we declare, certain that the sovereignty of the country resides with the States and that the States are now no less sovereign than under the rule of the former princes.

[13] In August 1585 Queen Elizabeth concluded the treaty that concerned the matter in question. In January 1586 the States General appointed the earl of Leicester as governor-general.
[14] Since their meeting of 19 July 1572.

Adrian Saravia: The reasons why some of the magistrates of Leyden have conceived a bad opinion of me and caused me to be suspected by the States of Holland, 6 October 1588[1]

Adrian Saravia (born 1530) was a chaplain in the service of the prince of Orange in 1568. He had been a minister since 1582 and later a professor at Leyden. As a staunch supporter of the earl of Leicester he was involved in the unsuccessful attempt to take Leyden for Leicester in October 1587, and was later to emigrate to England. In his Apology he sets forth Wilkes's constitutional point of view (see Document 65).

Thereupon after about six months[2] people began to discuss sovereignty, in order to reduce the authority of His Excellency[3] and to make it inferior to that of the States, as if he were only the lieutenant of the States and they the sovereign. Conversing familiarly with a burgomaster on this topic one day, I told him my sincere opinion, which I was sure was the truth. I said firstly that those called the States had never been sovereign, were not sovereign and could not be sovereign. The reason is clear: where he reigns a sovereign acknowledges only God over him, and he has to account for his actions to none except God. The States have as their masters the town-councils, whose attorneys and commissaries they are, from whom they have instructions which limit their power, and to whom they have to report and account for their actions. Their title of representative States is also sufficient indication that they are not the true States, but only their servants pending the assembly and only for those affairs with which they are especially charged. This is entirely contrary to the nature of sovereignty. And I concluded that the governor-general of the country is not the lieutenant of the representative States, but of the county of Holland itself, which is the true state composed of all the towns and

---

[1] 'Les causes pourquoy certains du magistrat de Leide ont conceu mauvaise opinion de moy et fait que i'ay esté tenu suspect des Estats de Hollande' (British Museum, Cotton Mss, Galba D III, copied by Miss F. G. Oosterhoff in her doctoral thesis – unpublished –'The Earl of Leicester's Governorship of the Netherlands, 1586–1587', London, 1967, pp. 378ff.).
[2] At the beginning of 1587.   [3] Leicester, at that time temporarily in England.

the nobility. The governor-general possesses his office not for a single day when the States meet, but till his commission is revoked by the special command of all the towns and the nobility. I added that the States have no power to deprive the governor of his power or to limit or modify it without a special charge and command of their masters. From them and not from the States the governor takes his authority. His Excellency took his oath to the county of Holland and to the body of the other provinces, and not to the representative States who were invested with authority in some special cases to-day but not for to-morrow. The body of the county keeps its authority for ever, losing it only when it is resigned and handed over to a single count or seignior.

As to the sovereign authority, I let this matter rest, but I told my friend that neither King Philip nor any of his predecessors was sovereign seignior of Holland, Gelderland, Friesland, Brabant etc., with the exception of the Emperor Charles in his capacity as emperor. It is true that King Philip is the sovereign prince of Flanders and Artois because the emperor acquired the sovereignty of these countries by the sword and King Francis and his successor King Henri renounced it several times in peace treaties.[4] Thus King Philip is not only count of Flanders and Artois but sovereign prince and truly king, though he does not bear the title; he holds these countries directly from God and recognises Him alone as his superior. But he pays homage and service to the empire and is a liegeman of the emperor, for the duchies of Brabant and Gelderland, and for Holland and Friesland and the emperor is the true sovereign prince of these duchies and counties. And though King Philip forfeited the right and title of count of Holland,[5] he could not forfeit the sovereignty, since he never had it. It could give rise to some misunderstanding, I said, should the authority of the Emperor Charles be associated with that of his son King Philip, for the case is quite different. The former derived his authority from being an emperor as well as from being a count, and thus he was sovereign not in his capacity as count but as emperor. And though King Philip succeeded his father, he succeeded him only in his capacity as count. Thus when he gave up the empire and all his seigniories,[6] the Emperor Charles had two successors, the one his brother Ferdinand who succeeded to the empire and to sovereignty over all the lands and seigniories held from the empire, the other King Philip, who succeeded to Spain and to the lands and seigniories of the Netherlands,

[4] The treaties of Madrid (1526), of Cambrai (1529), of Crépy (1544) and of Cateau-Cambrésis (1559).
[5] In 1581 by the edict of the States General: Document 49.   [6] In 1555-6.

to each of them in accordance with their differing condition. If it is true that the emperor did not leave the sovereignty to King Philip – and I have never heard the contrary – and if, as seems to be the case, the emperor and the empire have nowadays abandoned it, we must conclude that as long as the towns of Holland remain as united as before, sovereignty devolved on all the town-councils together and on no one of them in particular, for they constitute one body, one state or county. Whenever a state is dissolved by the death of a sovereign who leaves no successor or in any other way, the power and authority, whether sovereign or not, comes into the possession of the whole of that state, unless regulations have previously been made about the government to be established during an interregnum, as in the Roman Empire and in elective kingdoms. When the kings had been expelled from Rome, the consuls and the senate thought that the sovereign authority had devolved on them, but the people understood it differently. When they saw that the senate appropriated all the royal and sovereign power that the kings had had formerly, they realised that they had been deceived when they were told that once the kings had been expelled they would be a free people. They had a rude awakening when instead of one king they saw two hundred. They rebelled against the senate and introduced reforms to give the state a popular form of government in which the people had the principal authority in matters of sovereign power, though the senate had the first rank and after them the equites. As for Holland, this can only be a popular state because the nobles have no prerogative either in voting or in state-affairs. In fact all of them together have but one vote, no more than the smallest town-council of Holland.[7] In consequence I am greatly surprised at what your lawyers advise for they should be aware of this and should acquaint you with the form of your government. As long as you are not acquainted with this, you cannot conduct your affairs properly and in keeping with public law but will continue to make many mistakes and blunders on this matter.

I have discussed these matters with only two or three persons. I do not know if my views have been reported to the gentlemen of the States. It is certain however that thereafter they held me in suspicion and thought that I had informed His Excellency of many things prejudicial to their authority and the country. However I have never held any conversation about the state of the country with His Excellency, in general or in particular. Once when he complained of the way in which the States

[7] See Document 66 note 11.

thwarted him I asked him for the love of God and of His church to have some patience and told him the States would of their own accord in the end listen to reason. And I said to His Excellency that the late prince of Orange, blessed be his memory, had won them over by such means and had brought them to the point where they undertook nothing without his permission and counsel, and in fact decided shortly before his death to give him the whole government of the country and to make him count of Holland.[8]

[8] The plan to raise the prince to the rank of count of Holland (and Zeeland) was ready to be put into effect when he was murdered (July 1584). The prince was to hold Holland as an independent county without feudal ties with the Empire.

Bibliography

The number of publications relating to the Revolt of the Netherlands is enormous. We restrict ourselves to mentioning in section 1 the pamphlet catalogues and in section 2 some works on the subject dealt with in the Introduction. We draw special attention to the works of Dr J.K. Oudendijk which we have used so extensively in some passages of our Introduction that it was impossible to acknowledge our debt by means of the usual references.

1

P. A. Tiele, *Bibliotheek van Nederlandsche pamfletten. Verzameling van Frederik Muller te Amsterdam, naar tijdsorde gerangschikt en beschreven*, 3 vols. (Amsterdam, 1858–61).

H. C. Rogge, *Catalogus der pamflettenverzameling van de boekerij der Remonstrantsche Kerk te Amsterdam*, 5 vols. (Amsterdam, 1862–5).

J. K. van der Wulp, *Catalogus van de tractaten, pamfletten enz. over de geschiedenis van Nederland ... aanwezig in de bibliotheek van Isaac Meulman*, 3 vols. (Amsterdam, 1866–8). Most of this material is now in the University Library at Ghent.

L. D. Petit and H. J. A. Ruys, *Bibliotheek van Nederlandsche pamfletten. Verzamelingen van de bibliotheek van Joannes Thysius en de bibliotheek der Rijks-Universiteit te Leiden*, 4 vols. (The Hague, 1882–1934).

W. P. C. Knuttel, *Catalogus van de pamflettenverzameling berustende in de Koninklijke Bibliotheek*, 9 vols. (The Hague, 1889–1920).

J. F. van Someren, *Pamfletten in de Universiteits-bibliotheek te Utrecht niet voorkomende in afzonderlijk gedrukte catalogi der verzamelingen in andere openbare Nederlandsche bibliotheken*, 2 vols. (Utrecht, 1915–22).

G. van Alphen, *Catalogus der pamfletten van de bibliotheek der Rijksuniversiteit te Groningen, 1542–1853 (niet voorkomende in de catalogi van Broekema, Knuttel, Petit, Van Someren, Tiele en Van der Wulp)* (Groningen, 1944).

2

H. A. Enno van Gelder, *De Nederlandse Staten en het Engelse Parlement in verzet tegen vorstenmacht en gevestigde kerk* (Mededelingen van de Koninklijke Vlaamse Academie voor Wetenschappen, Klasse der Letteren, XXII, V, Brussels, 1960).

P. A. M. Geurts, *De Nederlandse Opstand in de pamfletten, 1566–1584* (Nijmegen, 1956).

G. Griffiths, *Representative Government in Western Europe in the Sixteenth Century* (Oxford, 1968).

H. G. Koenigsberger, *Estates and Revolutions* (Ithaca, 1971).

F. G. Oosterhoff, 'The Earl of Leicester's Governorship of the Netherlands, 1586–1587' (unpublished doctor's thesis, London, 1967).

286

H. Lademacher, *Die Stellung des Prinzen von Oranien als Statthalter in den Niederlanden von 1572 bis 1584* (Bonn, 1958).

J. K. Oudendijk, *Het 'contract' in de wordingsgeschiedenis van de Republiek der Verenigde Nederlanden* (Leyden, 1961).

J. K. Oudendijk, '"Den Coninck van Hispaengien heb ick altijt gheeert"', in *Dancwerc. Opstellen aangeboden aan Prof. Dr. D. Th. Enklaar* (Groningen, 1959), pp. 264–78.

J. W. Smit, 'The Netherlands Revolution', in R. Forster and J. P. Green eds., *Preconditions of Revolution in Early Modern Europe* (Baltimore, 1971), pp. 19–54.

A. C. J. de Vrankrijker, *De motiveering van onzen opstand* (Nijmegen, 1933).

Index

CAMBRIDGE STUDIES IN THE HISTORY
AND THEORY OF POLITICS

TEXTS

LIBERTY, EQUALITY, FRATERNITY, *by James Fitzjames Stephen.* Edited, with an introduction and notes, by *R. J. White*

VLADIMIR AKIMOV ON THE DILEMMAS OF RUSSIAN MARXISM 1895–1903. An English edition of 'A Short History of the Social Democratic Movement in Russia' and 'The Second Congress of the Russian Social Democratic Labour Party', with an introduction and notes, by *Jonathan Frankel*

TWO ENGLISH REPUBLICAN TRACTS, PLATO REDIVIVUS or, A DIALOGUE CONCERNING GOVERNMENT (*c.* 1681), *by Henry Neville* and AN ESSAY UPON THE CONSTITUTION OF THE ROMAN GOVERNMENT (*c.* 1699), *by Walter Moyle.* Edited by *Caroline Robbins*

J. G. HERDER ON SOCIAL AND POLITICAL CULTURE, translated, edited and with an introduction, by *F. M. Barnard*

THE LIMITS OF STATE ACTION, *by Wilhelm von Humboldt.* Edited, with an introduction and notes, by *J. W. Burrow*

KANT'S POLITICAL WRITINGS, edited with an introduction and notes, by *Hans Reiss*; translated by *H. B. Nisbet*

MARX'S CRITIQUE OF HEGEL'S 'PHILOSOPHY OF RIGHT', edited with an introduction and notes, by *Joseph O'Malley*; translated by *Annette Jolin* and *Joseph O'Malley*

FRANCOGALLIA, by *François Hotman.* Latin text by *Ralph E. Giesey*; translated by *J. H. M. Salmon*

STUDIES

1867: DISRAELI, GLADSTONE AND REVOLUTION. THE PASSING OF THE SECOND REFORM BILL, *by Maurice Cowling*

THE CONSCIENCE OF THE STATE IN NORTH AMERICA, *by E. R. Norman*

THE SOCIAL AND POLITICAL THOUGHT OF KARL MARX, *by Shlomo Avineri*